Inclusion in Tourism

Inclusion in Tourism provides examples of discrimination and marginalisation in tourism practices and avenues designed to recognise and overcome personal or institutional biases, setting a road map for researchers interested in establishing a more inclusive approach to tourism and tourism research.

Logically structured, multidisciplinary in approach, and compiled by a well-known scholar and leader in tourism theory, this volume comprises 13 chapters specially commissioned that provide concrete global examples of overcoming discrimination within tourism institutions, centred around examples of best practice, courses of action, and positive outcomes. Chapters outline, explain, and challenge the existing view of tourism theory as inclusionary, destroying the myth that tourism is an equal opportunity endeavour, bringing a new level of scrutiny to "stand-alone" concepts of "discrimination" and "marginalisation" as a long-existing phenomenon in tourism studies. The book begins with an institutionalised and global approach to discrimination, focusing on immigration policy, academic teaching, research, grant policies, and destination image in relation to minorities. The text then moves to the individual level, discussing aspects of institutionalised discrimination based on individual characteristics, such as sexual orientation, obesity, disability, and gender.

International in scope, this book will be of pivotal interest to graduate students, researchers, and practitioners interested in diversity and inclusion.

Susan L. Slocum, Associate Professor, Tourism and Event Management, George Mason University, Fairfax, Virginia, USA.

Contemporary Geographies of Leisure, Tourism and Mobility
Series Editor: C. Michael Hall
Professor at the Department of Management, College of Business and Economics, University of Canterbury, Christchurch, New Zealand

The aim of this series is to explore and communicate the intersections and relationships between leisure, tourism and human mobility within the social sciences.

It will incorporate both traditional and new perspectives on leisure and tourism from contemporary geography, e.g. notions of identity, representation and culture, while also providing for perspectives from cognate areas such as anthropology, cultural studies, gastronomy and food studies, marketing, policy studies and political economy, regional and urban planning, and sociology, within the development of an integrated field of leisure and tourism studies.

Also, increasingly, tourism and leisure are regarded as steps in a continuum of human mobility. Inclusion of mobility in the series offers the prospect to examine the relationship between tourism and migration, the sojourner, educational travel, and second home and retirement travel phenomena.

The series comprises two strands:

Contemporary Geographies of Leisure, Tourism and Mobility aims to address the needs of students and academics, and the titles will be published simultaneously in hardback and paperback.

Routledge Studies in Contemporary Geographies of Leisure, Tourism and Mobility is a forum for innovative new research intended for research students and academics, and the titles will initially be available in hardback only. Titles include:

Contemporary Advances in Food Tourism Management and Marketing
Edited by Francesc Fusté-Forné and Erik Wolf

Inclusion in Tourism
Understanding Institutional Discrimination and Bias
Edited by Susan L. Slocum

For more information about this series, please visit: www.routledge.com/Contemporary-Geographies-of-Leisure-Tourism-and-Mobility/book-series/SE0522

Inclusion in Tourism
Understanding Institutional Discrimination and Bias

Edited by Susan L. Slocum

LONDON AND NEW YORK

First published 2023
by Routledge
4 Park Square, Milton Park, Abingdon, Oxon OX14 4RN

and by Routledge
605 Third Avenue, New York, NY 10158

Routledge is an imprint of the Taylor & Francis Group, an informa business

© 2023 selection and editorial matter, Susan L. Slocum; individual chapters, the contributors

The right of Susan L. Slocum to be identified as the author of the editorial material, and of the authors for their individual chapters, has been asserted in accordance with sections 77 and 78 of the Copyright, Designs and Patents Act 1988.

All rights reserved. No part of this book may be reprinted or reproduced or utilised in any form or by any electronic, mechanical, or other means, now known or hereafter invented, including photocopying and recording, or in any information storage or retrieval system, without permission in writing from the publishers.

Trademark notice: Product or corporate names may be trademarks or registered trademarks, and are used only for identification and explanation without intent to infringe.

British Library Cataloguing-in-Publication Data
A catalogue record for this book is available from the British Library

ISBN: 978-1-032-18619-1 (hbk)
ISBN: 978-1-032-18620-7 (pbk)
ISBN: 978-1-003-25541-3 (ebk)

DOI: 10.4324/9781003255413

Typeset in Times New Roman
by Apex CoVantage, LLC

Contents

List of figures   vii
List of tables   viii
List of contributors   ix

1 **Introduction**   1
STEFANIE BENJAMIN AND ALANA DILLETTE

PART I
Discrimination policies in tourism   11

2 **Gastro-cultural identities for place branding: the forbidden fruit of minorities?**   13
STYLIANI (STELLA) KLADOU

3 **Canadian immigration policies: implications for discrimination and biases in tourism employment**   30
KELLY-ANN WRIGHT AND FREDERIC DIMANCHE

4 **Women in tourism employment: glass ceiling or gender equality?**   47
BUKET BULUK EŞITTI

5 **From Jim Crow to Black Lives Matter: a history of racism and tourism in the United States**   62
SUSAN L. SLOCUM AND LINDA J. INGRAM

6 **Overcoming institutional discrimination in USDA programmes: food and agricultural tourism**   78
KYNDA R. CURTIS, DEBRA TROPP, AND AMY D. HAGERMAN

7 Decolonising our curriculum: addressing the "miseducation" of tourism 94
SALLY EVERETT

PART II
The experiences of the "Other" in tourism 111

8 Othering in accessible tourism 113
SELIN ALTUN, GÜREL ÇETIN, AND İSMAIL KIZILIRMAK

9 Gay men's experiences of prejudiced attitudes and discrimination in tourism 129
CARLOS MONTERRUBIO AND CÉSAR CASELIN

10 Doing gender well and differently: the case of women managers in tourism 144
INÊS CARVALHO AND CARLOS COSTA

11 Exploring obese people's tourist experiences: a search for an accessible, bias-free experience 161
YANIV PORIA, ARIE REICHEL, AND JEREMY BEAL

12 50 Shades of discrimination: commercial kink in hospitality and tourism 176
CRAIG WEBSTER

13 But where is your wife? Reflections of a gay tourist in a heteronormative environment 189
AMIT KAMA

Index 203

Figures

2.1	Map of Gökçeada and Bozcaada, Turkey	19
6.1	2018 farm bill funding for selected programmes (ten-year totals in millions $US)	81
7.1	The 6C framework of decolonisation mapped against Hiatt's (2006) ADKAR model	97
8.1	The process model of othering	115
8.2	Othering factors in persons with disabilities	122
8.3	Participation Cycle of Persons with Disabilities in Tourism Activities model	123

Tables

4.1	Glass ceiling barriers for female managers	49
6.1	FMPP and SCBGP funding allocations, Fiscal Year (FY) 2008–2020	85
8.1	Factors affecting the travel participation of persons with disabilities	120
8.2	Groups that benefit from accessible tourism	121
10.1	Research participants	149
12.1	Kink events types and characteristics	182

Contributors

Selin Altun, PhD Student, Tourism Management, Istanbul University, Istanbul, Turkey. Selin graduated with a master's degree in tourism management from the Dokuz Eylül University. Her thesis was titled "Nonverbal Communication of Tour Guides and Its Impacts on Tourist Experience". She is active in several fields of study, tour guiding, travel agencies, disability, and accessibility tourism. She serves as a student evaluator at the Tourism Education Evaluation and Accreditation Board (TURAK).

Jeremy Beal is a former student at the Hospitality and Tourism Program, Pamplin College of Business, Virginia Polytechnic Institute, Blacksburg, Virginia, USA.

Stefanie Benjamin, Associate Professor, Department of Retail, Hospitality, and Tourism Management, University of Tennessee, Knoxville and Co-Director of Tourism RESET. Stephanie's research interests include social equity in tourism around the intersectionality of race, gender, sexual orientation, and people with disabilities. She also researches film-induced tourism, implements improvisational theatre games as innovative pedagogy, and is a certified qualitative researcher exploring collective storytelling, duo-ethnography, visual methodology, and social media analysis. Lastly, she serves as a Faculty Advisor on the Equity and Diversity Board for the Office of the Vice Chancellor for Diversity & Engagement at UTK.

Inês Carvalho, Assistant Professor, Universidade Europeia, Lisbon, Portugal. Inês's research interests include gender and languages within tourism studies. She holds a PhD in tourism from the University of Aveiro. She was a visiting PhD student at Tema Genus (gender studies) at the Linköping University in Sweden. She is an integrated member of GOVCOPP – Research Unit in Governance, Competitiveness and Public Policies from the University of Aveiro and has participated in research projects in the field of gender studies funded by the Portuguese Foundation for Science and Technology. She has published several articles in reputed journals, including the *Annals of Tourism Research*.

César Caselin, Universidad Autónoma del Estado de México, Texcoco, Mexico. César holds a bachelor's degree in tourism from the Universidad Autónoma del

Estado de México, Mexico. His research interest is sexual diversity in tourism and leisure.

Gürel Çetin, Professor, Faculty of Economics, Istanbul University, Istanbul, Turkey. Gürel earned his PhD in business administration from the Istanbul University in 2012. Since then, he has been teaching tourism and marketing courses in several institutions. His research interests include entrepreneurship, sustainable development, tourism, and marketing. He also serves as the co-editor of the *Journal of Tourismology*.

Carlos Costa, Professor and Head of the Department of Economics, Management Industrial Engineering and Tourism (DEGEIT), University of Aveiro, Aveiro, Portugal. Carlos has more than 25 years of academic and professional experience in tourism and planning. He is the head of the Tourism Research Group of the Research Center in Governance, Competitiveness and Public Policies (GOVCOPP) and the leader of the PhD tourism programme of the University of Aveiro. He is also the editor of the *Journal of Tourism & Development* (*Revista de Turismo e Desenvolvimento*). He is involved in several national and international tourism projects in the areas of tourism planning and development, policy and strategies, tourism management, tourism innovation, gender in tourism, and education and research in tourism.

Kynda R. Curtis, Professor and Extension Economist, Department of Applied Economics, Utah State University, Logan, Utah. Kynda received her PhD in Economics from Washington State University in 2003. Her research interests include agriculture/food marketing, direct-to-consumer marketing, as well as consumer demand for value-added, specialty, and differentiated foods. As an extension specialist, she assists small-scale growers in developing new markets for their products and assessing the feasibility of new food products and value-added processes. She has received extension group programme awards from the Agricultural and Applied Economics Association (AAEA) and the Western Agricultural Economics Association (WAEA), as well as the 2014 AAEA President's Award and the 2016 Food Distribution Research Society (FDRS) award for the best journal article.

Alana Dillette, Associate Professor, Payne School of Hospitality, and Tourism Management, San Diego State University and Co-Director of Tourism RESET. Originally from the islands of The Bahamas, Alana is always trying to maintain her connection to home through research on sustainable tourism initiatives for small island states. Her other research interests include issues around diversity and inclusion, more specifically looking at the intersection between tourism, race, gender, and ethnicity. Currently, she is working on research to gain a better understanding of the African-American travel experience.

Frederic Dimanche, Professor and Director, Ted Rogers School of Hospitality and Tourism Management, Ryerson University, Toronto, Canada. Fredric's research interests are about destination and tourism management and marketing. He has published numerous tourism-related research articles and has co-authored one book (in French) on hospitality management and another (in English) on tourism management in Russia. He has worked in New Orleans (USA) and Nice (France). He is a past president of the Travel and Tourism Research Association Europe and a member of the International Academy for the Study of Tourism.

Buket Buluk Eşitti, Associate Professor, School of Graduate Studies, Department of Tourism Management, Çanakkale Onsekiz Mart University, Çanakkale, Turkey. Buket received her master's degree from the Department of Tourism Management, Institute of Social Sciences, Çanakkale Onsekiz Mart University in 2016 and her PhD degree from Çanakkale Onsekiz Mart University in 2020. Her main fields of study are behavioural sciences, tourism marketing, sustainable tourism, food and beverage management, media and tourism, tourism and travel technology, travel agencies, and e-tourism.

Sally Everett, Professor and Vice Dean (Education), King's Business School, King's College London, England. Sally is the Academic Lead for Inclusive Education for King's College London. Sally was previously the Deputy Dean for the Business School at Anglia Ruskin University (2013–2018) and Chair of their inclusive working group. Sally is a National Teaching Fellow (2017), Principal Fellow of the Higher Education Academy (2013), Collaborative Award for Teaching Excellence award holder (2016), and is the Equality Officer for the Association of National Teaching Fellows. Sally is a member of the Chartered Association of Business School's Race Equality Working Group and their Equality and Diversity Committee. Before her role at Anglia Ruskin University, she was the Head of Department for tourism, events, and marketing at the University of Bedfordshire. Sally has published widely on inclusive education, student employability, diversity, and on the impacts of tourism.

Amy D. Hagerman, Assistant Professor, Department of Agricultural Economics, Oklahoma State University, Stillwater, Oklahoma, USA. Amy works on issues related to Agriculture and Food Policy. She completed her Bachelor of Science in agricultural economics at the Oklahoma State University in 2004, her Master of Science and her Ph.D. in agricultural economics at the Texas A&M University in 2005 and 2009, respectively, and her postdoc with the Foreign Animal and Zoonotic Disease Defense Center. Prior to joining Oklahoma State University, she spent seven years with the United States Department of Agriculture working on economic consequence assessments of trade and animal health policies on US agricultural industries. She focuses her integrated research and extension programme on understanding and management of the risks of agriculture, including animal health, extreme weather, and market fluctuations.

Linda J. Ingram, Adjunct Professor, Tourism and Event Management, George Mason University, Fairfax, Virginia, USA. Linda teaches sustainable tourism management and global issues in tourism. She earned her MS and PhD from the Texas A&M University. Her research interests include tourism, sustainability, gender studies, and historic preservation. She has published in several journals and released two edited books.

Amit Kama, Senior Lecturer, Department of Communication, Yezreel Valley Academic College, Yezreel Valley, Israel. Amit's research focuses on minority groups (LGBT, people with disabilities, and migrant workers) and cultural manifestations of the body. He has published around 40 peer-reviewed papers and book chapters and 6 books. He is the chair of the Israel Communication Association and of Gender and Sexuality Committee of The Academy of the Hebrew Language. He has been active in Israeli LGBT organisations since 1982.

İsmail Kizilirmak, Professor, Faculty of Economics, Istanbul University, Istanbul, Turkey. Ismail received his PhD degree from the Department of Tourism Management, Institute of Social Science, Istanbul University in 1996. He has 26 years of professional experience in lecturing, training, and coordinating scientific research in the tourism sector, supporting governmental and non-governmental institutions and the private sector. His research focuses on tourism marketing, tourism policy and planning, front office management, tourism and travel management, current issues in tourism, tourism management, and MICE.

Styliani (Stella) Kladou, Hellenic Mediterranean University, Crete, Greece. Stella is a postdoc researcher at the Hellenic Mediterranean University in Crete, Greece. She has served as an assistant professor in the Tourism Administration Department at the Boğaziçi University in Istanbul, Turkey and a senior lecturer at the Sheffield Hallam University in the United Kingdom. Her PhD research was realised in cooperation with the Hellenic Open University in Greece, the Istanbul Bilgi University in Turkey, and the University of Rome La Sapienza. She has published in prominent academic journals and has co-edited books relating to tourism (peer-to-peer accommodation and community resilience). She is an International Place Brand Specialist for the Place Brand Observer and is on the editorial board of the *Journal of Qualitative Research in Tourism*. Her research mainly pertains to place branding, cultural and wine tourism, and digital marketing.

Carlos Monterrubio, Lecturer, Universidad Autónoma del Estado de México, Texcoco, Mexico. Carlos holds a PhD in tourism from the Manchester Metropolitan University, UK. He is a researcher and lecturer in tourism at the Universidad Autónoma del Estado de México, Mexico. His main research interests are tourism impacts and sexuality and gender diversity in tourism and leisure.

Yaniv Poria, Academic Director and Professor, Department of Hotel and Tourism Management, Ben-Gurion University, Be'er Sheva, Israel. Yaniv is the academic director of Eilat Campus and a professor at the Department of Hotel and Tourism Management, Ben-Gurion University in Israel.

Arie Reichel, Professor Emeritus, Guilford Glazer Faculty of Business and Management, Ben-Gurion University, Be'er Sheva, Israel. Arie is the founding

Contributors   xiii

dean of the BGU's southern campus at the resort city of Eilat and the founding head of the Department of Hotel and Tourism Management on BGU's main campus in Be'er Sheva.

Susan L. Slocum, Associate Professor, Tourism and Event Management, George Mason University, Fairfax, Virginia, USA. Susan has worked on regional planning and development for 15 years and worked with rural communities in Tanzania, the United Kingdom, Belarus, and the United States. Her primary focus is on rural sustainable development, policy implementation, and food tourism, specifically working with small businesses and communities in less advantaged areas. Sue received her doctoral education from the Clemson University and was a Fulbright Scholar in 2020. She has published 11 books and numerous academic articles. She is also on the editorial boards of several tourism journals.

Debra Tropp, Principal, Debra Tropp Consulting, Kensington, Maryland, USA. Debra spent more than 26 years at the USDA Agricultural Marketing Service's Transportation and Marketing Program, retiring from federal service in early 2019. Over the course of her career, she served in a variety of roles, including agricultural economist, interim staff officer for the Federal-State Marketing Improvement Program, team leader and chief of the Farmers Market and Direct Farm Marketing Research Branch, and finally, deputy director of AMS's Marketing Service Program. In this capacity, she served as the primary editor for the AMS-sponsored report "The Economics of Local Food Systems: A Toolkit to Guide Community Discussions, Assessments and Choices" (March 2016). Debra holds a bachelor's degree in political science from the Bryn Mawr College and an MS in international relations/economic and political development from the Columbia University.

Craig Webster, Associate Professor, Department of Applied Business Studies, Ball State University, Muncie, Indiana, USA. Craig received an MA and a PhD in political science from the Binghamton University in New York State and an MBA from the Intercollege, Cyprus. He has taught at the Ithaca College, the College of Tourism and Hotel Management, and the University of Nicosia. His research interests include the political economy of tourism, event management, and robots in tourism and hospitality. He has published in many peer-reviewed journals internationally and is the co-editor of two books.

Kelly-Ann Wright, Recreation and Leisure Studies, University of Waterloo, Ontario, Canada. Kelly-Ann is a PhD student. Her research is currently situated at the intersections of climate change, disasters, racial capitalism, and the rights and livelihoods of tourism-dependent communities and workers. She aims to apply a critical approach to tourism research to disrupt the status quo and to reimagine tourism futures. She obtained a Master of Environmental Studies in geography at the University of Waterloo and holds a Bachelor of

Science in hospitality and tourism management. Alongside her academic work, she is an urban sketcher and watercolourist. She enjoys gardening, farming, hiking, and backcountry canoeing. She lives and works on the traditional territory of many First Nations, including the Wyandot peoples, Mississaugas of the Credit, the Anishnabeg, the Chippewa, and the Hauden.

1 Introduction

Stefanie Benjamin and Alana Dillette

Understanding diversity, equity, and inclusion

Interest in diversity, equity, and inclusion (DEI) has gained momentum amongst academics and practitioners across the hospitality and tourism industries in recent years (Benjamin et al., 2020). With good reason, some of the benefits of DEI to organisations include diversified talent recruitment, enhanced customer service, and positive organisational culture (Manoharan & Singal, 2017). This, along with significant societal events highlighting a historically capitalistic and racist system, brings to light some of the major inequities that still exist within the tourism realm. For example, COVID-19 has severely affected numerous industries, with hospitality and tourism being one of the hardest hit (Benjamin et al., 2020). Along with this global pandemic, new strands of the virus, along with other viruses like monkeypox, only highlight and amplify the systems of oppression and marginalisation at work in tourism sites and tourism research (Benjamin & Laughtner, 2022). To be truly transformational, tourism must bring an actionable focus on equity and inclusion.

A resilient tourism industry must be more equitable and just, in terms of how it operates and how it affects people and places. Thus, a commitment to inclusion requires specific changes in practices and decisions at multiple levels, along with growing a more comprehensive ethical framework (Kalargyrou & Costen, 2017). This mindset pivot requires us, as tourists, corporations, and educators, to step away from a selfish, hedonistic perspective and critically examine our perceptions and understandings of tourism with a truly inclusive focus. Taking action to deconstruct racism, dismantle white supremacy and bigotry, and move towards social equality requires strategic planning and practice. As such, the scholars in *Inclusion in tourism: Understanding institutional discrimination and bias* help to expose and engage in difficult conversations regarding race, gender, sexual orientation, accessibility, and additional inequities intertwined within the institutions of tourism and pedagogy. Armed with awareness, understanding, knowledge, and empathy from these difficult conversations, the authors of this book have used their research, networks, and daily encounters to speak up, stand up, and intervene against inequality.

The term "research" is inextricably linked to European imperialism and colonialism (Tuck & Yang, 2014), which endorses and privileges Western knowledge systems and their epistemologies (Denzin et al., 2008). However, tourism scholars can disrupt hegemonic Eurocentric research design by adopting critical theory-informed methodologies like counter-narratives (Benjamin & Laughtner, 2022). The potential of counter-narratives as a transformative methodology can contribute towards the development of Critical Race Tourism – helping to curate scholarship with the potential to change how people understand issues of race and racism, sex and sexuality, disability, and gender; to help empower marginalised communities; and to infuse joy into tourism landscapes. In tourism studies specifically, this focus on healing and justice requires changes in practices and decisions at multiple levels with support from a wide ethical framework (Benjamin et al., 2020). Changing the narrative, inviting the community into the research design and analysis, and "planning a tourism future not fuelled solely by demand but guided by an ethics of care, social and environmental justice, and racial reconciliation" (Benjamin et al., 2020, p. 5) may serve as a dynamic explainer of institutional and structural racism in tourism studies – where our discipline and industry can face and centre marginalised voices with the goal of achieving social justice. Before we begin, let us first ground ourselves in common language around terms and concepts that revolve around inclusion, diversity, and implicit bias to assist with the interpretation of the work presented in this book.

Over its history, tourism has normalised a series of systemic inequalities that contribute, in part, to the dilemma in which the industry and its communities now find themselves (Higgins-Desbiolles, 2010). There is an opportunity – if not an outright necessity – not just to regain travel and tourism dollars and market position but to reform and repair the industry in meaningful ways. Inclusion is the intentional, open embrace of diversity by a community so that each individual feels not only included but accepted, connected, understood, supported, and valued. True inclusion acknowledges and works to dismantle systems of discrimination and oppression by dominant social groups. This includes understanding what diversity actually means and how institutionalised and systemic inequities work to uphold power and privilege of dominant identities. For instance, white supremacy is a historically based, institutionally ingrained system of exploitation and oppression of continents, nations, and people of colour by white people and nations of the European continent. Race and racism are endemic, permanent, and ingrained in the cultural landscape; consequently, racism looks and feels ordinary and natural to society and promotes a culture and history where whiteness is the norm (Benjamin & Laughtner, 2022).

As the world becomes more diverse, companies must adapt and welcome a greater range of diversity. Diversity refers to the range of human characteristics and socially constructed identities (typically, as reflected in a group of people), potentially including, but not limited to, age, body size, ethnicity, gender, gender identity, intellectual or political perspective, language, life experience, national origin, physical or cognitive ability, race, religious belief, relationship or family status, sexual orientation, socioeconomic status, and other intersecting identities.

Additionally, diversity has a direct impact on corporate success, the economy, and the world at large. Such diversity brings greater innovation and creativity as different perspectives contribute to success. Narrowly focused companies miss enormous opportunities in engaging their workforce, reaching a greater customer base, making companies stronger, and helping to reduce absenteeism and turnover.

We all have unique ways of viewing and understanding the world around us. These perspectives are often influenced by the sum of our cultures, our educational backgrounds, our personal experiences, and our upbringings. Our interactions with various people groups – or lack thereof – may negatively affect our perceptions of specific individuals and cause us to develop biases towards them. Our natural tendency towards categorising people into social groupings (Crisp & Meleady, 2012) further exacerbates this issue because it may lead us to make assumptions about people, and thereby shut down opportunities to address critical issues that prevent mutual understanding. This phenomenon is known as *implicit bias*, and it is something that we all have as a result of our life experiences. However, tourism studies have yet to embrace these deeper, more difficult concepts around identity, be it from the perspective of the researcher or the researched (Benjamin & Laughtner, 2022). Consequently, the tourism scholars in this book continue to work on unpacking and critically examining discrimination and bias in the hospitality and tourism industries, which are highlighted below in five themes: representation in tourism marketing and branding; race-based discrimination in tourism; unpacking gender and sexual orientation challenges; overcoming institutional discrimination in industry and education; and accessible and inclusive tourism.

Representation in tourism marketing and branding

Tourism promotional materials exist in diverse forms, including travel brochures, rack cards, websites, and online booking platforms that influence a visitor's perception of a destination (Benjamin et al., 2021). These advertising and promotional materials are used by visitors for a variety of reasons, ranging from finding activities to learning about the culture of their destination (Pritchard & Morgan, 2000). As texts are interspersed with images, they can also perform a social role by shaping the tourist imagination – they provide their readers an opportunity to escape their everyday life and imagine life as a tourist in an exotic destination (Burton & Klemm, 2011; Francesconi, 2011). These promotional images are not just about displaying products and attractions, they also convey representations of social groups and societies. However, marketing and branding still remain very homogenous, consisting of dominant ideologies and identities representative of white, heteronormative, and non-disabled images (Benjamin & Dillette, 2021; Dillette & Benjamin, 2022).

Embracing and understanding the counter-history and narratives of destinations help to create and curate authentic, unique, and local touristic experiences. However, dismantling power structures and dynamics can be difficult when trying to incorporate minoritised perspectives into destination branding, marketing, and representation. In Chapter 2, Kladou helps to unpack the ways in which two small islands, Gökçeada and Bozcaada, located in contemporary Turkey, primarily focus on the gastro-cultural attributes of local populations. Their work suggests that featuring local cultural identity in branding strategies can boost civic identity and help to support inclusion, sustainability, and multiculturalism in states. Furthermore, their exploratory research serves as an example of how institutions may collide with the priorities and efforts of tourism stakeholder groups in a response to regulatory, normative, and cognitive institutional characteristics and destination branding. Incorporating and co-collaborating with minoritised populations when branding or marketing a destination is essential to the sustainability and authenticity of the travel and tourism landscape. By doing so, difficult dialogues and complicated histories can be better understood through the lens of underrepresented populations, helping to curate holistic, authentic, and truthful narratives and experiences.

Race-based discrimination in tourism

Unfortunately, tourism has operated under a white-dominant hierarchy since its inception. As Wright and Dimanche highlight in Chapter 3, it originally stemmed from European colonial expansion in the 1500s, which supplied agricultural commodities and slave or cheap labour to European countries (Amin, 1976). Thus, it is no surprise that racial discrimination and bias continue to deeply impact the industry. Wright and Dimanche take us to the North, where they examine how Canada's immigration policy has supported the racialisation of immigrants as cheap labour that face institutionalised de-skilling, discrimination, and exploitation in various sectors, including hospitality and tourism. Sadly, the authors reveal that Canada's immigration policy is inherently racist, the consequences of which are far-reaching. They highlight the immigration pathway as "perpetuating white cultural domination established during colonial times, and racist stereotypes about the social position of black and brown bodies, as labourers and entertainers for white tourist consumption". Suggestions to address these deep inequities include an overhaul of local labour laws and immigration policies by the Canadian government.

However, it is not until recently that this has begun to make its mark in the tourism literature. As Goodwin (2020) points out:

> The travel industry tends to think of itself as a space of leisure, fun, and escape where such things like racism are left behind for good times. The problem is, for Black individuals and people of colour, escaping racism is not something they can do by taking a vacation. Racism, like in many other sectors of society, has been built into the travel industry, both knowingly and unknowingly
>
> (p. 910).

Furthermore, it is no secret that Black people in the United States have been plagued with racial inequalities, segregation, and discrimination for centuries (Foster, 1999).

In Chapter 5, Slocum and Ingram discuss US Black history, from the Jim Crow era (1954–1968) through the present Black Lives Matter movement. They highlight the ways in which American history has perpetuated racism and discrimination against African Americans, specifically in the tourism industry. During Jim Crow, there were many legalised "separate but equal" spaces in the travel and tourism industries – buses, restaurants, hotels, and motels – thereby inhibiting the physical movement of African American travellers (Little, 2019; Thompson-Miller et al., 2015). Moving forwards into the civil rights era where the Civil Rights Act of 1964 abolished Jim Crow (Hall, 2014), the struggle for freedom was now transforming into a struggle for true equality within a system that was still steeped in institutionalised racism. This era did, however, make way for the Great Migration when many African American families moved to the North to escape the deep seeded racism in the Southern United States. Fast forward to the present day, the Black Lives Matter movement, which is grounded in the civil rights movement, bears witness to the fact that while progress has been made, the promises of equality across racial lines, unfortunately, remain unfulfilled (McKersie, 2021).

In conclusion, Slocum and Ingram challenge us to rethink the way tourism stakeholders conduct business, both formally and informally in order to produce authentic inclusive spaces. They suggest, "once an organisation has begun addressing racism from within, it should begin to showcase its achievements, ensuring that African American visitors are welcome and that they feel akin to the organisation through visible commitments to diversity". The result is a continued and ever-evolving celebration of the diversity of our unique life experiences and perspectives, growth in market share, and truly inclusive access to the world's largest industry.

Unpacking gender and sexual orientation challenges

It is no secret that organisational leadership and management have traditionally been hierarchically gendered with a preference for cisgender male individuals (Hearn, 2001). In Chapter 4, Eşitti provides an examination of gender equality and career barriers that female employees face in the tourism sector. Providing a thorough literature review, Eşitti highlights the various "glass ceiling" categories, which include (1) barriers caused by individual factors such as taking on multiple roles or personal preferences and perceptions; (2) barriers caused by organisational factors such as culture, policies, and lack of mentorship; and (3) barriers caused by social factors, such as occupational distinction and gender-based stereotypes. Enhancing the discussion around gender equity in tourism is Chapter 10, where Carvalho and Costa unpack the nuances of the lived experiences of 24 female senior managers in Portuguese hotels and travel businesses. Interestingly, their work reveals that the women interviewed feel they do in fact have individual agency to accept or reject traditional gender role expectations. While the authors point out that although women cannot truly "undo" gender, this should still be viewed as a "step forward" for gender equity and inclusivity. They provide evidence that women can unsettle gender stereotypes which, over time, will have a net positive benefit for gender equity. As the authors argue "capturing how gender is done well and differently allows for the recognition of the fluid and paradoxical nature of doing gender". Heading back to Chapter 4, Eşitti concludes with a set of meaningful suggestions for the tourism industry to take into consideration while stirring for greater gender equality. Some highlights include developing legal structures and regulatory mechanisms to eliminate gender discrimination, along with providing equal investment and financing opportunities for female investors and entrepreneurs. Furthermore, Eşitti encourages women to feel empowered while chasing after roles that have traditionally been out of reach, establishing networks of support, and taking risks to seek new opportunities.

Perhaps it goes without saying that, similar to other traditionally marginalised populations, people with sexual identities outside of the mainstream heteronormative "cis-man and cis-woman" combination encounter a plethora of biases based on either forthright or implicit homophobia or sheer ignorance. And, while the visibility and social acceptance of gay people have generally improved, gay men continue to experience the negative consequences of ingrained cultural conditions and social prejudice in the form of discrimination and violence. In Chapters 9 and 13, we gain a deeper understanding of these experiences specific to gay men and consider the future of travellers with this sexual identity in a traditionally heteronormative world. In Chapter 9, Monterrubio and Caselin provide us with an in-depth qualitative study where they conducted interviews to explore the lived experiences of gay male travellers in Mexico.

In Chapter 13, Kama takes us through an auto-ethnography sharing his personal experiences navigating sexuality and identity as a gay man in predominantly heterosexual and heteronormative circumstances. Kama poses a question that may seem obvious but is not often broached – why is sexual orientation relevant to being a tourist at all? In his vignette, he shares unique perspectives around these questions so often faced by same-sex couples: do we really need to come out? When? At the time of booking a room or upon checking in? Will we be unwelcome or frowned upon? In the chapter, Kama reveals ways in which being a gay tourist has implications across numerous spaces, including lodging, transportation, events, venues, festivals, and food and beverage establishments. Kama also makes the connection that some of his experiences with homophobia have often been ironically clouded by the intersectionality of racism as his partner is quite dark-skinned. Thus, bringing to light an important note that intersectionality amongst marginalised groups should not be ignored in this ongoing right for true equity. Unfortunately, both chapters reveal that gay men, particularly those that display affection in public and those that are perceived as effeminate, are more vulnerable to discrimination and verbal and physical abuse, thereby asserting that gay men's participation in tourism is conditional on not being too overtly gay, and therefore, denying their own sexual identity. In conclusion, Kama reminds us that "homophobia and heterosexism – like other forms of prejudice and discrimination – cannot end instantaneously" but that changing mindsets will require the longevity of commitment and authentic care within and outside of the LGBTQIA population.

Introduction 7

Lastly, BDSM (bondage and discipline, dominance and submission, sadism, and masochism) practitioners face similar challenges, both in events where kink is practiced and in more casual social circles. In Chapter 12, Webster shows how anonymity remains vital to the acceptance of their social groups, as a necessity to avoid harassment, violence, and discrimination. While there is a great deal of speculation about the commercialisation of kink events for the travel and leisure industries, the stigma of being associated with this lifestyle has resulted in "a tendency for members of the community to remain in the closet".

Overcoming institutional discrimination in industry and education

In many ways, the policies, laws, social structures, and institutions in Western society have operated to perpetuate the preservation of historical legacies of numerous inequities with or without the intention of individuals and groups in society. Tourism and higher education are two such existing structures that impose social, economic, and health costs on minoritised populations that influence their well-being and human dignity (Elias & Paradies, 2021). In Chapters 6 and 7, scholars unpack the ways in which institutional bias and discrimination have impacted the United States Department of Agriculture (USDA) and the challenges behind decolonising tourism curriculum in higher education.

Tourism projects, including food and agricultural tourism, are supported by many USDA programmes. USDA programmes have always been and are still homogeneous, which means that socially disadvantaged minoritised populations such as women, people of colour, the LGBTQ community, and veterans have been disenfranchised. However, in Chapter 6, Curtis, Hagerman, and Tropp discuss the ways in which the USDA works on overcoming institutional biases and discrimination by providing assistance to socially disadvantaged groups seeking to develop food and agricultural-based tourism projects. This framework is working towards creating an equitable landscape for marginalised communities in government-based programmes. Best practices, likely to increase the probability of success in other government-based programmes, are also provided in the chapter.

As educators, it is our responsibility to facilitate difficult conversations that encourage an "unlearning" of the old "normal" of tourism and a re-learning of what might be possible and more equitable (Benjamin & Dillette, 2021). This starts with revising and critiquing the current tourism curriculum and pedagogy. In Chapter 7, Everett argues for looking beyond Western epistemologies with the decolonisation of tourism education. Informed by Hiatt's (2006) ADKAR model of change management, this chapter structures decolonisation using six "C words", moving from challenge, consciousness, conversations, co-conspirators, and construction to how this might ultimately shape the curriculum. The chapter provides a framework that acts as a starting point for reflection and prompts consideration about how tourism instructors might disrupt the educational scaffolding that has ostracised marginal voices and dominated our teaching. Furthermore, Everett contributes to the "critical turn" literature where the tourism curriculum recognises tourism as more than an industry, instead as a social force capable of positive and just impacts (Higgins-Desbiolles, 2006).

Accessible and inclusive tourism

Underrepresented populations in society, including people of colour, LGBTQIA, and people with disabilities (PWDs), are growing markets in hospitality and tourism and make a significant economic contribution to the industry. Focusing specifically on PWDs, globally one billion people, or 15 percent of the world's population, experience some form of disability, and this number is increasing due to an ageing population, the spread of chronic diseases, and improvements in measuring disabilities (World Health Organization, 2019). The recognition of PWDs in the tourism industry has been discussed in relation to access to tourism venues and services but has yet to embrace an inclusive perspective where PWD travellers are recognised and actively involved in the ethical production, consumption, or sharing of tourism benefits (Benjamin et al., 2021). In Chapter 8, Altun, Çetin, and Kizilirmak offer a model of an accessible tourism cycle that serves as a framework for determining *othering* factors in accessible tourism. Their ongoing research explores the obstacles faced in the decision-making processes of persons with disabilities in tourism activities, helping to create the Participation Cycle of Persons with Disability in Tourism Activities model. Advocating for accessible tourism calls on service providers and destination managers to ensure that "all persons, regardless of their physical or cognitive needs, are able to use and enjoy the available amenities in an equitable and sustainable manner" (United Nations, 2019, paragraph 11).

Small and Harris (2012) claimed that tourism settings seem to attract "beautiful people" and that those who do not fit this image are not "welcome in paradise" (p. 687). This image of Eurocentric beauty traditionally excludes tourists who do not "fit this mould" of bodily perfection and perpetuates a non-inclusive touristic atmosphere. In Chapter 11, Poria, Reichel, and Beal explore the lived touristic experiences of obese people (OP) in relation to flights, hotels, restaurants, theme parks, and museums in the United States. Interviewing 36 self-identifying OP, their findings revealed that in most cases, OP felt safer in their home environment due to the uncomfortable and unwelcoming *gaze* from other people, often resulting in self-afflicted seclusion. Creating an inclusive touristic experience starts with designing a welcoming environment. As such, one of the major implications of their study suggests that tourism and travel organisations should provide OP with information about accessibility.

Conclusion

The scholarship reviewed in this book illuminates many of the ways that racism, sexism, ableism, homophobia, and nationalism manifest in higher education, industry, and touristic landscapes. As co-directors of Tourism RESET, an initiative made up of scholars and industry partners advocating for equitable spaces in tourism, we hope to see more touristic inclusivity scholarship in the future. Leaning in towards the discomfort of difficult dialogue and dark histories helps to sustain an authentic touristic landscape that is advocating for equity. However, working towards inclusive tourism requires constant awareness of institutional discrimination and bias. We believe it is important that advocates of equity do not become overly focused on these daily experiences but also maintain a focus on the systemic ways in which power, politics, and dominant ideologies operate and must be addressed.

Conceiving tourism as a social force (rather than just a capitalistic venture) and empowered by critical thought epistemologies, one can see how tourism has the power to change people and societies (Benjamin et al., 2021). This shift in mindset requires a "critical turn" in order to critically challenge and critique our perception and understanding of tourism towards an equitable focus. The scholars in this book have worked towards curating a truly inclusive tourism landscape by calling for decolonisation of curriculum to amplify marginalised travellers' lived experiences. The way forward is to encourage more of this critical thinking, research, and teaching that supports space for a scholarship that challenges dominant ideologies. However, producing critical and diverse research also calls for scholars to continuously work on unpacking their own implicit biases. For scholars who hold dominant identities, we encourage taking time to truly reflect on how they can use such privileges for actionable change, as well as working on strategies to co-collaborate with minoritised communities and disseminate such research beyond academic landscapes. Working together to disrupt and dismantle Western, Eurocentric-centred methods, theories, pedagogy, and ways of conducting research can help establish a more inclusive and rich touristic discipline.

References

Amin, S. (1976). *Unequal development: An essay on the social formations of peripheral capitalism*. Harvester Press.

Benjamin, S., Bottone, E., & Lee, M. (2021). Beyond accessibility: Exploring the representation of people with disabilities in tourism promotional materials. *Journal of Sustainable Tourism, 29*(2–3), 295–313.

Benjamin, S., Dillette, A., & Alderman, D. H. (2020). "We can't return to normal": Committing to tourism equity in the post-pandemic age. *Tourism Geographies, 22*(3), 476–483.

Benjamin, S., & Dillette, A. K. (2021). Black travel movement: Systemic racism informing tourism. *Annals of Tourism Research, 88*, 103169.

Benjamin, S., & Laughtner, J. (2022). Toward critical race tourism: Valuing counter-narratives and endarkened storywork. *Journal of Sustainable Tourism*, 1–17.

Burton, D., & Klemm, M. (2011). Whiteness, ethnic minorities, and advertising travel brochures. *The Service Industries Journal, 31*(5), 679–693.

Crisp, R. J., & Meleady, R. (2012). Adapting to a multicultural future. *Science, 336*(6083), 853–855.

Denzin, N. K., Lincoln, Y. S., & Smith, L. T. (Eds.). (2008). *Handbook of critical and indigenous methodologies*. SAGE Publications.

Dillette, A., & Benjamin, S. (2022). The black travel movement: A catalyst for social change. *Journal of Travel Research, 61*(3), 463–476.

Elias, A., & Paradies, Y. (2021). The costs of institutional racism and its ethical implications for healthcare. *Journal of Bioethical Inquiry, 18*(1), 45–58.

Foster, M. S. (1999). "In the face of Jim Crow": Prosperous blacks and vacations, travel and outdoor leisure, 1890–1945. *Journal of Negro History, 84*(2), 130–149.

Francesconi, S. (2011). Images and writing in tourist brochures. *Journal of Tourism and Cultural Change, 9*(4), 341–356.

Goodwin, M. (2020). Lessons in race and racism in the legal academy: Notes on Pauli Murray. *Rutgers University Law Review, 73*, 913.

Hall, P. (2014). *Cities of tomorrow: An intellectual history of urban planning and design since 1880*. John Wiley & Sons.

Hearn, J. (2001, March). Men and gender equality: Resistance, responsibilities and reaching out. In *Men and gender equality conference* (Swedish EU Presidency Calendar of Meetings) (pp. 15–16).

Hiatt, J. (2006). *ADKAR: A model for change in business, government, and our community*. Prosci.

Higgins-Desbiolles, F. (2006). More than an "industry": The forgotten power of tourism as a social force. *Tourism Management, 27*(6), 1192–1208.

Higgins-Desbiolles, F. (2010). The elusiveness of sustainability in tourism: The culture-ideology of consumerism and its implications. *Tourism and Hospitality Research, 10*(2), 116–129.

Kalargyrou, V., & Costen, W. (2017). Diversity management research in hospitality and tourism: Past, present and future. *International Journal of Contemporary Hospitality Management, 29*(1), 68–114.

Little, B. (2019). *Before the green book, these resorts offered hidden safe havens for Black Americans*. Retrieved December 12, 2021, from www.history.com/news/green-book-black-travel-resorts-jim-crow

Manoharan, A., & Singal, M. (2017). A systematic literature review of research on diversity and diversity management in the hospitality literature. *International Journal of Hospitality Management, 66*, 77–91.

McKersie, R. B. (2021). The 1960s civil rights movement and black lives matter: Social protest from a negotiation perspective. *Negotiation Journal, 37*(3), 301–323.

Pritchard, A., & Morgan, N. (2000). Constructing tourism landscapes – gender, sexuality, and space. *Tourism Geographies, 2*(2), 115–139.

Small, J., & Harris, G. (2012). Obesity and tourism: Rights and responsibilities. *Annals of Tourism Research, 39*(2), 686–707.

Thompson-Miller, R., Feagin, J. R., & Picca, L. H. (2015). *Jim Crow's legacy: The lasting impact of segregation*. Rowman & Littlefield.

Tuck, E., & Yang, K. W. (2014). Unbecoming claims: Pedagogies of refusal in qualitative research. *Qualitative Inquiry, 20*(6), 811–818.

United Nations. (2019). *Promoting accessible tourism for all*. Department of Economic and Social Affairs: Disability. www.un.org/development/desa/disabilities/issues/promoting-accessible-tourism-for-all.html

World Health Organization. (2019). www.who.int/

Part I
Discrimination policies in tourism

2 Gastro-cultural identities for place branding

The forbidden fruit of minorities?

Styliani (Stella) Kladou

Introduction

Place branding experts and scholars emphasise how place brands should focus on "plans that define the most realistic, competitive, and compelling strategic vision for the country, region, or city" (Anholt, 2003, p. 212). Institutions in fields affiliated with place branding have only recently been investigated in the tourism literature (see Fong et al., 2018; Lavandoski et al., 2013). Relevant efforts predominantly focus on resident communities' perceptions in relation to tourism institutions (Nunkoo et al., 2012, 2013), yet these do not seem to provide an explicit investigation nor a holistic approach to all resident groups, including minorities. This exclusion contradicts the importance of tourism and place branding initiatives to reflect policies that accommodate different minority cultures in order to support multiculturalist states[1] (Hellyer, 2006).

In place branding, the stakeholder groups are, by nature, much more diverse and complex than those in corporate branding. In place branding and marketing, "co-creation occurs and is sustained by institutions that form open systems (service ecosystems) that interact with one another" (Brown, 2018, p. 106). In the tourism industry, actors have been found to respond to the changes of institutional factors by adopting an institutional logic of coopetition. Actors collaborate and ally with strategic partners while, at the same time, competing to achieve coopetition through exploiting, exploring, bridging, sharing, and boundary spanning with other actors (Fong et al., 2018). This generic co-creative approach, although relevant to place branding, only presents part of the picture. Paraphrasing from Warnaby (2009, p. 411), "the [place] and its institutions become the forum in which the various (place) stakeholders communicate and (hopefully) reach some consensus as to their future development – through the articulation and offer of place value propositions to consumers". Such a forum could further inspire identification with a civic identity regardless of the resident group's diversified cultural identities, thereby moving beyond dimensions of difference and towards national inclusion (Dovidio et al., 2010; Pehrson et al., 2009). However, the consideration of different actors and stakeholder groups, when developing branding strategies and the inclusiveness of institutions, is subject to power relations (e.g. Paul et al., 2004)

DOI: 10.4324/9781003255413-3

in the effort to move from the multicultural state status to the multiculturalist one (Hellyer, 2006).

Culture emerges as an institution that influences, and is influenced by, various macro- and micro-environmental factors, including history, branding, and actors' power. Especially since the 19th and 20th centuries, the decisions regarding the transition of Turkey from the Ottoman Empire to diverse nation states, which seek to emphasise ethnic similarities over differences, have often been troublesome. Such decisions transformed populations into minorities, specifically those whose ancestors lived, thrived, and developed various cultural representations in given geographies. Specifically, the establishment of the Turkish Republic in 1923 meant replacing the common culture and "sense of belonging" of the populations previously residing in the former Ottoman Empire with a new homogenised republican community called "the nation" (Babul, 2012). Following the First World War and the resulting unrest in the region, the Lausanne Convention foresaw, amongst others, the compulsory mutual exchange of religious minority groups between the newly founded Turkish Republic and neighbouring Greece.

Such political decisions failed to comprehend the role and characteristics of culture. Although tangible culture was transferred beyond national borders, in terms of architectural and artistic influences, intangible culture is more difficult to conform to national borders. Cuisine emerges as an example of a (gastro-) cultural characteristic that extends beyond borders and unites people – either those who used to live together prior to being separated by nation-state developments or those who developed similar gastro-cultural attributes in response to akin geographical and climate conditions. However, institutional approaches can either reinforce the (gastro-) cultural bridges and local identities or seek to nationalise culture and promote a nation-wide identity. This chapter explores the case of two small islands located in contemporary Turkey and serves as an example of how institutions may collide with the priorities and efforts of tourism stakeholder groups in a response to regulatory, normative, and cognitive institutional characteristics and destination branding.

Literature review

Culture, identity, and inclusion in place branding

Culture is the key element mirroring place identity. The uniqueness of a local culture, paired with relevant physical resources, can create a unique value proposition (e.g. Anholt, 2003) and should include a variety of resources which, in pursuit of destination competitiveness, are difficult for other localities to duplicate. Such resources can be traced in the unique natural environment and cultural heritage of a region, which includes physical heritage and elements that reflect rich history, religion, or other cultural expressions. Cultural resources can be both tangible (e.g. heritage reflected in arts and architecture) and intangible (e.g. music), and include elements such as – in the words of Govers and Go (2009) – the largely unchanging DNA of the place (e.g. location and history), infrastructure, superstructure, heritage, and festivals representing the inner mentality of the population. Cultural heritage, especially its intangible forms, has been marginalised in the development of contemporary places (Perry et al., 2019), although empowering face-to-face interactions (e.g. in festival settings) can stimulate initiatives that represent the diversity of a community, which is, nowadays, extant in most localities (Derrett, 2020).

Diversities are usually evident in localities, either due to historic events and relations (e.g. Jones, 1997) and the transformation of former multinational states into ethnic ones (e.g. the Ottoman Empire) or due to the immigration and refugee flows which transform localities into multicultural societies. Respect for multiculturalism and diversity goes hand in hand with anti-discrimination and inclusive policies, minority rights, and the maintenance of the identity of the minority group. European states link integration of minorities to assimilation (Berry, 2012), yet minorities should not have to "forgo their cultural identity in the name of integration; rather their distinct identity should be nurtured" (Berry, 2012, p. 5).

People have two identities: a civic identity and a cultural identity (Bruter, 2005). Civic identity represents the relationship that a person has with the state and their sense of belonging within that state; however, cultural identity relates to other elements, such as ethnicity, language, or religion that separates individuals from mainstream society. Cultural identity may also include the identity of origin, family identity, and intellectual, political, religious, social, and professional identities of each person. Extant studies on the dimensions of difference have identified two dimensions of national inclusion: ethnic nationalism and civic nationalism (Pehrson et al., 2009). Ethnic nationalism highlights biology and views national inclusion in terms of shared ancestry, reflected by physical appearance, language, and heritage (Dovidio et al., 2010). On the other hand, civil nationalism prioritises ideology and defines national group members in terms of commitment to the ideals and standards perceived to define a nation (Dovidio et al., 2010). In response to nationalism approaches, this chapter argues that strengthening the civic identity boosts the co-existence and respect of multiple cultural identities – an element of truly pluralistic, multiculturalist, and coherent multicultural societies, where nationality and culture are not mutually exclusive.

For specific places, as well as in national contexts, Kavaratzis and Ashworth (2015) identify the significance of synergies when culture *in, of,* and *for* the place is incorporated in place branding: culture *in* the place commonly refers to the culture of the place that is being projected and promoted; culture *for* the place refers to those cultural elements that can foster cultural exchange between people; and culture *of* the place refers to those characteristics which actors perceive to be place- or country-specific attributes and which link people together as a community. In practice, place branding strategies may, to some degree, incorporate culture *in, of,* and *for* the place. Yet, whether or not minorities and distinct cultural identities are taken into consideration and embraced in cultural and branding initiatives is subject to the objectives of branding actors and their realisation of how inclusive branding policies might strengthen the civic identity and reflect the true identity of the place.

As Lucarelli (2017, p. 192) puts it, place branding patterns may be "structured in ways that deviate markedly from articulations of citizen sovereignty". This might be particularly true in locations where the macro-environmental pressures lead to shifting demographics. Moreover, political shifts and power struggles (Paul et al., 2004) may influence even the largely unchanging DNA of a location (i.e. the external ethnic borders or the regional prefectural limits), as well as the interpretation and representation of history in order to serve the objectives of governing bodies. At the same time, private actors may influence the place branding process and relevant visions, missions, and priorities as they try to interpolate their own perceptions of place identity and how to communicate it. Governments (at the national, regional, and local levels), together with the private sector, are the main actors in developing the place branding strategy. In this effort, actors influence extant institutions and vice versa; actors (their knowledge, skills, intention, and motivation) are also influenced *by* institutions (Edvardsson et al., 2014). Culture is a clear example of something that changes over time, although some of its elements may be maintained, depending on the power of the actors involved in developing branding strategies.

Institutions in place branding

Institutions can be seen as "a set of rules governing interpersonal governance" (North, 1990, p. 70) and shared patterns of cognition at the individual and societal levels that guide behavioural rules and practices of actors (Friedland & Alford, 1991). As such, institutions are based upon three pillars: the regulative pillar, which consists of regulation, observation, and sanctioning (if necessary) and includes all formal rules that ensure that actors' behaviour aligns with certain standards; the normative pillar, which consists of norms and values and refers to both actors' objectives and how these could or should be achieved; and the cognitive pillar, which is connected to the perceptions and representations of reality (Edvardsson et al., 2014).

In line with the first regulative pillar, studies in the place and destination domain have adopted an institutional approach to research public administration, public policy, and, more rarely, marketing (Lucarelli, 2017). Still, such efforts can be further developed by adopting an approach of ethics in marketing and power in place branding by explicitly discussing the ethics of marketing in relation to strategies and practices applied in place branding. The Hunt-Vitell model (1986, 2006), among others, provides a general theory and process model of ethical decision-making in corporate branding. Once individuals involved in decision-making perceive the set of alternative choices, both the deontological and teleological evaluation processes are initiated. The Hunt-Vitell model (1986, 2006) concludes that corporate "branding is ethically right because of brandings' highly positive societal consequences" (Hunt, 2019, p. 415) by including improvements in the quality of products and the increased ability of society to hold accountable the producers of shoddy or unsafe goods. As Hunt (2019, p. 45) argues, "anti-branding critics ignore (or are ignorant of) such positive consequences of branding as a societal institution", which are valid for all stakeholders. Institutions are particularly relevant when trying to understand whether place branding is ethical or to attempt to apply the corporate branding's rationale in a place perspective because of improvements in the quality of life and place experiences. Such positive consequences in place branding would be reflective of different ethical and normative worldviews that are at play (Lucarelli, 2017) and guide the decisions of place branding actors.

Place branding literature only recently began investigating institutions in relevant fields, adopting primarily a tourism perspective (see Fong et al., 2018; Lavandoski et al., 2013), which focuses on resident communities' perspective in relation to tourism institutions (Nunkoo et al., 2012, 2013). The aforementioned deontological and teleological evaluations conceptually relate to normative and cognitive institutional pillars and seem particularly relevant when focusing on cultural and gastro-cultural attributes. Place and tourism value propositions often build upon cultural elements, sometimes in an attempt to develop sustainable strategies pairing the identity-based approach to place branding with destination branding. Culture is a sensitive area that is frequently perceived differently by various place actors, thereby leading place actors to varying perceptions and evaluations of the role of culture and to the hijacking of culture.

In line with the identity-based approach to place branding (Kavaratzis & Ashworth, 2015), this chapter views culture *of* the place as particularly connected to normative institutional thinking. Culture *of* the place reflects the cultural values and norms that place actors (at the local, regional, and national levels) identify within a given place. As such, culture *of* the place reflects predetermined deontological local norms and hypernorms. Culture *in* and *for* the place should be bundled with culture *of* the place in order to efficiently and sustainably correspond to cognitive institutions and feed into positive teleological evaluations to boost the positive consequences of place branding as a societal institution. Culture *in*, *for*, and *of* the place takes place according to how culture (among other regulative institutions) emerges, maintains, and decays in place branding.

Despite the danger of oversimplifying the process according to which institutions set the place ecosystem in which resources are integrated and exchanged to create value, a specific example can facilitate the understanding of culture as regulative, normative, and cognitive institutions in place branding and gastro-cultural identity. In line with Scott (2010), religion/religious beliefs (as a domain of culture) are reflected in spaces (temples, mosques, churches, cemeteries, etc.), rituals and practices, and religious events, among others. In various cultures and countries, religion may help locals construct their culture (i.e. part of their cultural identity, including local/national dress codes or diets). Through the joint participation of visitors and locals (of varying religious and cultural beliefs) in religious festivities and events, religion can also facilitate "outsiders" understanding and experiences with the local culture and identity (i.e. the place brand). Identifying, extracting, and expressing specific aspects of religion, relevant to the culture *in*, *for*, and *of* the place, can facilitate the strategic development of place branding through the proliferation of specific events, symbols, landmarks, infrastructure, and services. As an example, in 2017, based on the Hindu belief that cows are sacred (normative institutions), the federal government in India ordered a ban on the sale of cattle at livestock markets (regulative institutions). Depending on local actors' own perceptions and representations of the holy (cognitive institutions), some restaurants may choose (not) to serve beef even in those states that considered disregarding the ban. This differentiation could be relevant to other dimensions of the place brand (e.g. *tourism* if these states differentiate themselves because they wish to appear more "welcoming" to visitors who include beef in their diet; *people* and *culture/heritage* if locals in these states hold different beliefs; or *immigration/investment* depending on the profile of the people each state wishes to attract). In any case, the decision to follow the ban on beef facilitates state actors to co-create value with other actors who share corresponding perceptions and/or beliefs. While not an all-encompassing indicator of culture, there are many similar interactions between religion and dietary restrictions the world over.

In this context, it is paramount to underline food as an important domain of culture that is also interconnected with other cultural counterparts. In an attempt to define various functions of food, aside from its nutritional value, Bessière (1998) suggests that food can be considered a symbol, an indicator of social connectedness, a socio-economic differentiator, or an umbrella for geographical or social belonging. From a tourism-centric perspective, the gastronomical features of specific areas or communities can be utilised as a potential tool to increase visitation (Shortridge, 2004) and to enhance tourism experiences (Sims, 2009); yet, it is imperative to remember that residents' perception of tourism is of utmost importance for their engagement with activities that foster the branding initiative and tourism product development (Kwon & Vogt, 2010). The integration of gastronomy into the place branding initiative is especially realised in rural areas, which are striving to compete with their urban counterparts (e.g. Lee et al., 2015). In fact, cuisine itself can be considered an institution. Through an analysis of historic changes in French cuisine (i.e. the paradigm shift from classical to nouvelle cuisine), Rao et al. (2003) suggest that identity movements potentially trigger an institutional change.

It is proposed in this chapter that the uniqueness of resource integration, and elements of this uniqueness, could and should be reflected in the place branding strategy. For this to be made possible, this chapter seeks to provide a better understanding of institutions and the role of culture, or more specifically, its gastronomy-related subdomain. Culture influences, and is influenced by, actors in policymaking, tourism, hospitality, and other place-related fields, as well as the beliefs and priorities of stakeholders, as institutional logic guides behavioural rules and collective practices of policy and branding actors (Friedland & Alford, 1991). If organisations are likely to encounter contradicting institutional logics (because of being embedded in multiple institutions that constituent diverse beliefs, perceptions, values, and expectations (Fong et al., 2018)) and, therefore, face important challenges to maintaining prevalent institutional orders (e.g. Tidström & Hagberg-Andersson, 2012), then the situation becomes even more complicated in the case of places, where a larger number of actors, at all levels, are sought to actively engage in the ecosystem. Moreover, culture and the place, as an ecosystem, include a variety of elements and dimensions, some of which may be place specific, whereas others may be national or transnational.

The islands of Gökçeada and Bozcaada in Turkey

Gökçeada and Bozcaada (Imbros and Tenedos, respectively, in Greek) are two small islands in Turkey's Çanakkale province, in the North-eastern Aegean Sea (lying between Greece and Turkey) (see Figure 2.1). Gökçeada hosts the westernmost point of Turkey, and with a few thousand permanent residents, it is triple the size of Bozcaada. Until the latter half of the 20th century, *Rums* (i.e. a Greek-speaking Orthodox minority holding a Turkish or dual Greek-Turkish nationality) were the main inhabitants of both islands. Yet, this changed due to the Turkish

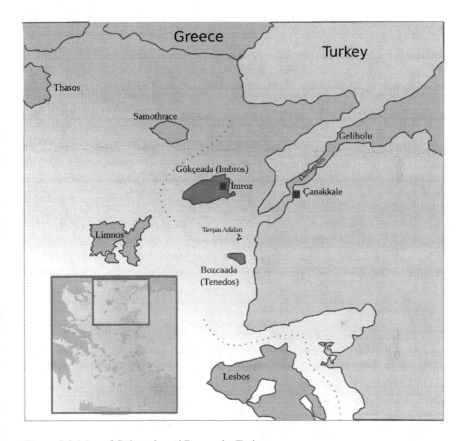

Figure 2.1 Map of Gökçeada and Bozcaada, Turkey.

Source: Future Perfect at Sunrise, Creative Commons Attribution-Share Alike 3.0 Unported license.

nationalisation processes (Babul, 2012). The Greek Orthodox populations residing in Istanbul, Gökçeada, and Bozcaada (as well as the Muslim populations residing in Western Thrace, which conventions recognised as a Greek territory) were exempted from the exchange of populations foreseen by the Lausanne Convention (Babul, 2012). Therefore, in the aftermath of the Lausanne Convention, a Greek Orthodox minority continued to live in the newly founded Turkey and, in the case of the islands, to constitute the majority of the local population. However, later nationalisation processes (see Babul, 2012) have led, in the second half of the 20th century and the beginning of the 21st century, to a decrease of over 90% of the *Rum* (Orthodox Greek) population of the islands (Kahraman, 2005). The effect of these shifting demographics is reflected in the changing patterns of the sociocultural and economic life of the islands. For instance, when *Rums* constituted the majority of the local population, the local economy relied largely on viticulture and wine production activities, especially in Bozcaada (Akpınar et al., 2011).

The characteristic that initially made the islands stand out as unique lies in the harmony between the two different ethnic groups and religions (Akpınar et al., 2011), a characteristic upon which early tourism development was built. Travellers would visit friends and relatives on the islands or would attend *panigiria* (*panayır* in Turkish, i.e. the centuries-old traditional and cultural festival organised to celebrate the patron saint of the place) and general cultural and social activities (particularly activities relevant to viticulture in Bozcaada). Agriculture largely drove everyday life on the islands, with families producing various goods, primarily for their own consumption, and their own house wine and *raki* (i.e. a distilled alcoholic drink, popularly consumed in Turkey and Greece). Especially in the 21st century, sun-sand-sea tourism development started gaining ground, turning the islands into popular mass tourist destinations (Ayhan & Kladou, 2022). At the same time, descendants of the *Rum* minority started visiting the islands for longer periods of time, whereas several parameters (i.e. international pressures, the efforts of the expatriate community, and the Greek debt crisis of 2009) led to some positive changes on the islands, including the re-opening of Greek schools, which motivated some *Rum* natives to return, especially back to Gökçeada (e.g. Akyol, 2015).

Methodology

This study investigates how institutions, which influence place branding efforts, reflect the dominant (national) culture and whether they are inclusive and embrace a deeper understanding of local heritage and dimensions of difference (Dovidio et al., 2010). In order to address this gap, this study focuses on two small islands and examines the cultural domain of gastronomy. Findings primarily build on a thematic analysis of (online and offline) documents, booklets, and information prepared by actors with some branding authority in Bozcaada and Gökçeada (Turkey) as no official destination management organisation exists on the islands. This analysis included online material made available through June 2021, in both written and audio-visual format, although the latter was extremely limited when excluding social media from the analysis (i.e. actors with official branding authority do not currently have social media accounts). Analysis further incorporated papers and proceedings relevant to the gastrostomy and tourism experience or destination branding of either island, published commonly in English or Turkish. Semi-structured interviews were then performed in September 2021 with local authorities, incorporating the views of mayors and three *muhtar*s (elected local representatives).

Extant theory on institutions, the identity-based approach to place branding, and the dimensions of difference help identify *a priori* themes within the data. Specifically, initial coding and the organisation of the themes were built upon Scott's (2010) classification of institutions in place branding, Kavaratzis and Ashworth's (2015) framework of culture *in, for, of* the place, and Dovidio et al.'s (2010) approach to dimensions of difference. Multiple rounds of coding, copying, re-organising, and comparing thematic categories facilitated the development of interrelated themes. The predetermined deontological norms reflect decision-makers' personal values (i.e. general beliefs about moral behaviour, such as individual freedom), issue-specific beliefs (such as product safety or confidentiality of data), local norms (i.e. context-specific or community-based norms, such as the legal and political system), and hypernorms (i.e. reflecting religious, philosophical, and cultural beliefs). In-depth thematic analysis identifies national and local actors' institutional influences in relation to relevant branding priorities, and inclusive and exclusive practices and examples.

Findings

Compared to normative and cognitive institutions, regulative institutions are more formalised, explicit, easily planned, and strategically manipulated (Scott, 2010). In the case of the islands, the standpoint of regulative institutions is reflected in funding and policy documents (including strategic documents and developmental plans). Gökçeada and Bozcaada are located in the TROY North Aegean cultural and thermal tourism development zone. The region, in general, hosts "a variety of plant species used in alternative medicine and produces olives, olive oil and wines" (Ministry of Culture & Tourism, 2007, pp. 46–47). However, strategic documents prioritise the creation of an Olive Corridor in the region, including the islands, and funding plans do not mention any support for local wine varieties.

According to the Tourism Strategy of Turkey 2023 (Ministry of Culture & Tourism, 2007, p. 52), the region is to be "developed as a destination for health and gastronomy tourism". The national strategy indicates that "tourism investments should safeguard, conserve, and improve the natural, historical, cultural, and social environment" (p. 7), and

> effective policies should: develop an understanding of tourism, which focuses on historical, cultural, and artistic assets and corresponds fully to the

demands and expectations of the local public and that enlivens, protects, and produces multiple activities and assets; and avoid causing adverse effects on nature, culture, and social structure

(Ministry of Culture & Tourism, 2007, p. 8).

The policy, particularly, supports local products and prioritises gastronomic, cultural, health, ecotourism, and agritourism (Ministry of Culture & Tourism, 2007; Republic of Turkey, 2019). Such priorities seem to align with the Slowfood movement, which views Gökçeada and Cittaslow in terms of "returning back to traditional values" (Yurtseven, 2006, p. 41) and prioritises the following: the unique lifestyle experienced in North Aegean Islands since the 15th century; old and historic villages, buildings, and archaeological areas; the natural beauty; and organic agriculture (Yurtseven, 2004). Moreover, the 11th Development Plan gives precedence to gastronomy tourism, cultural tourism, and agritourism and expresses support for activities relevant to viticulture, beekeeping, fishing, poultry farming, alternative agricultural products, and activities preserving the know-how of traditional production and storage of agricultural and food products (Republic of Turkey, 2019).

Wine had a dominant role in the everyday lives of *Rums* and their communities; wine culture and the role of food and wine dominated *panigiria*, various social-religious activities (e.g. weddings, baptisms), and everyday family gatherings. When *Rums* constituted the majority of those living on the islands, viticulture and wine production were central to house economics (i.e. families would produce their own wine) and, in Bozcaada, the local economy.[2] Yet, the 1982 constitution, ratified during a secular military junta, provides justification for restrictions on the production, promotion, and distribution of alcoholic beverages, including wine and *raki* (i.e. in support of the state monopoly in Turkey, only the state-owned spirits company Tekel was legally allowed to distil and commercially distribute *raki* (Evered & Evered, 2016)). The Tobacco and Alcohol Market Regulatory Authority (TAPDK), established in 2002, led to increased control over the consumption of alcoholic beverages, whereas the tax on alcohol has raised the market price of wine by around 251% in the last 17 years (Tuncer, 2021). New laws ratified in 2013 further constrain the promotion and advertisement of alcoholic beverages (including wine) under all circumstances; these laws prohibit any campaign, promotion, or event that encourages or incentivises the consumption and sale of such products (such as wine festivals or open wine tastings). The brand name or logo of alcohol companies is not permitted appear as the sponsor to any type of event either. Such restrictions impact business activities surrounding wines and only allow the house production of wine and *raki* up to a specific volume.

The effect of such regulative elements on normative and cognitive institutions is evident. On one hand, the 11th Development Plan, in order to serve the aforementioned developmental objectives, supports certifications, including place labels and geographically marked products and ornamental plants, and asserts "to continue to support relevant initiatives and collaborations that will help preserve relevant activities for future generations" (Republic of Turkey, 2019, p. 182). On

Gastro-cultural identities for place branding 23

the other hand, nation-wide legislation contradicts regional and local reflections and affects everyday life and cognitive institutions. As a regional tourist brochure reports, minority populations "left or were forced to leave (by regulative institutions)", whereas in the past "(local groups) shared experiences and traditions . . . (for example) at Easter celebrations. Muslims and Christians had fun and painted eggs together; shopkeepers ate lunch together: barbequed meat from a Muslim butcher and wine from his Jewish craftsman neighbour" (Açanal, 2015, p. 8). Legislation further restricts the development of certifications and opposes protected designation of origin and activities promoting local varieties (e.g. Bozcaada *Çavuşu*, a white Turkish grape variety indigenous to Bozcaada).

Confusion is reflected in authorities' mistaken information as well. For example, despite legislation allowing the household production of alcohol for personal and family consumption (up to a certain volume), local representatives interviewed reported that the production of *raki* is still prohibited due to the state monopoly of Tekel.[3] Local *muhtars* shared inconsistent understandings on whether official permission is necessary to serve wine at *panigiria*, which is just one of the conflicts that came to light. Local Gökçeada *muhtars* inaccurately reported that in the past, pig breeding, which took place in nearly all *Rum* households (in order for each family to celebrate New Year's with a traditional pork-based recipe and then traditionally preserve the remaining pork to have access to meat throughout the year), was prohibited by law. One of the *muhtars* even claimed that prior to such (non-existent) legislation, cognitive institutions forbade pig breeding during the demographics shift in favour of Muslim populations because pig breeding could contaminate the water with pork particles, thereby making the water *haram* (i.e. forbidden due to religious beliefs) for Muslim residents.

Funding granted for agricultural activities does not clearly prioritise agricultural products that were central to local culture (olive oil and wine) but primarily sets nation-wide priorities on wheat and corn products, and in the case of Gökçeada, mostly refers to the importance of local organic farming. The agricultural products primarily emphasised represent national priorities rather than reflecting local food (see Yavuz & Özkanlı, 2019). Moreover, national policy sets production targets that do not correspond to the low production volumes of local organic farming. As a result, production and farming methods traditional to the islands, and supportive of local (organic) standards, are not, in practice, encouraged. Food-related cultural interaction is emphasised through the Organic Food Market and cooking classes serving mostly locals. Gökçeada Municipality points out social responsibility initiatives through webpages presenting the distribution of *aşure* and the organisation of *iftar* dinners (i.e. a dessert porridge served during Muharram, the first month of the Islamic calendar, and the evening meals with which Muslims break their daily fast at sunset during the month of Ramadan, respectively), thereby providing an additional example of the shift towards prioritising gastronomy of the religious majority. On the other hand, official travel brochures emphasise the Greek/*Rum* gastronomy and culture.

From the perspective of tourism regulatory institutions, the Tourism Strategic Plan raises the issue of building awareness among public, private, and non-governmental organisations to support alternative tourism development (particularly agricultural tourism and ecotourism) (Ministry of Culture & Tourism, 2007). In order to achieve this, actors should seek to integrate tourism types specific to each place and region while actors "create tourism products based on tourist profiles" (Ministry of Culture & Tourism, 2007, p. 5). Still, the Strategic Plan does not openly refer to either island or specific local (gastro-) cultural elements nor does it address minority populations and minority culture. Analysing local and regional websites indeed matches such institutional influences and reveals that local and regional actors (e.g. residents, farmers, hospitality entrepreneurs, Gökçeada Municipality, and Northern Marmara Development Agency) may receive funding or participate in activities and projects but do not actively contribute to the creation of the gastro-cultural place brand and relevant tourism experiences. In fact, Gökçeada Municipality, which joined Cittaslow International in 2011 (Yurtseven & Karakaş, 2013) (i.e. a project which currently gives the impression of being on hold), seems to be the only normative institution reflecting sustainable and inclusive co-creation opportunities. Overall, correspondence to tourists' profiles seems to be a more relevant tourism priority in the case of the islands: Gökçeada and Bozcaada appear to be moving towards mass tourism development and away from former tourism initiatives that more accurately reflect the island's identity. Especially in Bozcaada, local actors have expressed their discomfort and disappointment because local tourism development has moved away from wine tourism and wine identity, which locals continue to value despite shifting demographics (Ayhan & Kladou, 2022).

Conclusion and implications

The identity and gastro-cultural brand of Gökçeada and Bozcaada, relating to minority populations and relevant co-creation initiatives in practice, appear largely absent, although such synergies could boost the civic identity (Bruter, 2005) despite extant dimensions of difference (Dovidio et al., 2010; Pehrson et al., 2009). This minority heritage is mentioned in booklets and through food and wine experiences available to the visitor. *Rum* and Turkish populations have lived in harmony on the islands (Andarabi & Hassan, 2018; Özdemir & Ayhan, 2019), and despite the effects of the minority displacement which mainly started in the 1960s (Burkay, 2016), local actors continue to associate the culture, identity, and sense of place with elements of the *Rum* culture (e.g. wine in Ayhan & Kladou, 2022).

For specific places, as well as national contexts, Kavaratzis and Ashworth (2015) identified the significance of synergies when the culture *in, of,* and *for* the place is incorporated in place branding. In the case of the islands, the culture *in* the place commonly refers to cultural elements considered by the "event hallmarking" technique, such as well-known food events and festivals, or cultural and social events (e.g. *panigiria*). Such events on the islands, however, appear to primarily address visitors or same-group resident interactions rather than inspire different resident groups' co-creation. The culture *for* the place refers to elements fostering cultural exchange between people, that is, agricultural activities or cooking classes in the case of the islands – although both largely reflect food and agricultural goods representing national or regional priorities, rather than local food culture (e.g. wheat over wine production and traditional Turkish rather than *Rum* recipes). Lastly, the culture *of* the place refers to those gastro-cultural characteristics that place actors perceive as place- or country-specific attributes linking them together as a community. Culture *of* the islands, at the local level, largely reflected the *Rum* minority food culture, for instance cognitive institutions are reflected in well-known *panigiria* and, in Bozcaada, wine festivals and activities. These are developed by private and civil actors as regulatory and top-down normative institutions have added pressure on such expressions of locality. In fact, more recent regulatory institutions in Turkey (e.g. Ministry of Culture & Tourism, 2007) seek to inspire culture *in, for*, and *of* the place that will link the local community to country-specific characteristics and those populations residing on mainland Turkey. These regulative institutional pillars, in recent years, influence normative and cognitive pillars and take branding efforts away from the islands' distinct identity. This is particularly evident through policy and funding alternatives that prioritise (tourism and agricultural) development that moves away from food, wine, local heritage and culture.

When founded, the Turkish Republic was set to be a secular state. Still, in the early years of the Republic, the nationalisation processes led to a shifting demographic based on religious attributes. In the last few decades, political efforts to move the state away from its secular foundations more openly emphasise religion. Such a religious character might not always be reflected in regulative institutions but can influence normative and cognitive institutions. By not explicitly communicating regulative tolerance or exemptions (such as the case of cows in India), policies lead to exclusive practices more specific to gastro-cultural attributes (e.g. pig breeding is extinct on the islands). Giving more space to regional and local decision-making, embracing both secular policymaking, in practice, and diversifying cognitive institutions when developing regulatory institutions could lead to more inclusive branding practices that boost civic identity. Creating the place brand strategy involves the "evaluation, (re)assembling, (re)positioning, and (re)formulation of the identity of the place" (Govers & Go, 2009, p. 49). Thus, a sustainable place brand strategy does not result from assimilating the local culture with the national one but from nurturing a civic identity that builds on the local cultural identity resulting from the ongoing dialogue between resident groups' different cultural identities.

For instance, a starting point could be identifying the gastro-cultural elements of the culture *in, for*, and *of* the islands that reflect local *Rum* identity and using those universally/locally accepted features as a bridge to boost the sense of belonging to the island. The island culture *per se* can act as the connection between the different identities, provided that locals learn, appreciate, and embrace the distinct local culture and heritage and are encouraged to interact in everyday life (e.g. at local *panigiria*) (Derrett, 2020). To this date, however, legislation might not prohibit the house production of alcohol or pork, but local and regional efforts to highlight what unites locals, and to boost their sense of belonging to the island, are limited compared to national efforts emphasising religious and ethnic differences.

Currently, the "struggle" to disengage the local identity from its links with an ethnic, religious minority and align it more with the national culture is evident in top-down (and subsequently regional) funding and strategic priorities that do not align with local identification of the place distinctiveness. Such efforts to eliminate cultural differences (Dovidio et al., 2010) and varying degrees of discrimination (as per Ruhanen & Whitford, 2018) impact the sustainability of branding efforts and locals' engagement with the projected sense of place (Ayhan & Kladou, 2022). It would, therefore, be wise to differentiate between national contexts (and preconceptions) and local divergences that may be observed within national borders and seek to detect and develop sustainable, co-creative synergies. Local food has a diverse value, including local, ethnic, national, or transnational traditions, as well as history, customs, culture, and eating habits beyond gastronomic and dietary values (in line with Hall et al., 2003). Food experiences have an experiential value and holistic nature, an ability to bond people through its consumption and production (Boswijk et al., 2007). Moreover, ethnic and cultural differences and gastronomic tourism have sociocultural implications for society, place, and identity (Kesimoğlu, 2015). Using food experiences and food culture to boost the distinct cultural place identity can support the civic identity and eliminate dimensions of difference (Dovidio et al., 2010) at a local level.

Future research could, therefore, seek to feed into the application of the ethics of place branding efforts and build on additional research methods, embracing more actors through *in situ* primary data collection and analysis of documents and publications. An in-depth analysis of the role of institutions and how they emerge, maintain, and decay can help better understand the underlying reasoning of institutional pressures towards conflicting policies. Such an in-depth analysis may help assess differences and similarities across developing and developed destinations, as the maturity and confidence of the place, the nation, and relevant actors might be a determining factor influencing institutional thinking. Still, this exploratory chapter provides a preliminary discussion on how institutions at different levels may be in conflict, adding pressures towards different policy directions, specifically when top-down decision-makers influencing regulatory institutions are not at ease with the local history and traditions of ethnic and religious minorities. When this is the case, pressures on normative and cognitive institutions are evident, and the question arising is what will prevail in the future, the power and influence of regulative, normative, or cognitive institutions.

Notes

1 The term multicultural state describes states within which a number of cultures exist, whereas multiculturalist states pursue a policy of accommodation of these cultures (Hellyer, 2006).
2 In Bozcaada, the local economy was traditionally based on viticulture and wine production activities, and vineyards covered one-third of the island; 13 wineries operated as opposed to the 6 wineries still operating to this day (see Ayhan & Kladou, 2022; Çavuşoğlu, 2012).
3 This state monopoly ended in the early 2000s with the privatisation of Tekel, thereby allowing other private companies to distil and sell *raki*

References

Açanal, H. (2015). *Food in Çanak: About the food history and culture of Çanakkale*. Çanakkale History and Culture Foundation.

Akpınar, F., Saygın, N., & Karakaya, E. (2011). Evaluation of the conservation activities in the historical settlement Tenedos Bozcaada Island. In C. A. Brebbia & E. Beriatos (Eds.), *Sustainable development and planning V* (pp. 329–343). WIT Press. http://doi.org/10.2495/SDP110281.

Akyol, K. (2015). *For Turkey's Greek minority, an island school provides fresh hope*. Retrieved July 27, 2021, from www.al-monitor.com/pulse/originals/2015/10/turkey-greece-minority-island-school-escape-extinction.html

Andarabi, F. F., & Hassan, A. T. (2018). The impact of service performance in package tours to slow cities on tourists' satisfaction and behavioral intention: The Gökçeada case. *Uluslararası Türk Dünyası Turizm Araştırmaları Dergisi, 3*(2), 171–188.

Anholt, S. (2003). *Brand new justice: The upside of global branding*. Butterworth Heinemann.

Ayhan, N., & Kladou, S. (2022). Moving away from wine tourism and sustainable tourism development: The paradox in the case of Bozcaada (Tenedos), Turkey. In S. Kladou, A. Farmaki, K. Andriotis, & D. Stylidis (Eds.), *Tourism policy and development in the Middle East* (pp. 95–110). CABI Tourism Series.

Babul, E. (2012). *Belonging to Imbros: Citizenship and sovereignty in the Turkish Republic (PDF)*. Bogazici University. Retrieved July 28, 2021, from https://web.archive.org/web/20120219230918/http:/www.sant.ox.ac.uk/esc/esc-lectures/babul.pdf

Berry, S. E. (2012). Integrating refugees: The case for a minority rights based approach. *International Journal of Refugee Law, 24*(1), 1–36.

Bessière, J. (1998). Local development and heritage: Traditional food and cuisine as tourist attractions in rural areas. *Sociologia Ruralis, 38*(1), 21–34.

Boswijk, A., Thijssen, T., & Peelen, E. (2007). *The experience economy: A new perspective*. Pearson Education.

Brown, J. (2018). A service ecosystem approach to representing a place's unique brand. In M. Kavaratzis, M. Giovanardi, & M. Lichrou (Eds.), *Inclusive place branding: Critical perspectives on theory and practice* (1st ed., pp. 104–126). Routledge.

Bruter, M. (2005). Political identities and public policy: Institutional messages and the politics of integration in Europe. *Refugee Survey Quarterly, 24*, 43–46.

Burkay, H. Ö. (2016). *The olive as an object of rural development: The cultural politics of organic food and the making of the local* [Unpublished PhD dissertation, Carleton University]. Retrieved July 27, 2021, from https://curve.carleton.ca/874526e7-796a-4e9f-a9c6-a997592d5c8b

Çavuşoğlu, M. (2012). Gökçeada e-koagro turizm projesi. *Karamanoğlu Mehmetbey Üniversitesi Sosyal Ve Ekonomik Araştırmalar Dergisi, 2012*(2), 123–128.

Derrett, R. (2020). Community festivals reveal tangible and intangible bounty: Lismore NSW Australia. In L. J. Ingram, S. L. Slocum, & C. T. Cavaliere (Eds.), *Neolocalism & tourism: Understanding a global movement* (pp. 100–122). Goodfellow.

Dovidio, J. F., Gluszek, A., John, M. S., Ditlmann, R., & Lagunes, P. (2010). Understanding bias toward Latinos: Discrimination, dimensions of difference, and experience of exclusion. *Journal of Social Issues, 66*(1), 59–78.

Edvardsson, B., Kleinaltenkamp, M., & Tronvoll, B. (2014). Institutional logics matter when coordinating resource integration. *Marketing Theory, 14*(4), 1–19.

Evered, E. Ö., & Evered, K. T. (2016). From rakı to ayran: Regulating the place and practice of drinking in Turkey. *Space and Polity, 20*(1), 39–58.

Fong, V. H., Wong, I. A., & Hong, J. F. L. (2018). Developing institutional logics in the tourism industry through coopetition. *Tourism Management, 66*, 244–262.

Friedland, R., & Alford, R. R. (1991). Bringing society back in: Symbols, practices, and institutional contradictions. In W.W. Powell & P. J. DiMaggio (Eds.), *The new institutionalism in organizational analysis* (pp. 232–267). University of Chicago Press.

Govers, R., & Go, F. (2009). *Virtual and physical identities, Constructed, imagined and experienced*. Palgrave Macmillan.

Hall, C. M., Sharples, L., Mitchell, R., Macionis, N., & Cambourne, B. (Eds.). (2003). *Food tourism around the world, development, management and markets*. Routledge.

Hellyer, H. A. (2006). Muslims and multiculturalism in the EU. *Journal of Muslim Minority Affairs, 26*, 329–351.

Hunt, S. D. (2019). The ethics of branding, customer-brand relationships, brand-equity strategy and branding as a societal institution. *Journal of Business Research, 95*, 408–416.

Hunt, S. D., & Vitell, S. J. (1986). The general theory of marketing ethics. *Journal of Macromarketing, 6*(Spring), 5–15.

Hunt, S. D., & Vitell, S. J. (2006). The general theory of marketing ethics: A revision and three questions. *Journal of Macromarketing, 26*(2), 1–11.

Jones, J. M. (1997). *Prejudice and racism* (2nd ed.). McGraw-Hill.

Kahraman, S. Ö. (2005). Gökçeada'da göçlerin nüfus gelişimi ve değişimi üzerine etkileri. *Coğrafi Bilimler Dergisi, 3*(2), 39–53.

Kavaratzis, M., & Ashworth, G. J. (2015). Hijacking culture: The disconnection between place culture and place brands. *The Town Planning Review, 86*(2), 155–176.

Kesimoğlu, A. (2015). A reconceptualization of gastronomy as relational and reflexive. *Hospitality & Society, 5*(1), 71–91.

Kwon, J., & Vogt, C. A. (2010). Identifying the role of cognitive, affective, and behavioral components in understanding residents' attitudes toward place marketing. *Journal of Travel Research, 49*(4), 423–435.

Lavandoski, J., Silva, J., & Vargas-Sánchez, A. (2013). *Institutional theory in tourism studies: Evidence and future directions*. Discussion Papers N°13, Spatial and Organizational Dynamics. University of Algarve, Faro.

Lee, A. H., Wall, G., & Kovacs, J. F. (2015). Creative food clusters and rural development through place branding: Culinary tourism initiatives in Stratford and Muskoka, Ontario, Canada. *Journal of Rural Studies, 39*, 133–144.

Lucarelli, A. (2017). Place branding as political research: From hidden agenda to a framework for analysis. In M. Kavaratzis, M. Giovanardi, & M. Lichrou (Eds.), *Inclusive place branding: Critical perspectives on theory and practice* (pp. 185–199). Routledge.

Ministry of Culture & Tourism. (2007). *Strategy of Turkey 2023*. Ankara. Retrieved November 12, 2020, from www.ktb.gov.tr/Eklenti/43537,turkeytourismstrategy2023pdf.pdf?0&_tag1=796689BB12A540BE0672E65E48D10C07D6DAE291

North, D. C. (1990). *Institutions, institutional change and economic performance. Series: Political economy of institutions and decisions*. Cambridge University Press.

Nunkoo, R., Ramkissoon, H., & Gursoy, D. (2012). Public trust in tourism institutions. *Annals of Tourism Research, 39*, 1538–1564.

Nunkoo, R., Smith, S. L. J., & Ramkissoon, H. (2013). Residents' attitudes to tourism: A longitudinal study of 140 articles from 1984 to 2010. *Journal of Sustainable Tourism, 21*(1), 5–25.

Özdemir, E., & Ayhan, Ç. K. (2019). Gökçeada Örneğinde Kültürel Peyzajın Korunması Açısından Sakin Şehir Hareketinin Önemi. *Yüzüncü Yıl Üniversitesi Sosyal Bilimler Enstitüsü Dergisi*, 291–310.

Paul, T. V., Wirtx, J., & Fortmann, M. (2004). *Balance of power: Theory and practice in the 21st century*. Stanford University Press.

Pehrson, S., Vignoles, V. L., & Brown, R. (2009). National identification and anti-immigrant prejudice: Individual and contextual effects of national definitions. *Social Psychology Quarterly*, *72*, 24–38.

Perry, B., Ager, L., & Sitas, R. (2019). Festivals as integrative sites, valuing tangible and intangible heritage for sustainable development. https://realisingjustcities-rjc.org/reports-and-briefings

Rao, H., Mohin, P., & Durand, R. (2003). Institutional change in Toque Ville: Nouvelle Cuisine as an identity movement in French gastronomy. *American Journal of Sociology*, *108*(4), 795–843.

Republic of Turkey. (2019). *11th development plan (2019–2023)*. Retrieved December 8, 2020, from www.sbb.gov.tr/wp-content/uploads/2019/07/OnbirinciKalkinmaPlani.pdf

Ruhanen, L., & Whitford, M. (2018). Racism as an inhibitor to the organisational legitimacy of Indigenous tourism businesses in Australia. *Current Issues in Tourism*, *21*(15), 1728–1742.

Scott, R. W. (2010). Reflections: The past and future of research on institutions and institutional change. *Journal of Change Management*, *10*(1), 5–21.

Shortridge, B. (2004). Ethnic heritage food in Lindsborg, Kansas, and New Glarus, Wisconsin. In L. Long (Ed.), *Culinary tourism* (pp. 268–296). The University Press of Kentucky.

Sims, R. (2009). Food, place and authenticity: Local food and the sustainable tourism experience. *Journal of Sustainable Tourism*, *17*(3), 321–336.

Tidström, A., & Hagberg-Andersson, Å. (2012). Critical events in time and space when cooperation turns into competition in business relationships. *Industrial Marketing Management*, *41*(2), 333–343.

Tuncer, G. (2021). 17 yılda rakı yüzde 1200 zamlandı: Vergi arttıkça kayıtdışı artıyor, çiftçi gelirini, insanlar hayatını kaybediyor. *Independent Türkçe*. Retrieved July 27, 2021, from www.indyturk.com/node/296931/ekonomi%CC%87/17-y%C4%B1lda-rak%C4%B1-y%C3%BCzde-1200-zamland%C4%B1-vergi-artt%C4%B1k%C3%A7a-kay%C4%B1td%C4%B1%C5%9F%C4%B1-art%C4%B1yor-%C3%A7ift%C3%A7i

Warnaby, G. (2009). Towards a service dominant place marketing logic. *Marketing Theory Articles*, *9*(4), 403–423.

Yavuz, M., & Özkanlı, O. (2019). Yöresel Yiyecek ve İçeceklerin Gastronomi Turizmine Etkileri: Gökçeada Örneği. *Güncel Turizm Araştırmaları Dergisi*, *3*(2), 279–301.

Yurtseven, H. R. (2004). Küçük adalara ilişkin alternatif turizm biçimlerinin geliştirilmesinde bir stratejik planlama modeli: Gökçeada (Imbros) örneği. *1. Balıkesir National Tourism Congress*, 201–215.

Yurtseven, H. R. (2006). *Slow food ve Gökçeada: Geleneksel değerlere dönüş*. Detay Yayıncılık.

Yurtseven, H. R., & Karakaş, N. (2013). Creating a sustainable gastronomic destination: The case of Cittaslow Gokceada, Turkey. *American International Journal of Contemporary Research*, *3*(3), 91–100.

3 Canadian immigration policies

Implications for discrimination and biases in tourism employment

Kelly-Ann Wright and Frederic Dimanche

> The nonrecognition of foreign credentials amounts to the systematic exclusion of immigrant workers from the upper segments of the labour market. In particular, I suggest that institutionalised processes of cultural distinction contribute to the segmentation of immigrant labour.
>
> (Harald Bauder, *"Brain Abuse," or the Devaluation of Immigrant Labour in Canada*)

Tourism: a thriving sector

Prior to 2020, when COVID-19 brought the global economy to a halt, hospitality and tourism was one of the world's leading and fastest growing economic sectors (United Nations World Tourism Organization (UNWTO), 2020). The global hospitality and tourism sector grew for the ninth consecutive year in 2018, with international visitor arrivals increasing by 5% to 1.4 billion, two years ahead of the UNWTO's forecast (2019). In the same year, the sector generated US$1.7 trillion in worldwide tourism receipts and supported 10% of global employment, highlighting strong economic clout (UNWTO, 2019).

Despite the tourism sector's growth and expansion, the vast majority of workers have not benefitted from this prosperity due to the unequal distribution of resources and because the hospitality and tourism sector is riddled with inequalities and the rampant exploitation of tourism workers (Baum et al., 2016; Bianchi, 2018; Bianchi & de Man, 2021; Hickel, 2019). It is widely known (some would even say accepted) that most jobs within the sector are classified as "undignified" (Baum et al., 2016; Winchenbach et al., 2019). In fact, tourism is one of the lowest paying sectors in the world (Birgier, 2017), where jobs are considered to be low-paid, low-skilled, and temporary or part-time in nature. In addition, most workers "in the lower tier of the employment spectrum predominately consists of women, immigrants and young people" (Zampoukos & Ioannides, 2011, p. 25).

As a result, the sector has gained such a poor reputation for its treatment of workers that, in some countries, only people with few other options and job opportunities are willing to accept employment within the sector (Steiner, 2006).

DOI: 10.4324/9781003255413-4

While international tourist arrivals and spending break industry records each year, workers within the sector must contend with poor working conditions (Bianchi & de Man, 2021). It is no surprise that the sector often experiences labour shortages, as it is competing with other industries that offer better conditions and compensation. One argument for the low pay and low status of many hospitality and tourism jobs is that the work requires limited skills and knowledge to perform tasks and, as such, is to be expected to be low paying (Lacher & Oh, 2012). However, it could be stated that the hospitality and tourism sector has been built upon the exploitation and inequitable treatment of workers to attain its decades of economic prosperity and growth (Hickel, 2019).

Reliance on cheap labour

Researchers have contended that the growth and development of the hospitality and tourism sector relies upon cheap labour, and without it, the entire sector may indeed collapse (Bianchi & de Man, 2021; Hickel, 2019; Massidda et al., 2017). As such, the principle underpinning the sector, and its well-documented growth across the globe, is the continued exploitation of its workers, particularly society's poor and marginalised. Indeed, the intersectionality of workers has a bearing on their level of exploitation in the hospitality and tourism sector, with women, racial minorities, and migrants bearing the brunt of the mistreatment (Abassah-Oppong & Holmes, 2020; Benjamin & Dillette, 2021; Li et al., 2020). Although women account for 54% of tourism employees globally, the wage gap between men and women remains around 15% (UNWTO, 2019). Globally, women within the tourism sector not only earn less (Fleming, 2015; Santos & Varejão, 2007) but continue to be overlooked for management roles that are largely occupied by men (Abassah-Oppong & Holmes, 2020; Akbar, 2019). Minorities and racialised women face more disadvantages due to their intersectional identities. According to a Canadian study, white women earned 20% more than racialised women (Tastsoglou & Preston, 2005). Racism and discrimination are undeniably rampant in tourism (Kipp et al., 2021; Yu & Hyun, 2021). In a Canadian study, Abassah-Oppong and Holmes (2020) found that 8% of the participants reported experiencing workplace discrimination, 27% reported seeing racial discrimination, 27% reported witnessing gender discrimination, and 18% reported witnessing sexual harassment. It has been shown that racism affects all tourism stakeholders, including workers, communities, and tourists (Costen et al., 2002; Hudson et al., 2020). In fact, there is evidence that racialised tourists have experienced racism while on vacation (Dillette et al., 2019; Lee & Scott, 2017).

Race has a significant impact on every aspect of a worker's experience, from job duties and responsibilities to where they work, their pay level, and even in which department they are promoted. Studies (Mirchandani & Bromfield, 2021) show that tourism is highly segregated by race and that a racialised hierarchy exists in the sector. Although the overwhelming majority of frontline workers in hospitality and tourism are racialised, they remain under-represented in the middle and higher echelons of management (Costen et al., 2002; Somerville & Walsworth, 2009). The US Bureau of Labor Statistics (2020) reported that 43.1% of workers within hospitality and tourism are racialised minorities, whereas Costen et al. (2002), examining the racial make-up of 5,549 hotel managers in 552 properties in the United States, found that only 20% were represented in managerial positions, the majority of which were found in housekeeping, a role where "key decision-making and financial authority is infrequent" (p. 65).

Hospitality and tourism sector also has a history of race-typing, where a particular race or minority group is perceived to be more suitable to undertake certain jobs, which are usually low paying and of low status (Costen et al., 2002). Race-typing occurs as a result of the development of stereotypes about a particular racial group, and then racialised workers are offered jobs that fit ethnic stereotypes while being passed over for other jobs. This means that racialised workers are consistently relegated to, and clustered in, certain departments, leading to job racialisation, defined as jobs that are predominantly made up of, used by, and concerned with racialised and ethnic minority workers (Collins, 1997). For example, Filipinos make up the majority of cruise ship workers: they are seen as "readymade workers for subordinate positions rather than for roles as leaders on the ship" (Terry, 2014, p. 73).

Several studies have found that many departments within the sector are segregated by race (Costen et al., 2002; Efthymiou et al., 2020). Collins (1997) stated that departments with a high concentration of racialised workers can lead to occupational ghettos, which are departments that have little to no influence on the firm's key financial and decision-making functions and often entail laborious, repetitive, and underpaid jobs. Worse, these departments frequently serve as occupational voids, preventing workers from being promoted to more lucrative job positions that play a more significant role in decision-making and financial operations, such as accounting, sales and marketing, and human resources. Racialised employees who are trapped in occupational ghettos, unable to gain additional skills, knowledge, and job experience, are thus unable to advance and frequently leave the sector.

This issue does not only affect frontline employees but also racialised people promoted to management positions, who often oversee occupational ghettos with little to no upward mobility into important high-level decision-making roles. When racialised people are elevated to management positions, it seems as if their primary skills and duties are to oversee and manage Other racialised and ethnic employees who do repetitive activities in substandard working conditions, have low status, and receive low wages (Costen et al., 2002). In fact, Costen et al. (2002) found that within the lodging sector, managerial roles are largely White, except in housekeeping. Other studies consistently show that White workers are overrepresented in management, and one argument for this overrepresentation is that Whites are largely in charge of the hiring process and, therefore, have dominant access to the selection processes (Birgier, 2017; Costen et al., 2002). These racialised people face discrimination and exploitation within hospitality and tourism sector.

A sector that is inherently inequitable

From its inception, the tourism sector can be seen as working to maintain a White-dominant hierarchy. It originated with European colonial expansion in the 1500s, which produced a core-periphery structure in which the global south (periphery) supplied agricultural commodities and slave or cheap labour to European countries (core) (Amin, 1976). Thus, the periphery acts as a source of resource extraction (including human resources) from which the core benefits at little or no cost (Peters, 1969). Following the Second World War, tourism grew rapidly worldwide with many developing countries exchanging one resource of extraction (i.e. agriculture) with another (i.e. pleasure tourism) (Weaver, 1988). The global south quickly became the world's "pleasure periphery" (Weaver, 1988, p. 319), a recreational haven for people residing in core areas (Baldacchino, 2016; Hall & Tucker, 2004). This core-periphery dynamic, on which global tourism is built, works to sustain the dynamic of poor and racialised "foreigners" serving wealthy White tourists (Flint, 1983). Thus, we could consider the tourism sector in the West as working to recreate the racial structure of the core periphery, which can only be recreated in core regions if racialised people can be extracted from periphery regions and used as cheap labour.

Tourism is increasingly reliant upon cheap migrant labour for its growth and expansion in many regions. In Italy, Massidda et al. (2017) found that regions with a higher share of migrants had more tourism-related businesses. In addition, immigrant labourers, being paid lower wages, help to sustain the expansion of firms and the labour market outcomes of native Italians in those regions. Tan and Lester (2012) had similar findings in Australia. These and other studies (e.g. Joppe, 2012) indicate that cheap immigrant labour is essential not only to the growth of tourism but to the overall economic growth of countries as well. To guarantee the growth of companies and, indeed, the economies of developed nations, it is essential to procure a cheap labour force, and immigration policies work to provide productive workers whose labour can be inexpensive. One strategy for acquiring cheap labour is for developed countries to attract workers from periphery regions with promises of prosperous lives, then make professional work difficult to obtain, and forcing the newcomers to settle for survival jobs, the majority of which are in the service sector.

Brain drain

Skilled migrants are valuable for OECD (Organisation for Economic Co-operation and Development) member nations, such as the United States, Canada, and the United Kingdom, as demand for such workers has increased significantly since 2010 in comparison to other categories (e.g. unskilled migrants and refugees) (Bailey & Mulder, 2017). Many skilled immigrant programmes are geared towards attracting trained workers from developing countries. Skilled immigrants contribute significantly to the development, wealth, and innovation of industrialised nations by offering a broader range and diversity of skills and knowledge, given their domestic ageing population and declining birth rates (Bailey & Mulder, 2017; Caplan, 2008). Countries such as Canada profit because they benefit from competences they did not invest time or money in developing, as skilled migrants arrive fully equipped to be integrated into the labour market (Caplan, 2008). Since they have talents that will allow them to become economically viable, these immigrants are also regarded as being less likely to become welfare reliant, making them even more appealing to the OECD countries (Bailey & Mulder, 2017). While immigration undoubtedly benefits developed countries, it also benefits skilled immigrants and their families, as they are sometimes escaping difficult situations to seek a better life in a new country while often sending remittances to families back home. However, as numerous studies demonstrate, finding an occupation that fits their expertise is not a given, with some skilled workers frequently experiencing poor labour market outcomes once they arrive in their new home countries (Jeeva, 2018; Somerville & Walsworth, 2010).

Although skilled immigrants provide many benefits to the State and the economy, they are often considered less valuable than native-born citizens, and they are subjected to a plethora of social, cultural, and economic barriers that prevent them from entering certain professions, even if they have the required abilities (Bailey & Mulder, 2017; Birgier, 2017). Among these barriers are language, other competencies, or the lack of recognition of their professional accreditations. Furthermore, many professions require the acquisition of locally sourced credentials or local work experience, which takes time and resources that newcomers may not have since they must concentrate on making a living in their adopted countries. For Bauder (2003, p. 699), "the nonrecognition of foreign credentials and dismissal of foreign work experience systematically excludes immigrant workers from the upper segments of the labour market". Indeed, Bhuyan et al. (2017) have argued that the requirement for a "Canadian experience" is one way that racism operates. Skilled migrants are, therefore, forced into accepting low-skilled work in lower-status and exploitative sectors, such as tourism (Bailey & Mulder, 2017; Birgier, 2017).

Tourism in Canada

Before the pandemic, Canada's tourism sector saw continued growth with a record 22.1 million international travellers in 2019 (Destination Canada, 2020). In 2019, tourism represented 6.4% of Canada's GDP and accounted for 9.3% of total employment (World Travel and Tourism Council, 2020). Despite this high contribution to national employment, it is not enough, as the tourism sector experiences a well-documented labour gap. White Canadians and older immigrants (i.e. living more than 5 years in Canada) avoid working in the sector, preferring to take jobs with better remuneration elsewhere, resulting in tourism's well-documented labour shortage (Jeeva, 2018; Tourism HR Canada, 2021). In 2018, Tourism HR Canada assessed the gap as 240,000 jobs and recommended immigration as one of the strategies to reduce the shortfall. The sector has been especially hard hit during the COVID-19 pandemic, when many workers left tourism to seek work in other sectors, effectively widening the labour gap (Tourism HR Canada, 2018).

Before the pandemic, national tourism and hotel associations worked with the government to design immigration programmes aimed at recruiting immigrants to work in tourism to narrow the gap. But Canada's existing immigration policy, though not designed to do so, was already working to funnel immigrants, many of whom are highly skilled and educated, into low-skill, low-paying industries such as tourism.

Canadian immigration policy

On May 1, 1947, William Lyon Mackenzie King, Canada's 10th prime minister, addressed parliament with a speech, which made clear that it was the intention of Canada to arrange its immigration policy so that Canada's population remained White (Triadafilopoulos, 2013). King stated:

> With regard to the selection of immigrants, much has been said about discrimination. I wish to make quite clear that Canada is perfectly within her rights in selecting the persons whom we regard as desirable future citizens. There will be general agreement with the view the people of Canada do not wish, as a result of mass immigration, to make a fundamental alteration in the character of our population. Large-scale immigration from the orient would change the fundamental composition of the Canadian population. Any considerable oriental immigration would, moreover, be certain to give rise to social and economic problems of a character that might lead to serious difficulties in the field of international relations.
> (House of Commons Debates, 1947, p. 2646).

Based on these requirements, Canada's immigration policy was grounded on admitting White immigrants, largely western and northern European, who made up the vast majority of immigrants before the 1960s, as they were perceived as more "desirable". This meant the active exclusion of other ethnicities and racial groups who were seen as undesirable (Triadafilopoulos, 2013). It is critical to acknowledge that this is the foundation upon which Canada's immigration policy was built and forms the basis on which Canada perceives and values different races, ethnicities, and nationalities.

Following various social, economic, and political pressures, Canada replaced its overtly racist policy with the Immigration Act of 1967 (later updated to the Immigration and Refugee Protection Act in 2002). The policy no longer prioritised race and pivoted to fulfil economic, social, and humanitarian objectives (Triadafilopoulos, 2013). Currently, Canada has three categories of immigrants: the family migrant category, the refugee migrant category, and the economic migrant category.

Economic migrants to Canada and their employment outcomes

Economic migrants are admitted on the basis of educational attainment, skills, and professional work experience. Since the inception of the Immigration Act of

1967, economic migrants have consistently been the largest immigrant class, representing at least 55% of new immigrants admitted to Canada each year. According to Immigration, Refugees and Citizenship Canada (IRCC) (2020), immigrants make an impact: 26% of Canadian workers are immigrants; they fill gaps in the labour force, and there are over 600,000 self-employed immigrants. In addition, immigrants are increasingly well educated: in 2019, 56% of very recent immigrants had a university degree.

In addition to being skilled, economic migrants are more attractive than other immigrant categories because they must have economic resources to immigrate. A Canadian requirement for economic migrants is the need to demonstrate that they will be able to sustain themselves financially once they settle (IRCC, 2021). Unlike other migrant groups who are perceived to be potential burdens to the welfare system, economic migrants will inject capital into the economy as soon as they arrive.

The selection of economic migrants in Canada is based on a points system centred on education attainment, fluency in one of Canada's official languages, work experience, age, adaptability, and arranged employment (Immigration, Refugees and Citizenship Canada (IRCC), 2021). IRCC places premium points for human and social capital and emphasises to candidates that these resources are transferable, sought after in the labour market, and enhance economic integration (Reitz, 2005). While the Canadian government maintains that the economic migrant category is intended to attract productive and equipped individuals into Canada's labour market, this is not always the case. Many immigrants are caught off-guard when they arrive and find a disconnect between expectations and reality. They face diminished employment outcomes, including lower earning power, unemployment, and high rates of poverty (Grant & Sweetman, 2004; Picot, 2004). In fact, Somerville and Walsworth (2010) found that the employment outcomes of economic class migrants in Canada were worse than their counterparts in the United States and continue to deteriorate.

Barriers: a disconnect between the federal and provincial governments

Newcomers to Canada experience discrimination, and there are barriers that prevent them from gaining access to quality work and equal pay (Akbar, 2019; Mirchandani & Bromfield, 2021). There are two main factors contributing to the poor outcomes for economic migrants in Canada: skill-discounting and discrimination (Reitz, 2005). Skill-discounting "refers to the devaluation of foreign experience and credentials" (Somerville & Walsworth, 2010, p. 152). Treuren et al. (2021, p. 31) found in Australia that the hospitality sector provides "refuge employment" and that skill-discounted immigrants "found hospitality employment in disproportionately high numbers, compared to all other industries".

In Canada, skill-discounting happens both at the government level and in the workplace. Newcomers encounter skill-discounting as soon as they arrive, and this may be due to a disconnect between the federal and provincial government employment standards (Reitz, 2005). The issue lies in the fact that there are no federal professional standards; rather, provincial governments regulate provincial labour markets. Provinces determine what credentials, skills, and experiences are required for skilled labour within the provinces, and as such, professional standards vary by province (Bauder, 2003; Reitz, 2005). Nonetheless, the federal government has been recruiting immigrants based on educational attainment and accreditations that may not align with provincial standards. For Somerville and Walsworth (2010, p. 155), "The immigration process for highly-skilled workers under the Economic Class in Canada is saturated with overly optimistic messages implicit in the Canadian point system that foreign earned credentials are recognized and valued in the Canadian labour market". Thus, the federal government has been giving economic migrants the false impression they will be able to smoothly transition into the labour market with their international credentials and work experience.

However, when newcomers settle in a province, they discover that provincial standards must be met, rendering their education and professional credentials completely or partially insufficient. Newcomers in such situations are left vulnerable and report being frustrated and angry for being misled (Bauder, 2003; Somerville & Walsworth, 2010). In order to work in their specialty, they must gain educational and professional accreditation from Canadian institutions. This is a time-consuming and expensive barrier for many newcomers who must focus on supporting themselves and their families when they arrive. As a result, many newcomers, who find themselves in this situation, get jobs that are below their skill and experience levels, often in hospitality and tourism sector, because the barriers to entry are quite low.

Skills discounting also occurs at the market level, where employers devalue international accreditation and work experience (Picot, 2004). Employers do not understand the quality of education systems outside of Canada and may falsely believe that international education and work experience may not be *on par* with Canada (Somerville & Walsworth, 2010). As a result, Canadian employers either give hiring preference to people with Canadian education and experience or recruit immigrants with international experience at a discounted wage (Vosko et al., 2017). Sweetman (2004) argued that Canadian employers may be justified in being cautious of some international accreditations since the professional and education systems in some countries are indeed subpar. On the other hand, Somerville and Walsworth (2010) suggested that perhaps Canadian employers are simply being risk-averse and may not be deliberately discriminatory when they give preference to Canadian workers. However, it could be stated that Canadian employers have no incentive to hire equitably, as they benefit from the underpayment of the labour of newcomers who may be highly educated and skilled. When the earnings of economic migrants and native-born individuals with the same credentials are compared, there is a huge wage gap (Ali & Newbold, 2020; Banerjee et al., 2019; Ferrer et al., 2020; Grant & Sweetman, 2004; Picot, 2004). According to Bauder (2003, p. 713):

> immigrants suffer from occupational downgrading, are forced to switch careers and experience loss of social status. Many immigrants feel that they

have been tricked into this situation by Canadian immigration policies and labour-market regulations that do not disclose to immigrants prior to their arrival in Canada that their human capital will be devalued.

Canada's points system no longer works as new immigrants are faring worse than previous cohorts (Akbar, 2019). The disparity in earnings between immigrants and their Canadian-born counterparts is increasing despite improved educational attainment amongst immigrants (Akbar, 2019). Increasingly, immigrants with university degrees face challenges in securing employment. One way new immigrants can avoid the issues that limit their employment is to become self-employed. In fact, the entrepreneurship rate for immigrants is higher than for Canadian-born, and immigrant-owned firms make a disproportionate contribution to job creation in the private sector (Picot & Rollin, 2019).

Canada's racially segregated labour markets

Canada's policies and history of systemic racism have led to segregated labour markets (Evans & Moore, 2015). In Canada, race, gender, education, and length of residency all act as social factors that influence access to quality work (Akbar, 2019; Picot, 2004). First, Canada's labour markets are stratified by race, meaning there is a racial hierarchy in access to higher status jobs and decent working conditions (Block & Galabuzi, 2011, 2020; Block et al., 2014; Lightman & Good Gingrich, 2018; Picot, 2004). Block and Galabuzi (2020) found that in Ontario, Canada, racialised women were more likely to work in low-income occupations (25.1%) compared to White women (23.6%), racialised men (17.8), and White men (15.1). Interestingly, these patterns are reversed for occupations paying at or above the top 10% of the median income. Block and Galabuzi (2020) found that 11% of White men were employed in these higher status and higher paying jobs, while 8.8% of racialised men and only 5.5% of racialised women occupy these jobs.

Racialised people who immigrate to Canada from African, Asian, and other non-European countries have worse outcomes than their European counterparts, as they face double discrimination: first for having international credentials and experience and second because they are not White (Bauder, 2003; Wilson-Forsberg, 2015). Bernhardt (2015) confirmed that the Canadian job market is stratified by race, and according to Preston and Murnaghan (2005, p. 69), "recent visible minority immigrants are much more likely to be living in poverty". Block et al. (2014) also demonstrated that a pay gap exists between White and racialised workers, with many facing barriers to promotion. Block et al. (2014) found that racialised Canadians had a higher labour market participation rate (67.3%) compared to White Canadians (66.7%). Despite this willingness to work, racialised men were 24% more likely to be unemployed and earn 31.3% less than White men. Racialised women fare worse as the study also found they were 48% more likely to be unemployed and earn 55.6% less than White men. Akbar (2019) indicated that Bangladeshis' and other visible minority immigrants' educational qualifications do not provide an earning advantage. This has led researchers to conclude that educational attainment is not the issue; the problem is that the Canadian labour market is shaped by not only race but also gender, as racialised women face even more hardships. Since White Canadian-born workers earn higher wages than racialised workers (Schirle & Sogaolu, 2020), this leads to a persistent wage gap based on skin colour.

Research also shows that length of time in Canada is a factor. Newcomers, needing to get adjusted to their new homes quickly, are forced into "bad" jobs with the rationale being that newcomers need "Canadian experience" (Bauder, 2003). This means that racialised newcomers fare worse than racialised immigrants who have been in Canada for a longer time, who then fare worse than White immigrants (Jeeva, 2018). To illustrate, racialised newcomers are more likely to be employed in low-level jobs, have access to fewer working hours, be relegated to seasonal and part-time work, or have precarious work compared to older racialised immigrants.

According to Mirchandani and Bromfield (2021, p. 40), "racialized workers are often funneled into jobs that are prone to have employment standards violations". Vosko et al. (2017) discovered that between 2014 and 2015, the lodging and food services industry had the highest rate of monetary Employment Standard (ES) complaints in Ontario, surpassing the construction industry. According to Vosko et al. (2017), "the majority of complainants from this industry (54%) are employed in full-service restaurants, and a quarter (25%) are found in limited service eating places, such as fast-food restaurants" (p. 265). Unfortunately, workers have limited recourse as labour laws in Canada are geared towards unionised employees or collective agreements, but low-level jobs, such as those within the hospitality and tourism sector, are often non-union and, therefore, not well protected (Mirchandani & Bromfield, 2021; Oxfam Canada, 2017). The vulnerabilities of immigrants, particularly racialised ones, are engineered in such a way that their skills and experiences are discounted, forcing them into jobs for which they may be overqualified.

Policy changes are needed

Canada, a country with one of the world's oldest populations and one of the world's lowest birth rates, continues to need immigrants, particularly as the country rebounds from the COVID-19 pandemic. The government has confirmed its commitment to attract over 400,000 new permanent residents per year from 2021 through 2023. In light of the problems discussed earlier, Canada needs immigration policy changes. Currently, work assignments by racial stereotyping generate the perception that racialised immigrants are only suitable for certain jobs and tasks. Though these jobs are essential to the economy, government policies (i.e. through their actions and inactions) ensure these jobs remain "undignified". Stereotypes and racist practices have become normalised within the Canadian labour force (Jeeva, 2018), past racist policies entrenched ideas and practices that persist today. These policies underscore Canada's role in channelling workers, particularly racialised workers, into labour markets that are stratified by race and a continued reluctance to recognise international credentials and work experiences. Canada's immigration policy works by promising easy labour market and economic integration for many racialised immigrants, but it does not deliver on the promise

The main policy recommendation that can be made is about recognising and validating degrees, professional credentials, and experience earned abroad and making sure that these credentials lead to employment in the desired sector. In parallel, some national and provincial professional associations should relax their requirements, or at least synchronise job requirements across regions, to allow the hiring of qualified foreign workers. A third recommendation is to help immigrants start their own businesses. Currently, the federal government, which provides language support and education to prepare immigrants to become employees, does not provide support and entrepreneurship training (Kalu & Okafor, 2021). This is a missed opportunity, especially for the tourism sector, where many opportunities exist for entrepreneurs. A fourth recommendation, specific to the tourism and hospitality sector, is to implement better employment experiences for workers. As Winchenbach et al. (2019) noted, job dignity (respect, self-respect, professional identity, autonomy, etc.) has received too little attention in tourism research.

Policymakers and industry leaders must work together to agree on better employee management practices and to respond to employees' requests for fairness, better scheduling, and benefits. As part of these practices, efforts to control and eradicate discrimination, racism, and harassment, which remain significant in the sector, should be included. Finally, and following the previous recommendations, industry leaders and professional associations must make a conscious effort to improve the reputation of the sector. It must be recognised that the solution to the labour gap in Canada is not to attract more immigrants: it is first to provide decent work environments and career growth options for Canadian-born and immigrants alike.

Conclusion

The consequences of the current immigration policies are far-reaching. They contribute to perpetuating the perception that it is the natural order of things for racialised people to serve the White, dominant clientele. Tourism, as an international phenomenon, has been an important instrument in perpetuating White cultural domination established during colonial times and racist stereotypes about the social position of Black and brown bodies, as labourers and entertainers for White tourist consumption, continue to be reinforced.

Government action regarding policy development is critical to creating decent working conditions and protecting tourism workers. The Canadian immigration policy knowingly or unknowingly acts as a supplier of cheap labour to exploitative sectors, such as tourism. As such, Canada's immigration policies work to consolidate racism and a White supremacist dynamic within hospitality and tourism, whereby racialised frontline workers, overseen by their White superiors, labour to serve a mainly White clientele. Canada's immigration policy is inherently racist because it attracts immigrants to a system that sees immigrant workers as cheap labour. It also underscores Canada's role in plundering low- and middle-income countries for their most productive and brightest, only to use them as cheap labour. For the hospitality and tourism work issues to be addressed, local labour laws, as well as immigration policies must be addressed and revisited. All levels of Canadian government must work to eradicate the policies and practices that serve to uphold racism. As Price (2013, p. 637) wrote, "the legacies of White supremacy and colonialism continue to haunt Canada", and Canada's hospitality and tourism sector continues to be affected by those legacies.

The case of Canada is exemplary: it is among the countries that rely the most on immigration to respond to their economic needs. Its policies, however, contribute to discrimination and racism and keep alive the racial hierarchy that exists within its tourism sector. While policy reforms are needed at the national and provincial levels, practices must also change within the tourism sector to reduce inequalities and to provide better and more desirable working conditions for all workers, with a particular focus on racialized immigrants. According to Baum (2018, p. 875), "There is growing recognition of ineffectual engagement with workforce issues in tourism policy and planning and, arguably, also in the priority it is accorded by practice in the private sector". Industry leaders have the responsibility to change the image and reputation of the sector if they want to attract and retain good prospects and reduce the ever-expanding labour gap. Fair treatment of workers and opportunities for all to grow and gain access to management positions are essential for tourism to be sustainable, successful, and competitive. The COVID-19 crisis has pointed to precarious employment and has increased negative public perceptions towards hospitality jobs. It is the industry's responsibility to change this for Canada and its tourism businesses to remain competitive. As tourism comes out of the pandemic, it has a unique opportunity to change "what 'normal' is and what it should be. We, tourism academics, together with industry partners and governments, can design a path toward a new era" (Della Lucia et al., 2021, p. 265).

References

Abassah-Oppong, S., & Holmes, M. R. (2020). *The persistent gender gap in Canadian hotel operations*. Travel and Tourism Research Association Annual Conference: Advancing Tourism Research Globally. 6. Innsbruck, Austria. https://scholarworks.umass.edu/ttra/2020/research_papers/6https://scholarworks.umass.edu/ttra/2020/research_papers/6

Akbar, M. (2019). Examining the factors that affect the employment status of racialised immigrants: A study of Bangladeshi immigrants in Toronto, Canada. *South Asian Diaspora*, *11*(1), 67–87. https://doi.org/10.1080/19438192.2018.1523092.

Ali, W. K., & Newbold, K. B. (2020). Geographic variations in precarious employment outcomes between immigrant and Canadian-born populations. *Papers in Regional Science*, *99*(5), 1185–1213. https://doi.org/10.1111/pirs.12528

Amin, S. (1976). *Unequal development: An essay on the social formations of peripheral capitalism*. Harvester Press.

Bailey, A., & Mulder, C. H. (2017). Highly skilled migration between the Global North and South: Gender, life courses and institutions. *Journal of Ethnic and Migration Studies*, *43*(16), 2689–2703. https://doi.org/10.1080/1369183X.2017.1314594

Baldacchino, G. (Ed.). (2016). *Archipelago tourism: Policies and practices*. Routledge.

Banerjee, R., Verma, A., & Zhang, T. (2019). Brain gain or brain waste? Horizontal, vertical, and full job-education mismatch and wage progression among skilled immigrant men in Canada. *International Migration Review, 53*(3), 646–670. https://doi.org/10.1177/0197918318774501

Bauder, H. (2003). "Brain abuse," or the devaluation of immigrant labour in Canada. *Antipode, 35*(4), 699–717. https://doi.org/10.1046/j.1467-8330.2003.00346.x

Baum, T. (2018). Sustainable human resource management as a driver in tourism policy and planning: A serious sin of omission? *Journal of Sustainable Tourism, 26*(6), 873–889. https://doi.org/10.1080/09669582.2017.1423318

Baum, T., Cheung, C., Kong, H., Kralj, A., Mooney, S., Ramachandran, S., Ružic, M. D., & Siow, M. L. (2016). Sustainability and the tourism and hospitality workforce: A thematic analysis. *Sustainability, 8*(8), 809. https://doi.org/10.3390/su8080809

Benjamin, S., & Dillette, A. K. (2021). Black travel movement: Systemic racism informing tourism. *Annals of Tourism Research, 88*. https://doi.org/10.1016/j.annals.2021.103169

Bernhardt, N. S. (2015). Racialized precarious employment and the inadequacies of the Canadian welfare state. *Sage Open, 5*(2), 2158244015575639. https://doi.org/10.1177/2158244015575639

Bhuyan, R., Jeyapal, D., Ku, J., Sakamoto, I., & Chou, E. (2017). Branding "Canadian experience" in immigration policy: Nation building in a neoliberal era. *Journal of International Migration and Integration, 18*(1), 47–62.

Bianchi, R. V. (2018). The political economy of tourism development: A critical review. *Annals of Tourism Research, 70*, 88–102. https://doi.org/10.1016/j.annals.2017.08.005

Bianchi, R. V., & de Man, F. (2021). Tourism, inclusive growth and decent work: A political economy critique. *Journal of Sustainable Tourism, 29*(2–3), 353–371. https://doi.org/10.1080/09669582.2020.1730862

Birgier, D. P. (2017). Immigration, occupations, and native wages: Long time trends in the US. *Research in Social Stratification and Mobility, 51*, 41–55. https://doi.org/10.1016/j.rssm.2017.07.002.

Block, S., & Galabuzi, G. E. (2011). *Canada's colour coded labour market: The gap for racialized workers*. Canadian Centre for Policy Alternatives. Retrieved October 7, 2021, from www.policyalternatives.ca/sites/default/files/uploads/publications/National%20Office/2011/03/Colour%20Coded%20Labour%20Market.pdf

Block, S., & Galabuzi, G. E. (2020). *Persistent inequality*. Research and Studies on Race Relations in Canada, 127. Retrieved October 7, 2021, from www.researchgate.net/profile/Kon-Madut/publication/330480802_How_Nationalism_influenced_Settlements_and_Integration_of_Racialized_Migrants_in_Canada/links/5e99d2a2299bf13079a2287a/How-Nationalism-influenced-Settlements-and-Integration-of-Racialized-Migrants-in-Canada.pdf#page=127

Block, S., Galabuzi, G. E., & Weiss, A. (2014). *The colour coded labour market by the numbers*. Wellesley Institute. Retrieved October 7, 2021, from www.wellesleyinstitute.com/wp-content/uploads/2014/09/The-Colour-Coded-Labour-Market-By-The-Numbers.pdf

Caplan, G. L. (2008). *The betrayal of Africa*. Groundwood Books Ltd.

Collins, S. M. (1997). *Black corporate executives: The making and breaking of a Black middle class* (Vol. 71). Temple University Press.

Costen, W. M., Cliath, A. G., & Woods, R. H. (2002). Where are the racial and ethnic minorities in hotel management? Exploring the relationship between race and position in hotels. *Journal of Human Resources in Hospitality & Tourism, 1*(2), 57–69. https://doi.org/10.1300/J171v01n02_05

Della Lucia, M., Giudici, E., & Dimanche, F. (2021). Lessons for shared value creation in tourism: The pandemic challenge. In M. Della Lucia & E. Giudici (Eds.), *Humanistic management and sustainable tourism: Human, social and environmental challenges* (pp. 255–268). Routledge.

Destination Canada. (2020). *Canada experiences third consecutive record-breaking year for tourism in 2019*. www.destinationcanada.com/en/news/canada-experiences-third-consecutive-record-breaking-year-tourism-2019

Dillette, A. K., Benjamin, S., & Carpenter, C. (2019). Tweeting the black travel experience: Social media counternarrative stories as innovative insight on #TravelingWhileBlack. *Journal of Travel Research*, 58(8), 1357–1372. https://doi.org/10.1177/0047287518802087

Efthymiou, L., Orphanidou, Y., & Panayiotou, G. (2020). Delineating the changing frontstage and backstage segregation in high-end and luxury hotels. *Hospitality & Society*, 10(3), 287–312. https://doi.org/10.1386/hosp_00025_1

Evans, L., & Moore, W. L. (2015). Impossible burdens: White institutions, emotional labor, and micro-resistance. *Social Problems*, 62(3), 439–454. https://doi.org/10.1093/socpro/spv009

Ferrer, I., Lee, Y., & Khan, M. N. (2020). Understanding the lived experiences and financial realities of older immigrants. *Canadian Ethnic Studies*, 52(2), 53–78. https://doi.org/10.1353/ces.2020.0013

Fleming, S. S. (2015). Déjà vu? An updated analysis of the gender wage gap in the US hospitality sector. *Cornell Hospitality Quarterly*, 56(2), 180–190. https://doi.org/10.1177/1938965514567680

Flint, J. (1983). Scandal at the Bristol Hotel: Some thoughts on racial discrimination in Britain and West Africa and its relationship to the planning of decolonisation, 1939–47. *The Journal of Imperial and Commonwealth History*, 12(1), 74–93. https://doi.org/10.1080/03086538308582651

Grant, H., & Sweetman, A. (2004). Introduction to economic and urban issues in Canadian immigration policy. *Canadian Journal of Urban Research*, 1–24. www.jstor.org/stable/44320793

Hall, C., & Tucker, H. (2004). *Tourism and postcolonialism contested discourses, identities, and representations*. Routledge.

Hickel, J. (2019). Degrowth: A theory of radical abundance. *Real World Economics Review*, 87, 54–68. www.paecon.net/PAEReview/issue87/Hickel87.pdf

House of Commons Debates. (1947). Immigration. *20th Parliament, 3rd Session*, 3, 2644–2647. Retrieved October 7, 2021, from https://parl.canadiana.ca/view/oop.debates_HOC2003_03/657?r=0&s=4

Hudson, S., So, K. K. F., Meng, F., Cárdenas, D., & Li, J. (2020). Racial discrimination in tourism: The case of African-American travellers in South Carolina. *Current Issues in Tourism*, 23(4), 438–451. https://doi.org/10.1080/13683500.2018.1516743

Immigration, Refugees and Citizenship Canada. (2020). *2020 Annual report to parliament on immigration*. www.canada.ca/en/immigration-refugees-citizenship/corporate/publications-manuals/annual-report-parliament-immigration-2020.html#immigration2019

Immigration, Refugees and Citizenship Canada. (2021). *Proof of funds – Skilled immigrants (Express Entry)*. www.canada.ca/en/immigration-refugees-citizenship/services/immigrate-canada/express-entry/documents/proof-funds.html

Jeeva, A. (2018). Newcomer women and the workforce: A critical policy analysis of employment and labour legislation in Ontario. *Social Justice and Community Engagement*, 30. https://scholars.wlu.ca/brantford_sjce/30

Joppe, M. (2012). Migrant workers: Challenges and opportunities in addressing tourism labour shortages. *Tourism Management*, *33*(3), 662–671.

Kalu, K., & Okafor, O. N. (2021). Programming for immigrant women in Canada: Is entrepreneurship neglected? *International Migration*, *59*(1), 105–125. https://doi.org/10.1111/imig.12724

Kipp, A., Hawkins, R., & Gray, N. J. (2021). Gendered and racialized experiences and subjectivities in volunteer tourism. *Gender, Place and Culture*, *28*(1), 45–65. https://doi.org/10.1080/0966369X.2019.1708274

Lacher, R. G., & Oh, C. O. (2012). Is tourism a low-income industry? Evidence from three coastal regions. *Journal of Travel Research*, *51*(4), 464–472. https://doi.org/10.1177/0047287511426342

Lee, K. J., & Scott, D. (2017). Racial discrimination and African-Americans' travel behavior: The utility of habitus and vignette technique. *Journal of Travel Research*, *56*(3), 381–392. https://doi.org/10.1177/0047287516643184

Li, S., Li, G., Law, R., & Paradies, Y. (2020). Racism in tourism reviews. *Tourism Management*, *80*, 104100. https://doi.org/10.1016/j.tourman.2020.104100

Lightman, N., & Good Gingrich, L. (2018). Measuring economic exclusion for racialized minorities, immigrants and women in Canada: Results from 2000 to 2010. *Journal of Poverty*, *22*(5), 398–420.

Massidda, C., Etzo, I., & Piras, R. (2017). The relationship between immigration and tourism firms. *Tourism Economics*, *23*(8), 1537–1552. https://doi.org/10.1177/1354816617708660

Mirchandani, K., & Bromfield, S. M. (2021). The entrenchment of racial stratification through the colour-blind employment standards enforcement regime in Ontario. *Canadian Ethnic Studies*, *53*(1), 23–45. https://doi.org/10.1353/ces.2021.0001

Oxfam Canada. (2017). *Tourism's dirty secret: The exploitation of hotel housekeepers*. https://oxfamilibrary.openrepository.com/bitstream/handle/10546/620355/rr-tourisms-dirty-secret-171017-en.pdf?

Peters, M. (1969). *International tourism: The economics and development of the international tourist trade*. Hutchinson.

Picot, G. (2004). The deteriorating economic welfare of Canadian immigrants. *Canadian Journal of Urban Research*, *13*(1), 25–46. www.jstor.org/stable/44320794

Picot, G., & Rollin, A. M. (2019). Immigrant entrepreneurs as job creators: The case of Canadian private incorporated companies. *Analytical Studies – Research Paper Series*, Catalogue no. 11F0019M – No. 423. https://www150.statcan.gc.ca/n1/pub/11f0019m/11f0019m2019011-eng.htm

Preston, V., & Murnaghan, A. M. (2005, Spring). Immigrants and racialization in Canada: Geographies of exclusion? *Canadian Issues*, 67–71.

Price, J. (2013). Canada, white supremacy, and the twinning of empires. *International Journal*, *68*(4), 628–638. https://doi.org/10.1177/0020702013510675

Reitz, J. G. (2005). Tapping immigrants' skills: New directions for Canadian immigration policy in the knowledge economy. *Law & Business Review of the Americas*, *11*, 409–432.

Santos, L. D., & Varejão, J. (2007). Employment, pay and discrimination in the tourism industry. *Tourism Economics*, *13*(2), 225–240. https://doi.org/10.5367/000000007780823186

Schirle, T., & Sogaolu, M. (2020). *A work in progress: Measuring wage gaps for women and minorities in the Canadian labour market*. CD Howe Institute Commentary, 561. https://ssrn.com/abstract=3517443

Somerville, K., & Walsworth, S. (2009). Vulnerabilities of highly skilled immigrants in Canada and the United States. *American Review of Canadian Studies*, *39*, 147–161. https://doi.org/10.1080/02722010902848169

Somerville, K., & Walsworth, S. (2010). Admission and employment criteria discrepancies: Experiences of skilled immigrants in Toronto. *Journal of International Migration and Integration*, *11*, 341–352. https://doi.org/10.1007/s12134-010-0138-4

Steiner, C. (2006). Tourism, poverty reduction and the political economy: Egyptian perspectives on tourism's economic benefits in a semi-*rentier* state. *Tourism and Hospitality Planning & Development*, *3*(3), 161–177. https://doi.org/10.1080/14790530601132286

Sweetman, A. (2004). *Immigrant source country educational quality and Canadian labour market outcomes* [Unpublished manuscript]. School of Policy Studies, Queen's University, Kingston, Canada.

Tan, Y., & Lester, L. H. (2012). Labour market and economic impacts of international working holiday temporary migrants to Australia. *Population, Space and Place*, *18*(3), 359–383. https://doi.org/10.1002/psp.674

Tastsoglou, E., & Preston, V. (2005). Gender, immigration and labour market integration: Where we are and what we still need to know. *Atlantis: Critical Studies in Gender, Culture & Social Justice*, *30*(1), 46–59.

Terry, W. C. (2014). The perfect worker: Discursive makings of Filipinos in the workplace hierarchy of the globalized cruise industry. *Social & Cultural Geography*, *15*(1), 73–93. https://doi.org/10.1080/14649365.2013.864781

Tourism HR Canada. (2018, March 28). *Bridging the labour gap: Latest labour supply report available*. https://tourismhr.ca/bridging-the-labour-gap-latest-labour-supply-report-available/

Tourism HR Canada. (2021, March 24). *Labour market information*. https://tourismhr.ca/category/labour-market-information/page/2/

Treuren, G. J., Manoharan, A., & Vishnu, V. (2021). The hospitality sector as an employer of skill discounted migrants. Evidence from Australia. *Journal of Policy Research in Tourism, Leisure and Events*, *13*(1), 20–35. https://doi.org/10.1080/19407963.2019.1655859

Triadafilopoulos, T. (2013). Dismantling white Canada: Race, rights, and the origins of the points system. In T. Triadafilopoulos (Ed.), *Wanted and welcome? Policies for highly skilled immigrants in comparative perspective* (pp. 15–37). Springer.

United Nation World Tourism Organization. (2019). *Tourism highlights, 2019 edition*. www.e-unwto.org/doi/pdf/10.18111/9789284421152

United Nation World Tourism Organization. (2020). *Covid-19 and tourism: Tourism in pre-pandemic times*. www.unwto.org/covid-19-and-tourism-2020

US Bureau of Labor Statistics. (2020). *Labor force statistics from the current population survey*. Retrieved from https://www.bls.gov/cps/cpsaat18.htm

Vosko, L. F., Grundy, J., Tucker, E., Thomas, M. P., Noack, A. M., Casey, R., Gellatly, M., & Mussell, J. (2017). The compliance model of employment standards enforcement: An evidence-based assessment of its efficacy in instances of wage theft. *Industrial Relations Journal*, *48*(3), 256–273. https://doi.org/10.1111/irj.12178

Weaver, D. B. (1988). The evolution of a "plantation" tourism landscape on the Caribbean island of Antigua. *Tijdschrift voor economische en sociale geografie [Journal of Economic & Social Geography]*, *79*(5), 319–331.

Wilson-Forsberg, S. (2015). "We don't integrate; we adapt": Latin American immigrants interpret their Canadian employment experiences in Southwestern Ontario. *Journal of International Migration and Integration*, *16*, 469–489. https://doi.org/10.1007/s12134-014-0349-1

Winchenbach, A., Hanna, P., & Miller, G. (2019). Rethinking decent work: The value of dignity in tourism employment. *Journal of Sustainable Tourism*, *27*(7), 1026–1043. https://doi.org/10.1080/09669582.2019.1566346

World Travel and Tourism Council. (2020). *Canada travel & tourism could reach pre-pandemic levels next year.* Retrieved from https://wttc.org/news-article/canada-travel-and-tourism-could-reach-pre-pandemic-levels-next-year

Yu, M., & Hyun, S. (2021). Development of modern racism scale in global airlines: A study of Asian female flight attendants. *International Journal of Environmental Research and Public Health, 18,* 2688. https://doi.org/10.3390/ijerph18052688

Zampoukos, K., & Ioannides, D. (2011). The tourism labour conundrum: Agenda for new research in the geography of hospitality workers. *Hospitality & Society, 1*(1), 25–45. https://doi.org/10.1386/hosp.1.1.25_1

4 Women in tourism employment
Glass ceiling or gender equality?

Buket Buluk Eşitti

Introduction

Tourism is a service sector that relies on labour-intensive employment. Women employees play an important role in tourism businesses and in the implementation of community development initiatives. However, it is noteworthy that gender inequalities still persist in tourism. Gender equality implies that women and men have equal opportunity to contribute to and benefit from economic, social, cultural, and political development. According to the United Nations (UN) (2021), gender equality means egalitarianism in rights, responsibilities, and opportunities for both women and men. Gender equality leads to improvements in working practices, an increase in the proportion of women in education and business life, a reduction in the wage gap created by gender differences, and participation in decision-making structures in business. However, according to the UN (2021), husbands can legally prevent their wives from working in 18 member-countries, boys and girls do not have equal inheritance rights in 39 member-countries, and 49 countries do not have laws protecting women from domestic violence.

Gender discrimination at regional, national, and global levels prevents women from using their capacity to contribute to the economy, political arena, and society in general (Baum, 2013). Women also appear to be restricted to the most vulnerable jobs, where they are more likely to experience poor working conditions, a lack of opportunity, violence, exploitation, stress, and sexual harassment (United Nations World Tourism Organization (UNWTO), 2010). Gender equality, especially in the workplace, is not only a fundamental human right but also a necessary foundation for a peaceful, prosperous, and sustainable organisational climate.

The underrepresentation of women employees in management stems from the inequality they encounter when vying for management positions which can be seen as gender and job discrimination (Kuhn & Shen, 2013, p. 287). Gender discrimination occurs both horizontally and vertically. In horizontal discrimination, while men and women employees have the same position and official title in an organisation, they assume different duties and responsibilities. This is because the same job does not contain equal responsibility, challenges, and opportunities (to move forward) for female employees. In vertical discrimination, female

DOI: 10.4324/9781003255413-5

employees begin in low-level positions that require longer employment tenure and more promotions to reach management positions (Boddy, 2002).

Women also encounter barriers to entering the work force. In the context of gender-based division of labour, housework and care services are expected to be done by women (Sharon, 2001). Making women responsible for these jobs, from which men are traditionally exempt, is an important factor affecting a woman's decision or ability to work outside the home. Moreover, being married is another factor that closely affects participation in the labour force. Evidence suggests that some women choose to work outside the home in order to escape male authority, although they often find themselves under the control of other men once they enter the workplace (Beauregard, 2006).

There are many career barriers and situations affecting the status of women in the workforce. These include (International Labor Service (ILO), 1998; Weyer, 2007) family responsibilities, which require women to devote time to both work and family, the long hours needed to be recognised and promoted in professional and managerial jobs, tokenism, organisational culture and climate, inequalities in educational opportunities and in-service training, deficiencies in legal regulations regarding the advancement of women, the inability to access informal communication networks (good old boys' network), traditional recruitment methods, lack of flexible working hours, expectations of society and family, inadequate childcare arrangements, prejudices, and the maternal wall (long hours spent managing home life and children). Often, businesses expect women to prioritise work over family obligations.

The 17 Sustainable Development Goals, developed by the UN, are vital for promoting global peace and harmony. Goal 5, gender equality and women's empowerment, is very important for the transformation of countries in order to provide equal opportunities for boys and girls in education and employment (UN, 2016). Gender equality requires not only equal access to skills (such as education), resources, and opportunities (such as property rights, health care, and employment) but also the ability to use these rights, talents, and resources. Tourism plays an important role at the heart of the 2030 Agenda for Sustainable Development as a way to deliver on commitments to gender equality and women's empowerment (United Nations World Tourism Organization (UNWTO), 2019). In the tourism sector, as in other sectors, it has been acknowledged that female employees are not adequately represented in leadership roles and that the glass ceiling remains in place (Chisholm-Burns et al., 2017). Therefore, this chapter explores the role of gender in relation to the glass ceiling concept.

Concepts in gender studies

The glass ceiling concept

According to Cotter et al. (2001), the glass ceiling can be defined as an invisible barrier that occurs around mid-management career levels and that prevents women from entering the higher echelons of an organisation despite having equal

Table 4.1 Glass ceiling barriers for female managers.

Barriers Caused by Individual Factors	Barriers Caused by Organisational Factors	Barriers Caused by Social Factors
• Taking on multiple roles • Women's personal preferences and perceptions	• Organisation culture • Organisational policies • Lack of mentorship • Inability to join informal communication networks	• Occupational distinction • Stereotypes (gender associated)

Source: Adapted from Barutçugil (2002), Deemer and Fredericks (2006), and Rosener (2011).

qualification, experience, and skills. The glass ceiling is a concept that emerged in the United States in the 1970s. It characterises the insurmountable barriers between women and senior management (Wirth, 2001) and occurs in government, industry, educational institutions, and non-profit organisations (Cotter et al., 2001). Table 4.1 presents gender-based glass ceiling barrier classifications (Barutçugil, 2002; Deemer & Fredericks, 2006; Rosener, 2011). From an integrative point of view, the elements that lead to the formation of a glass ceiling in organisations are derived from individual, organisational, and social factors (Dreher, 2003). Individual factors include the multiple roles a woman holds, such as family and work responsibilities, that do not allow for self-control of time commitments (Barutçugil, 2002). In turn, she is unable to dedicate the extra effort needed to advance in her career. In many organisations, male-dominated culture and values dictate measures of success for performance evaluations (Dodd, 2012), representing organisational barriers. Due to gender-based socialisation, stereotyped prejudices not only hinder women's working lives but also prevent the formation of female role models in managerial positions, precluding the idea that women are suitable for these roles (Deemer & Fredericks, 2006).

The gender equality concept

Demirel (2007, p. 29) defines gender equality as "the equal treatment of women and men based on the rule of law". Gender equality has a number of meanings, both qualitatively and quantitatively. In quantitative terms, it means ensuring equal representation of women employees and ensuring the balance of participation between men and women in all areas of society. Qualitatively, it shows that women and men have equal influence in the process of determining development priorities and that women and men benefit equally from the results (UN, 2008). Since women and men have different roles and responsibilities in the planning, decision-making, and implementation processes of social activities, it is also important to give equal value to the different perceptions, interests, needs, and priorities of women and men (UN, 2008).

Many academic studies in the literature draw attention to gender equality and strengthening women's employment opportunities. There are also many studies examining gender equality and the glass ceiling syndrome in tourism. For instance, Ferguson and Alarcón (2015) study gender equality within policymaking and projects. The study indicates that there is a highly political and contentious nature to gender in tourism. According to the authors, gender resistance emerged during projects related to sustainable tourism development initiatives, implying that gender equality approaches in society are important obstacles for the tourism sector. In this regard, the study calls for a re-evaluation of the concept of sustainable tourism to include gender analysis and gender equality as key components. Skalpe (2007) compares the gender pay gap between CEOs in the case of a Norwegian tourism firm and a manufacturing firm and finds that just over 20% of CEOs in the tourism industry are women, whereas only 6% are women in manufacturing firms. Moreover, this study highlights that female CEOs are subject to wage discrimination in both sectors. While female CEOs in the tourism sector are employed in relatively smaller companies, compared to the manufacturing sector, the gender-based wage gap is larger in the tourism sector. According to the author, this phenomenon may be more pronounced in other countries.

According to González-Serrano et al. (2018), the tourism sector's labour market has a strong female presence, although women employees have limited access to management positions. However, according to the study, a positive shift was observed in the Madrid sample in terms of female employees being promoted to higher positions. In another study, Carvalho et al. (2019) discuss the glass ceiling concept in the tourism sector by interpreting women's experiences in organisations from a gender-aware perspective. According to the authors, there are three main gender subtexts underlying the gendering of the workforce: the assumption of women's greater family orientation; the subjective expectation that women are less competent in management positions by nature; and male homo-social ties and exclusionary practices. The study indicates the importance of feminist theories in exposing the lack of gender neutrality in tourism organisations. Santero-Sanchez et al. (2015) explore gender inequality by addressing the lack of personal rights facing women, such as insecurity, unbenefits, and low wages, as well as the seasonal structure of the tourism sector.

Hutchings et al. (2020) emphasise that women are negatively discriminated against and segregated when it comes to managerial positions in their work. This situation is caused by invisible cultural barriers. According to this study, the tourism industry can create a work culture that supports women's inclusion and advancement in the workplace through innovative workplace policies and programmes and be a leader in the fight against discrimination faced by women. Damunupola and Sutha (2019) focused on the glass ceiling phenomenon by looking at specific tourism organisations. They find that there is a strong negative correlation between the presence of the glass ceiling and female career advancement in the Sri Lankan hotels. The researchers identified organisational barriers as the most influential factor for female career advancement. In the individual sense, tourism organisations are hindering the advancement of female employees with various subjective advancement criteria. It is possible to come across many studies in the global literature that deal with the issues of gender inequality and the glass ceiling faced by female employees, which confirm this phenomenon.

Gender in policymaking

Alarcón and Cole (2019) acknowledge that, without tackling gender equality in a meaningful and substantive way, tourism's potential to contribute to economies will be reduced, and it will be very difficult to ensure a sustainable form of tourism. Alrwajfah et al. (2020) state that women do not have a favourable view of tourism's economic impacts and that several barriers exist to female employment in the tourism sector. Tucker and Boonabaana (2012) point out that there is a relationship between tourism, gender, and poverty reduction, and the sector should consider the variable roles and conflicting career paths between men and women.

As in many sectors, development in tourism is not a spontaneous and easily achieved phenomenon, but a process that takes place in the context of global restructuring, where gender inequalities are a fundamental component. Particularly, the active participation of women in the tourism sector enhances developmental gains, such as the reduction of poverty faced by local societies, innovation, good governance, and sustainability (Harrison, 2008). According to the Equality in Tourism Organization report (2013), tourism is a sector with one of the lowest ratios of women on company board of directors, which is in stark contrast to the large number of women working in tourism companies (Equality in Tourism, 2013). The fact that tourism, itself, consists of gender-diverse activities necessitates gender diversity in the sector (Pritchard & Morgan, 2000). However, there are not enough studies in the literature on women's participation in policymaking, either at the organisational level or at the regional/national level (Ferguson, 2011).

Feminist theory

According to the relevant literature, women's participation in development policies or policymaking is generally theorised from a feminist perspective (Ferguson, 2011). Feminism is considered a political movement that questions the relationship between men and women in wide-ranging situations, such as family life, education, business, politics, culture, and history, and targets a change in the power relationship between women and men. It asks, "what is a woman?" Feminism aims to end male-centred social norms in the distinction between men and women and replace them with feminine values (Mitchell, 2015, pp. 1–10). Although feminism is, basically, a discourse about gender, it contains many different voices, such as liberal, radical, Marxist, and socialist ideologies. In this context, Gherardi (2005) provides three approaches that shape feminist theories:

- Body – Approaches that take the body as the main premise of male and female sexuality and childbearing capacity, in the context of biological and physical appearance, and uses the feminine body to define the qualities of a women. In addition, physical and emotional care and support, and the ability to empathise are considered female characteristics;
- Society, culture, or politics – According to this approach, the body is symbolic rather than the physical centre of the subject. Namely, it is true that

individuals have a masculine or feminine body, biologically and physiologically; however, individuals who have these bodies gain identity as men and women and are shaped in the context of the social culture in which they were born. In other words, within the framework of physical and biological differences, individual perceptions, attitudes, and behaviours will be shaped according to social and cultural beliefs (Demren, 2008); and

- Language – Language discussions, which started with postmodernism, have also affected the gender debates of feminist theories. Accordingly, the identity of an individual, as a subject, is formed within the framework of the language patterns in the society in which she was born and the ideologies shaped within that framework, which generally exhibit a patriarchal structure. Accordingly, feminist linguists identify women in male-dominated language patterns. They argue that her identity is "othered" against her male identity, thus legitimising the secondary position of women in society.

Feminist theories question the structure of gender and the causes of inequality between the sexes. Accordingly, within the framework of feminist theories, while gender is mostly placed on the body (liberal, radical, and psychoanalytic feminist theory), there are also positionings on culture and social relations (Marxist and socialist feminist theory), and language (postmodern feminist theory). Thus, although feminism is a discourse on gender in general, it deals with the secondary position of women in society from different perspectives and, as a result, develops different solutions (Irefin et al., 2012). Regardless of the point of view, the main goal of all feminist theories is to show that women should have equal rights with men in the economic, political, and social arena. Therefore, the ideas put forward from a feminist perspective also prioritise the situation in which women can obtain equal rights, positions, and wages with men in business circles (Çetinel & Yilmaz, 2016).

The entry of feminism into the policymaking area dominated by masculine thought naturally brings with it some difficulties. Feminist policymaking must, first of all, master the masculine policymaking processes and go beyond this to develop its own methods and strategies. The political methods feminism will adopt should differ from the existing masculine methods by engaging in a governance method in which women are actively involved. The concept of governance envisages the participation of relevant society in policy and decision-making processes in every possible field and form. In turn, the effective, efficient, and transparent presentation of services in a multi-actor structure must occur in an environment where the gap between ruler and subject begins to disappear (Sobaci, 2007). The phenomenon of governance has emerged as a pluralistic and interactive model by drawing attention to the inadequacy of management approaches based on the central power phenomenon (Merrien, 1998, p. 57).

The concept of feminist governance, on the other hand, expands the scope of governance and effectively includes women employees in the policymaking process (Halley et al., 2006, p. 340). The feminist governance model includes very different dynamics. In addition to activism against state and organisational policies for the protection of women's rights and the struggle for equality, it stipulates that the power of state mechanisms should not be ignored in ensuring these rights and equality. Feminist governance includes many different power relationships in the context of not only activist individuals, groups, local NGOs, or state practices but also international law and global NGOs in order to fulfil women's rights and equality at all levels of society. Any strategy should be viewed as a partnership between all stakeholders influenced by policy. Distinguishing this pluralistic approach, feminist governance sees many organisational, local, and global actors as partners who will work in cooperation for the protection of women's rights and the empowerment of women. It is precisely because of this multiple approach to policy that there is a single and clear definition of the concept of feminist governance, unique from contemporary governance.

Findlay (2018, p. 3) looks at management relations from a wider perspective and talks about the need to apply "femocratic management" when managing power relations in terms of gender, especially in the state, because state management is essential to the feminist transformation project. Walby (2002, p. 536) gives examples of two main areas of feminist politics. The first is the mainstreaming of gender in the economic field, particularly the legal regulation of equal treatment and employment in this area. The second is the attempt to stop male violence against women in society and in organisational structures. These two areas are important parts of feminist politics, and when translated into local adaptations, they form a common political network. Feminist governance plays an active role in both fundamental areas of feminist perspectives: activating it and forming an important component to advance feminist politics. Effective participation of women in policymaking is a great gain, both for society in general and for organisations. For this reason, gender equality should be ensured in the field of policymaking to ensure women participate in economic development and social progress.

Advantages of tourism employment for women

The tourism sector offers women more opportunities in the fields of labour force participation, entrepreneurship, and management compared to other sectors. In this direction, the number of women who become entrepreneurs is twice as high in the tourism sector when compared to other sectors (World Bank, 2017). Although research suggests that the tourism sector has a structure that reduces women to traditional gender roles and thus strengthens gender-based inequalities, tourism can enable women to be economically and socially empowered, especially in developing countries (Chant, 1997; Ferguson, 2011; Khatiwada & Silva, 2015; Lee & Kang, 1998; Sinclair, 1997). For example, Ferguson (2011) argues that tourism development can, theoretically, contribute to gender equality and women's empowerment and argues that relevant policies should maximise this potential. Similarly, Khatiwada and Silva (2015) examine the effects of tourism employment on gender inequality in Namibia, indicating that, due to the abundance of jobs that women can do, tourism provides certain advantages for women and that tourism employment helps reduce gender inequality.

According to some academic studies in Indonesia, Malaysia, the Philippines, and Thailand, more than half of tourism businesses are run by women, and in Panama, more than 70% of tourism businesses are owned by women entrepreneurs (World Bank, 2017). On the other hand, it is emphasised that tourism offers more opportunity in management compared to other sectors. For example, international accommodation businesses, such as Hilton and Marriott, support women employees through the Women Leaders Training Program. In this context, the main sector-specific features that facilitate the employment of women in the tourism sector can be listed as follows (Yetiş & Çalışkan, 2020, p. 11):

- Many jobs in the tourism sector do not require high skills and education. It is easier to employ women, and tourism, in turn, contributes to an increase in the number of women who gain their economic freedom in society;
- Tourism is a sector that values personal and hospitality skills. The compatibility of general female personal characteristics with most of the job skills required makes it easier for women to be employed in the tourism sector;
- Tourism offers seasonal and part-time work. Since employment relations in the tourism sector are established in direct proportion to tourism demand, it is easier to provide seasonal and part-time work opportunities for women with family responsibilities;
- Tourism does not necessarily require extensive financing for entrepreneurship. Subsequently, services provided in the tourism sector are labour-based, making it easier for women to start small- and medium-sized income-generating activities; and
- Women are provided with opportunity through the sharing economy. For example, it is easier for women to earn economic income in the tourism sector by renting their homes through online platforms, such as Airbnb and Vrbo, or driving opportunities through Uber and Lyft. As a result, tourism contributes to the economic and social empowerment of women and to the economic growth and development processes of countries by increasing women's registered employment.

Tourism employment in the context of glass ceiling and gender equality

In terms of working conditions, tourism is a sector that requires long workdays, often pays insufficient wages, and unionisation is low, largely due to the temporary/seasonal nature of tourism work (Riley et al., 2002). Accordingly, the tourism sector requires a less educated and qualified workforce compared to other sectors (Cheong, 2009; Cooper et al., 2005; Riley et al., 2002). Despite adversities, tourism plays an important role in providing employment opportunities to low-skilled people, immigrants, minority groups, the long-term unemployed, and women who enter the labour market for the first time or who have been removed from the work force or choose to work part-time due to family responsibilities (UNWTO and International Labor Organization, 2014).

According to the relevant literature, tourism jobs are accepted as an extension of housework, which is shown to belong to women based on traditional gender roles. For this reason, a large part of the workforce employed in the sector is comprised of women (Cave & Kılıç, 2010). Qin and Yang (2015) examined labour roles and gender equality in a five-star hotel in Beijing. It was determined that, while men were employed in the kitchen, security, and technical maintenance services, women employees were mostly concentrated in reception, housekeeping, and food and beverage service. The study also determined that, although the majority of hotel employees are women, only a few women were employed in the hotel's senior-level management positions. Similarly, in Cappadocia, Turkey, Elmas (2007) concluded that women were employed in housekeeping and food and beverage services, which are generally considered to be an extension of housework. It was also found that only one woman worked in a managerial position.

Kattara (2005) examined the profile of women managers working in 5-star hotels in Egypt. It was concluded that female managers work in departments such as housekeeping, marketing, and human resources, but their numbers are low in higher-level/higher-paying positions, such as general manager, finance, accounting, and food and beverage. In addition, there was a negative image associated with the advancement of women managers in hotels. Another study that assessed 30 hotel businesses found that only 13.9% of the total managers were women (Woods & Viehland, 2000). Li and Leung (2001) found that only two women were in the general manager position out of the 77 hotels in their study.

Brownell (1994) investigated gender differences in personal and career development among hotel general managers. He found that factors such as a determined stance, ambition, positive behaviours, personal skills, and hard work can help women overcome career barriers and career development obstacles. This supports research by Knutson and Schmidgall (1999), who show that women have to work harder and be more experienced than men in order to reach the general manager level in a hotel in the United States. Moreover, they have to make more personal sacrifices than men.

In summary, although the rate of women employed in the tourism sector is high (Cave & Kılıç, 2010), this density is mostly seen at lower levels, and the research presented shows that women are still excluded from top management positions in the sector. As in many other sectors, there is an important vertical and horizontal gender divide in terms of the labour market in tourism. Horizontally, men and women are in different jobs, with men possessing jobs with higher growth potential while women are concentrated in low-level jobs with few career advancement opportunities (Burgess, 2003). Vertically, women find it harder to advance because (Mann & Seacord, 2003, pp. 38–40) of the following reasons:

- Compared to other sectors, there are intense working hours in the tourism sector due to the obligation to provide service 24 hours a day, seven days a week. Working on weekends and holidays may mean neglecting family and private life, which creates an image that women may be unable to handle managerial responsibilities; and

- Certain obligations required by the management of tourism organisations, such as making agreements with agencies and tour operators or participating in various tourism fairs, can often lead to the necessity of travel or relocation. Such requirement brings with it the question of how women, especially married women with children, have this ability.

Conclusion

In light of the existing social structures, gender equality policies are far from promoting women's advancement and providing gender equality to women in employment. In fact, some legal regulations and practices regarding population growth discourage employed women from working, rather these practices encourage women to be mothers and wives. So, glass ceiling or gender equality? It can be said that the current answer to that question remains within the realm of the glass ceiling, that is, the negativities faced by women on the grounds of their gender still exist. The premise that women and men are given equal opportunities is false, as both formal and informal barriers exist (Kattara, 2005; Knutson & Schmidgall, 1999; Li & Leung, 2001; Woods & Viehland, 2000). While the number of women in the tourism labour force is significant, the glass ceiling remains a prominent obstacle for women in the tourism sector. Moreover, the tourism sector faces high rates of absenteeism and employee turnover (Pang et al., 2015). For these reasons, arrangements must be made to eliminate such inequity through the provision of flexible working hours, equal career opportunities, equal pay, equal training, and mentoring opportunities.

Arrangements that should be made, in terms of governance and tourism businesses, to improve employment opportunities for women, including their rise in management, can be listed as follows (Cole & Kelly, 2004; Eyring & Stead, 1998; ILO, 2004; Jackson, 2001; Mann & Seacord, 2003):

- Legal structures and regulatory mechanisms to eliminate gender discrimination;
- Guidelines for changing attitudes and eliminating bias in the workforce;
- Regulations that enforce equal labour laws and ensure staff are aware of their rights;
- A review of hiring and promotion policies that acknowledge equal merit for all departments within an agency;
- Development opportunities for women, which include flexible working hours, adequate child and elder care, and work-life balance;
- Mentoring to enable women to develop and advance their professional skills;
- Equal investment and financing opportunities for female investors and entrepreneurs;
- Use of recruitment resources that support the hiring of women in management positions; and
- Disclosure of promotion criteria in advance of open positions.

Suggestions for women who aspire to work in management positions and "break" the glass ceiling can be listed as follows (Davies-Netzley, 1998; Knutson & Schmidgall, 1999; Maxwell, 1997; Perrewe & Nelson, 2004; Veale & Gold, 1998):

- Take risks and seek out new opportunities, such as problem-solving;
- Believe in yourself;
- Develop your leadership skills;
- Find a strategic location where you can make a difference and be noticed;
- Consider earning professional certificates related to your profession;
- Establish professional networks;
- Develop your political skills and be self-confident;
- Find ways to advance the culture of your enterprise and to value fellow women's contributions to the organisation; and
- Find a mentor who has been successful in your field.

References

Alarcón, D. M., & Cole, S. (2019). No sustainability for tourism without gender equality. *Journal of Sustainable Tourism*, *27*(7), 903–919. https://doi.org/10.1080/09669582.2019.1588283

Alrwajfah, M. M., Almeida-García, F., & Cortés-Macías, R. (2020). Females' perspectives on tourism's impact and their employment in the sector: The case of Petra, Jordan. *Tourism Management*, *78*, 104069. https://doi.org/10.1016/j.tourman.2019.104069

Barutçugil, İ. (2002). *İş hayatında kadın yönetici* [Female manager in business]. Kariyer Publishing.

Baum, T. (2013). *International perspectives on women and work in hotels, catering and tourism, international labour organisation (No. 289)*. Gender Working Paper 1/2013, Sector Working Paper, International Labor Organization. www.ilo.org/gender/Informationresources/WCMS_209867/lang – en/index.htm

Beauregard, T. A. (2006). Predicting interference between work and home: A comparison of dispositional and situational antecedents. *Journal of Managerial Psychology*, *21*(3), 1–33. https://doi.org/10.1108/02683940610659588

Boddy, D. (2002). *Management: An introduction* (2nd ed.). Prentice Hall.

Brownell, J. (1994). Women in hospitality management: General managers' perceptions of factors related to career development. *International Journal of Hospitality Management*, *13*(2), 101–117.

Burgess, C. (2003). Gender and salaries in hotel financial management: It's still a man's world. *Women in Management Review*, *18*(1/2), 50–59. https://doi.org/10.1108/09649420310462325

Carvalho, I., Costa, C., Lykke, N., & Torres, A. (2019). Beyond the glass ceiling: Gendering tourism management. *Annals of Tourism Research*, *75*, 79–91. https://doi.org/10.1016/j.annals.2018.12.022

Cave, P., & Kılıç, S. (2010). The role of women in tourism employment with special reference to Antalya, Turkey. *Journal of Hospitality Marketing & Management*, *19*(3), 280–292. https://doi.org/10.1080/19368621003591400

Çetinel, E., & Yilmaz, S. E. (2016). Feminist theory: A critical approach to management and organization. *Journal of Ç. K. University Faculty of Economics and Administrative Sciences*, *6*(2), 119–148.

Chant, S. (1997). Gender and tourism employment. In M. T. Sinclair (Ed.), *Gender, work and tourism* (pp. 120–180). Routledge.

Cheong, W. M. (2009). Employment characteristics and trends of tourism-related industries. *Macao Monetary Research Bulletin, 13*, 67–89.

Chisholm-Burns, M. A., Spivey, C. A., Hagemann, T., & Josephson, M. A. (2017). Women in leadership and the bewildering glass ceiling. *American Journal of Health-System Pharmacy, 74*(5), 312–324.

Cole, G. A., & Kelly, P. (2004). *Management: Theory and practice*. Cengage Learning.

Cooper, C., Fletcher, J., Gilbert, D., Fyall, A., & Wanhill, S. (2005). *Tourism: Principles and practice*. Pearson Education.

Cotter, D. A., Hermsen, J. M., Ovadia, S., & Vanneman, R. (2001). The glass ceiling effect. *Social forces, 80*(2), 655–681.

Damunupola, A., & Sutha, J. (2019). Impact of glass ceiling on female career advancement; moderating role of female career aspirations: A study on hotel industry in Sri Lanka. *Asia Pacific Institute of Advanced Research (APIAR)*, 134–149.

Davies-Netzley, S. A. (1998). Women above the glass ceiling: Perceptions on corporate mobility and strategies for success. *Gender & Society, 12*(3), 339–355. https://doi.org/10.1177/0891243298012003006

Deemer, C., & Fredericks, N. (2006). *Dancing on the glass ceiling*. McGraw Hill Professional.

Demirel, S. (2007). Toplumsal cinsiyet [Gender]. In L. Taşkın (Ed.), *Doğum ve kadın sağlığı hemşireliği [Obstetrics/gynecology and women's health nursing]* (pp. 29–34). Sistem Ofset Publishing.

Demren, C. (2008). The subjectivity of masculinity through femininity. *C.U. Social Journal of Sciences, 32*(1), 73–92.

Dodd, F. (2012). Women leaders in the creative industries: A baseline study. *International Journal of Gender and Entrepreneurship, 4*(2), 153–178. https://doi.org/10.1108/17566261211234652

Dreher, G. F. (2003). Breaking the glass ceiling: The effects of sex ratios and work-life programs on female leadership at the top. *Human Relations, 56*(5), 541–562.

Elmas, S. (2007). Gender and tourism development: A case study of the Cappadocia Region of Turkey. In A. Pritchard, N. Morgan, & I. Atelyevic (Eds.), *Tourism and gender: Embodiment, sensuality and experience* (pp. 302–314). CABI Publishing.

Equality in Tourism. (2013, May 1). *Sun, Sand and Ceilings: Women in the boardroom in the tourism industry*. http://equalityintourism.org/wp-content/uploads/2013/07/Sun_Sand_Ceiling_F.pdf

Eyring, A., & Stead, B. A. (1998). Shattering the glass ceiling: Some successful corporate practices. *Journal of Business Ethics, 17*(3), 245–251.

Ferguson, L. (2011). Promoting gender equality and empowering women? Tourism and the third millennium development goal. *Current Issues in Tourism, 14*(3), 235–249. https://doi.org/10.1080/13683500.2011.555522

Ferguson, L., & Alarcón, D. M. (2015). Gender and sustainable tourism: Reflections on theory and practice. *Journal of Sustainable Tourism, 23*(3), 401–416. https://doi.org/10.1080/09669582.2014.957208

Findlay, T. (2018). *Femocratic administration*. University of Toronto Press.

Gherardi, S. (2005). Feminist theory and organization theory a dialogue on new bases. In H. Tsoukas & C. Knudsen (Eds.), *The Oxford handbook of organization theory: Meta-theoretical perspectives* (pp. 210–236). Oxford University Press.

González-Serrano, L., Villacé-Molinero, T., Talón-Ballestero, P., & Fuente-Cabrero, C. D. L. (2018). Women and the glass ceiling in the community of Madrid hotel industry. *International Journal of Human Resources Development and Management*, *18*(1–2), 91–111. https://doi.org/10.1504/IJHRDM.2018.10013649

Halley, J., Kotiswaran, P., Shamir, H., & Thomas, C. (2006). From the international to the local in feminist legal responses to rape, prostitution/sex work, and sex trafficking: Four studies in contemporary governance feminism. *Harvard Journal of Law and Gender*, *29*, 335.

Harrison, D. (2008). Pro-poor tourism: A critique. *Third World Quarterly*, *29*(5), 851–868. https://doi.org/10.1080/01436590802105983

Hutchings, K., Moyle, C. L., Chai, A., Garofano, N., & Moore, S. (2020). Segregation of women in tourism employment in the APEC Region. *Tourism Management Perspectives*, *34*, 100–655. https://doi.org/10.1016/j.tmp.2020.100655

International Labor Service (ILO). (1998, July 14). *World employment report, 1998–99*. http://ilo.org/wcmsp5/groups/public/–dgreports/–dcomm/documents/publication/dwcms_080628.pdf

International Labor Service (ILO). (2004, June 10). *Breaking Glass Ceiling Through the Women in Management*. www.ilo.org/wcmsp5/groups/public/–dgreports/ – dcomm/documents/publication/kd00110.pdf

Irefin, P., Ifah, S. S., & Bwala, M. H. (2012). Organizational theories and analysis: A feminist perspective. *International Journal of Advancements in Research and Technology*, *1*(1), 71–97.

Jackson, J. C. (2001). Women middle managers' perception of the glass ceiling. *Women in Management Review*, *16*(1), 30–41. https://doi.org/10.1108/09649420110380265

Kattara, H. (2005). Career challenges for female managers in Egyptian hotels. *International Journal of Contemporary Hospitality Management*, *17*(3), 238–251. https://doi.org/10.1108/09596110510591927

Khatiwada, L. K., & Silva, J. A. (2015). Mitigating gender inequality in rural regions: The effects of tourism employment in Namibia. *International Journal of Tourism Research*, *17*(5), 442–450. https://doi.org/10.1002/jtr.2010

Knutson, B. J., & Schmidgall, R. S. (1999). Dimensions of the glass ceiling in the hospitality industry. *Cornell Hotel and Restaurant Administration Quarterly*, *40*(6), 64–75.

Kuhn, P., & Shen, K. (2013). Gender discrimination in job ads: Evidence from China. *The Quarterly Journal of Economics*, *128*(1), 287–336. https://doi.org/10.1093/qje/qjs046

Lee, C., & Kang, S. (1998). Measuring earnings inequality and median earnings in the tourism industry. *Tourism Management*, *19*(4), 341–348.

Li, L., & Leung, R. W. (2001). Female managers in Asian hotels: Profile and career challenges. *International Journal of Contemporary Hospitality Management*, *13*(4–5), 189–196.

Mann, I. S., & Seacord, S. (2003). What glass ceiling. *Lodging Hospitality*, *59*(4), 38–40.

Maxwell, G. A. (1997). Hotel general management: Views from above the glass ceiling. *International Journal of Contemporary Hospitality Management*, *9*(5/6), 230–235. https://doi.org/10.1108/09596119710172624

Merrien, F. X. (1998). Governance and modern welfare states. *International Social Science Journal*, *50*(155), 57–67.

Mitchell, S. (2015). Feminism. *The Encyclopedia of Victorian Literature*, 1–10.

Pang, L., Kucukusta, D., & Chan, X. (2015). Employee turnover intention in travel agencies: Analysis of controllable and uncontrollable factors. *International Journal of Tourism Research*, *17*(6), 577–590. https://doi.org/10.1002/JTR.2025

Perrewe, P. L., & Nelson, D. L. (2004). Gender and career success: The facilitative role of political skill. *Organizational Dynamics, 33*(4), 366–378. https://doi.org/10.1016/j.orgdyn.2004.09.004

Pritchard, A., & Morgan, N. J. (2000). Privileging the male gaze: Gendered tourism landscapes. *Annals of Tourism Research, 27*(4), 88–905.

Qin, J., & Yang, Z. (2015). Perception of gender equality among female employees in Beijing five-star hotel. *Tourism Tribune, 30*(9), 63–71.

Riley, M., Ladkin, A., & Szivas, E. (2002). *Tourism employment: Analysis and planning*. Channel View Publications.

Rosener, J. B. (2011). Ways women lead. In P. H. Werhane & M. Painter-Morland (Eds.), *Leadership, gender, and organization* (pp. 19–29). Springer.

Santero-Sanchez, R., Segovia-Perez, M., Casto-Nunez, B., Figueroa-Domecq, C., & Talon-Ballestro, P. (2015). Gender differences in the hospitality industry: A job quality index. *Tourism Management, 51*, 234–246. https://doi.org/10.1016/j.tourman.2015.05.025

Sharon, M. (2001). Women's career in theory and practice: Time for change? *Women in Management Review, 16*(4), 183–192. https://doi.org/10.1108/09649420110392163

Sinclair, M. T. (1997). Gendered work in tourism: Comparative perspectives. In M. T. Sinclair (Ed.), *Gender, work and tourism* (pp. 219–233). Routledge.

Skalpe, O. (2007). The CEO gender pay gap in the tourism industry – Evidence from Norway. *Tourism Management, 28*(3), 845–853. https://doi.org/10.1016/j.tourman.2006.06.005

Sobaci, M. Z. (2007). Yönetişim kavramı ve Türkiye'de uygulanabilirliği üzerine değerlendirmeler [Assessments on the governance concept and its applicability in Turkey]. *Journal of Administrative Sciences, 5*(1), 195–208.

Tucker, H., & Boonabaana, B. (2012). A critical analysis of tourism, gender and poverty reduction. *Journal of Sustainable Tourism, 20*(3), 437–455. https://doi.org/10.1080/09669582.2011.622769

United Nations (UN). (2008, April 7). *The role of men and boys in achieving gender equality*. www.un.org/womenwatch/daw/egm/men-boys2003/Connell-bp.pdf

United Nations (UN). (2016, May 12). *17 goals to transform our world*. www.un.org/sustainabledevelopment/

United Nations (UN). (2021, May 14). *Concepts and definitions*. www.un.org/womenwatch/osagi/conceptsandefinitions.htm

United Nations World Tourism Organization (UNWTO). (2010, July 7). *Global report on women in tourism 2010*. www.e-unwto.org/doi/pdf/10.18111/9789284413737

United Nations World Tourism Organization (UNWTO). (2019, July 7). *Global report on women in tourism* (2nd ed.). www.unwto.org/publication/global-report-women-tourism-2-edition

United Nations World Tourism Organization and International Labour Organization. (2014). *Measuring employment in the tourism industries-guide with best practices*. UNWTO. www.e-unwto.org/doi/epdf/10.18111/9789284416158

Veale, C., & Gold, J. (1998). Smashing into the glass ceiling for women managers. *Journal of Management Development, 17*(1), 17–26. https://doi.org/10.1108/02621719810199527

Walby, S. (2002). Feminism in a global era. *Economy and Society, 31*(4), 533–557.

Weyer, B. (2007). Twenty years later: Explaining the persistence of the glass ceiling for women leaders. *Women in Management Review, 22*(6), 482–496. https://doi.org/10.1108/09649420710778718

Wirth, L. (2001). *Breaking through the glass ceiling: Women in management*. International Labour Office. https://labordoc.ilo.org/discovery/fulldisplay/alma993441173402676/41ILO_INST:41ILO_V2

Woods, R. H., & Viehland, D. (2000). Women in hotel management: Gradual progress, uncertain prospects. *Cornell Hotel and Restaurant Administration Quarterly*, *41*(5), 51–54.
World Bank. (2017). *Women and tourism: Designing for inclusion*. World Bank Group.
Yetiş, Ş. A., & Çalışkan, N. (2020). Turizm sektöründe kadın istihdamı: Mevcut duruma ilişkin bir değerlendirme [Female employment in tourism sector: An assessment of the current situation]. *Manisa Celal Bayar University Journal of Social Sciences*, *18*(3), 105–119. https://doi.org/10.18026/cbayarsos.601634

5 From Jim Crow to Black Lives Matter

A history of racism and tourism in the United States

Susan L. Slocum and Linda J. Ingram

> *The travel industry tends to think of itself as a space of leisure, fun, and escape where such things like racism are left behind for good times. The problem is, for black individuals and people of colour, escaping racism is not something they can do by taking a vacation. Racism, like in many other sectors of society, has been built into the travel industry, both knowingly and unknowingly*
>
> (Goodwin, 2020).

Introduction

The roots of discrimination and racism are embedded in the history of the United States. In the 1870s, a "social system of legal segregation" (Thompson-Miller & Feagin, 2007, p. 455), known as Jim Crow, emerged primarily in the southeast United States but was also prevalent in other areas of the country (Alderman & Inwood, 2014). Jim Crow was a method of promoting the segregation and oppression of minorities in society. Then, in 1896, the Supreme Court decision on *Plessy v. Ferguson* established the "separate, but equal" (p. 308) doctrine that made discrimination, economic subordination, and poor treatment legal (Hall, 2014). Homer Plessy of the *Plessy v Ferguson* ruling was arrested 130 years ago for sitting in the Whites-only section of a rail car and refusing to move to the one reserved for African Americans (Burnside, 2022). It took until January 5, 2022, to receive a posthumous pardon (he died in 1925) from the governor of Louisiana. The Jim Crow restrictions went beyond separate rail cars on trains by granting states the legal right to impose segregation on infrastructure, education, healthcare, the economy, and other aspects of life, including travel and tourism (Higginbotham & Smith, 1992). Although this racist doctrine ended around 1969, it is still very much alive in the bigotry African Americans face in many areas of their lives (Thompson-Miller et al., 2015), including travel and tourism.

The results of the 2020 census illuminated the United States as an increasingly diverse nation with a multiracial component that outpaced any other group in population growth from 2010 to 2020 (Jones et al., 2021). As of 2020, the African American/Black population in the United States was 41.1 million (up from 38.9 million in 2010), representing 12.4% of the total population (US Census,

2020), while the African American/Black population combined with other racial identities accounted for an additional 5.8 million (Jones et al., 2021). While the White population in the United States decreased by 8.6% between 2010 and 2020, the African American/Black population increased by 5.6%. The 2020 census numbers are in question as there is evidence the count was cut short, but these data will be accepted for the purposes of this chapter (Wang, 2022).

There is limited information about the travel practices of African Americans (Benavides, 2014). However, what is available reveals a tourism cohort "boldly traveling the globe", while the tourism industry has, overall, failed to address their travel needs and interests (Chen, 2020, para. 8). In 2020, MMGY Global, an integrated marketing company specialising in travel, tourism, and hospitality, undertook a dual-phased global study in order to analyse the travel needs and practices of African Americans (Buder, 2020). The first phase focused on African American leisure travel, while the second focused on the travel of African American professionals. They found that African Americans represent a significant segment of the US travel market, spending $109.4 billion in 2019. With an average of three overnight stays per year, 2.5 nights per trip, and spending of $600 per trip, the African American travel segment accounted for approximately 13% of US leisure travel expenditures. African American professionals spent over $900,000 on business travel, yet over 42% noted they have felt unwelcome at their destinations (Buder, 2020). Clayton Reid, CEO of MMGY Global, citing corporate responsibility and the need to work cooperatively to serve diversity called for the travel and tourism industry "to better understand the needs, behaviors, and concerns of underrepresented traveler communities". He also challenged companies to "begin to evaluate their approach to diversity, equity, and inclusion internally, they also need to create products, experiences, services and marketing campaigns that connect with the needs of diverse markets" (Chen, 2020, para. 7).

The purpose of this chapter is to examine the relationship between racism and tourism in the United States. In this chapter, we will focus on the ways Jim Crow was utilised to keep "African Americans under social, economic and political control through racial violence and terror" (Thompson-Miller et al., 2015, p. 3), then move on to the effects of Civil Rights on African American travel and tourism, and a brief look at the influence of the Black Lives Matter movement. From there, we will conclude with suggestions for academic, policy, management, and improvements to promote changes that would assist in moving towards equity and inclusion in both the production and consumption of tourism. While racism is common for all persons of colour (POC), the focus here will be on racism experienced by African American (Black) tourists, tourism business owners, and employees, particularly those African Americans who have battled, and still battle, racism in order to achieve the financial resources necessary to participate in tourism. African Americans did not stop travelling as a result of Jim Crow. Instead, they created their own conditions for safe tourism, outdoor recreation, rest, and relaxation experiences. The end of Jim Crow ended legally sanctioned racism, but socially sanctioned racism remains active in many quarters.

Racism

Racism is a fairly recent construct in human history. For thousands of years people of different cultural backgrounds occupied the same localities through migration, trade, war, and other endeavours. The variety of ethnicities that developed over time led to global diversities in agriculture, education, language, food, beliefs, values, religion, and place. While ethnocentrism and ethnic conflict have been ubiquitous throughout human history, they typically did not focus on physical characteristics as the determining factor of "Other" (Smedley & Smedley, 2005).

For centuries, the idea of race was synonymous with animal-related terms, such as type, breed, and species. Race, as a way of understanding peoples and assigning them a place within specific social categories, did not appear until the late 17th century in the American colonies (Smedley & Smedley, 2005). By the early 18th century, these categories had solidified to become a method of assigning status and value. In short, White men of power in the American colonies required a justification for enshrining the lifelong enslavement of Africans as just and appropriate. This pretext was used to reclassify African Americans as non-human – in spite of a lack of evidence of significant biological differences – which immediately relegated them to a lesser status and, therefore, a suitable form of cheap, mass labour (Smedley & Smedley, 2005).

Defining racism, however, has proven to be problematic, as it is often delineated according to the perspective from which it is being studied or examined (Schmid, 1996). However, there are similarities to be found in these various perspectives, such as the overarching belief that ethnicity and skin colour determine capabilities, traits, and value, automatically sanctifying the dominant culture as "superior". Those who are not members of the upper echelon are vulnerable to hostility, discrimination, and segregation with the accompanying housing, health, economic, educational, and employment disparities. Racism, then, can be understood as racial/ethnic discrimination based on membership in a specific culture/group deemed inferior or secondary by the dominant culture (Reskin, 2012).

Going a step further, structural racism (also known as institutional racism) focuses on the methods employed by societies to imbed and cultivate discrimination through formal or informal policies in employment, housing, education, healthcare, etc., which then strengthen intolerance and hate within a society (Bailey et al., 2017). Policies, often viewed as "colour blind" in nature, are in fact designed to limit participation or exclude certain behaviours without acknowledging that those behaviours may be culturally defined. Powell (2008) writes:

> Institutional racism shifts our focus from the motives of individual people to practices and procedures within an institution. Structural racism shifts our attention from the single, intra-institutional setting to inter-institutional arrangements and interactions. Efforts to identify causation at a particular moment of decision within a specific domain understate the cumulative impact of discrimination
>
> (p. 796).

Racist policies (or practices) in one sector can reinforce policies in other sectors, leading to an interconnected web of structural racism (Bailey et al., 2017). Take, for example, the current social issue of voting regulations in many US states. Fear of fraud in voting has led many states to restrict access to voting, either through a reduction in voting centres, limited voting hours, identification requirements, and/ or the elimination of absentee voting options. Opponents argue these restrictions disproportionately impact voters of colour, primarily because other policies, such as transportation policies or restrictions on identification processing, as well as the assumption that all voters are available from 9 am to 5 pm to vote, have already created an unequal playing field for African Americans (especially those in rural areas) (Brennen Center for Justice, 2021). Considering that many national and regional regulations are built on racist policies of the past, it is not hard to see that unravelling structural racism in the United States is a monumental task.

Jim Crow

In the 1830s and 1840s, Thomas Dartmouth, a white entertainer, performed a song-and-dance satire in blackface crudely depicting African Americans as lazy and stupid. Considered the "father of American minstrelsy", Dartmouth's routine was so popular with the audiences that he became one of the most renowned minstrel entertainers of the day. One of the songs he popularised was a slave song, "Jump Jim Crow", based on an African American folk character. How the name Jim Crow became attached to laws and practices discriminating against African Americans is largely unknown (Blackface! Minstrel Shows, n.d.; The Origins of Jim Crow, n.d.).

The tragedy of the Civil War, slavery, and Jim Crow and the resulting injustices inflicted upon African Americans have been well documented (e.g. Blackmon & Boutsikaris, 2009; Catton, 2004; Gunderson, 1974; Thompson-Miller & Feagin, 2007; Thompson-Miller et al., 2015; Woodward, 2002). Thousands of slaves fought under the Union flag during the Civil War in an effort to secure their freedom. The Civil War not only changed the status of African Americans from slaves to freedmen and freedwomen, it forced the United States to recognise the contributions and valour of African American soldiers, thereby redefining African Americans' roles in society (Foner, 1987). While the South remained entrenched in their ideologies surrounding slavery, the North continued their uneven progression towards some version of racial equality, leaving the country divided. Reconstruction began in 1865 as a way of bridging the divide between the North and South, making some economic, social, and other opportunities available to freedmen and freedwomen for a few, brief years. For example, African Americans were elected to the House of Representatives, Senate, and other government offices – until former Confederate (southern) politicians took power (Thompson-Miller et al., 2015). Yet, the hope of the Great Tradition – the belief that African Americans were an indispensable part of America and, thusly, were entitled to the same rights and privileges as White citizens – remained unfulfilled in spite of the passage of the Thirteenth Amendment (the abolition of slavery and involuntary servitude) and African American efforts to gain economic independence and social acceptance (Foner, 1987).

In 1866, Tennessee was the first Confederate State permitted to return to the Union after the Civil War. Many Tennesseans, and other southerners, would not accept that they had lost the war and resolved to preserve established power structures and social norms. In 1867, Tennessee passed a law prohibiting discrimination on railroads and commonly used carriers. This enraged Confederate Tennesseans, who then proceeded to create a solid Republican majority in state government. Over the next several years, statutes and laws enhancing discrimination and exploitation were passed as Republicans seized and consolidated power throughout the state. This move was echoed in many other states in an effort to block African Americans from full, non-discriminatory participation as citizens. Then, Congress passed the Civil Rights Act of 1875 guaranteeing equal treatment in public places and facilities. Many still remained opposed to the idea of equality, which led to the first Jim Crow law enacted in Tennessee in 1881. This new law upended the idea of equal treatment by requiring separate cars or compartments on trains for African Americans (Folmsbee, 1949).

The bravery and effectiveness exhibited by African American troops in contributing to the Union victory over the Confederates had quickly been forgotten. Any hope that African Americans would now secure equality, or at least improved status and living conditions, quickly evaporated in the face of the stifling racism of the Jim Crow doctrine (Foner, 1987). Laws designed to restrict African American participation in White society, through the heavy-handed application of segregation and oppression, quickly became ubiquitous, leaving Jim Crow to exert undue influence over the life circumstances of millions of African Americans (Woodward, 2002). Race-based disparities in opportunity, housing, education, healthcare, the criminal justice system, and economics – *all allowed and promoted by Jim Crow* – solidified African Americans' position as second-class citizens in the United States (Reskin, 2012). Violence against African Americans increased during this time, including urban violence prevalent in the North while lynchings became commonplace in the South (Olzak, 1990). As late as 1968, almost 20 years after it was abolished, the doctrine of Jim Crow continued to influence and encourage racist acts, such as the sign in Killeen, Texas, that read "'Killeen' meant 'Kill Each and Every Nigger'" (Thompson-Miller et al., 2015, p. 50).

In addition to the laws promoting segregation and racism, Jim Crow propaganda was also a formidable tool used to indoctrinate Whites against the "Others" in the society. For example, people were taught African Americans were inferior in almost every important way. Whites were "God's chosen people", so it was incumbent upon them to support and enforce segregation. Racist tropes held that equality would lead to interracial relationships, which would, in turn, destroy White purity. Consequently, there were stringent behavioural requirements for African Americans, which included dress, language, and mannerisms (Thompson-Miller & Feagin, 2014). Those who violated these requirements were punished (Pilgrim, 2000). As noted by Thompson-Miller and Feagin (2014), "The total institution of slavery was abolished in 1865; four years later, the total institution of Jim Crow replaced it" (p. 7). The notion of race as a determination of worth had not ended with the Civil War; Jim Crow enhanced and perpetuated the myth of White supremacy and purity until the mid-1960s.

Tourism during Jim Crow

In the first few years after the Civil War, most freedmen and freedwomen were forced to live off of subsistence wages and did not have the financial resources to participate in tourism. Those that did prosper enjoyed the newfound freedom to travel both in the United States and abroad. Soon, African American service and fraternal organisations from New Orleans began arranging excursions along the Gulf Coast that included music and entertainment, which became quite popular. Some Whites found this objectionable, so they forced the railroads to adhere to established segregation laws. African Americans countered by launching their own lawsuit, all of which contributed to *Plessy v. Ferguson* in 1896 (Foster, 1999) when the US Supreme Court determined that state-mandated segregation laws did not violate the equal protection clause of the Fourteenth Amendment. (No state shall make or enforce any law which shall abridge the privileges or immunities of citizens of the United States nor shall any state deprive any person of life, liberty, or property without due process of law.) The resulting "separate but equal" stance was rigorously enforced throughout the travel and tourism industry.

Jim Crow made travel in the United States both difficult and dangerous for African Americans through legal precedent and socially sanctioned racism. For example, African Americans were required by law to sit in "separate but equal" train cars. Whites would throw rocks at the windows of these passing train cars to make it clear to African Americans that they were not welcome. Travelling by bus often meant limited opportunities for obtaining food; African Americans were prohibited from going into many restaurants, so they would have to do without food until they reached an establishment that would serve them (Thompson-Miller et al., 2015). Many hotels, motels, and resorts would not allow African American travellers/tourists under Jim Crow (Little, 2019). For instance, world-renown entertainers of colour were a large draw for resort communities, such as Las Vegas and Reno in Nevada, and Atlantic City in New Jersey. Famous musicians and actors, such as Nat King Cole, Sammy Davis Junior, and Sidney Poitier, could not stay at the resorts in which they performed and often had to use the service entrance, as they were barred from entering through the front doors (Feldstein, 2013).

In response, Victor H. Green, a mailman in New York, and his wife, Alma, developed The Negro Motorist Green Book, more commonly known as The Green Book. In use from 1936–1964, The Green Book was a guidebook for African American travellers in the United States and abroad. The guidebook not only detailed accommodations and locations that were non-discriminatory, it also provided overviews of heritage sites and demographic profiles of places understood to be safe for African American travellers (Hall, 2014).

Exclusion from resorts, beaches, and other attractions led to the creation of towns, accommodations, sites, and activities specifically for African Americans, such as Highland Beach in Maryland, American Beach in Florida, Lincoln Hills in Colorado, and Idlewild in Michigan. Areas, such as Oak Bluffs and Saratoga Springs, became African American enclaves in White-dominated vacation spots, such as Martha's Vineyard in Massachusetts and Newport in Rhode Island, respectively (Little, 2019). One of the first African American resorts, Highland Beach in Maryland, was started in 1893 by Charles Douglas, a Civil War veteran, after being denied entry to an all-White resort (Little, 2019).

Established in 1912, Idlewild (the Black Eden) became one of the focal points for the burgeoning middle class of African Americans. While Idlewild was started by White businessmen, African Americans quickly adapted the community to accommodate their needs and began buying property in the area. Idlewild maintained its popularity during the Great Depression and beyond. By the 1950s, it was known as "the Summer Apollo of Michigan", attracting up to 25,000 people in a weekend (Dunn, 2020, para. 10) with performances by African American headliners, such as Aretha Franklin, the Temptations, Della Reese, and Jackie Wilson (Dunn, 2020). Lincoln Hills (established in the 1920s), outside of Boulder, Colorado, was the only African American resort west of the Mississippi and a popular destination for outdoor recreationists. Easily accessible by train, African Americans could purchase tracks of land in Lincoln Hills for use as a campsite or to build their own cabins. Camp Nizhoni (Navajo for "beautiful") hosted several dozen African American Girl Scouts every summer from 1927 to 1945, where they had the opportunity to learn about, and participate in, outdoor recreation (Encyclopedia Staff, n.d.). Most of the resorts provided a venue where middle- and upper-class African Americans could vacation safely. They often became property and/or business owners in the area (Encyclopedia Staff, n.d.; Little, 2019).

Somewhat ironically, the Civil Rights Act of 1964 led to the decline of these resorts. Legal prohibition of discrimination meant that African Americas could now enjoy the resorts, sites, activities, and experiences that had been denied them for decades. As a result, most resorts fell into a state of disrepair. Many are now in the process of revitalisation through preservation, grants, and other efforts to protect and promote these noteworthy sites of African American history (Dunn, 2020; Encyclopedia Staff, n.d.; Little, 2019).

Civil rights and increased mobility

In part, the civil rights movement of the 1950s and 1960s was a by-product of the Great Migration (between 1916 and 1970), when millions of black Americans headed North in search of economic freedoms, and the African American involvement in the armed services during the Second World War. Not only did the Great Migration began a new era of increasing political activism among African Americans, it also stimulated a cultural boom in cities, such as Chicago and New York. More than 1.1 million African American soldiers served in the Second

World War, and while the US military was segregated, once in Europe, for many African Americans

> Post-Nazi Germany was hardly a country free of racism. But for the black soldiers, it was their first experience of a society without a formal Jim Crow color line. Their uniform identified them as victorious warriors and as Americans, rather than "Negroes".
>
> (Höhn, 2018, n.p.)

Before 1916, nine in ten blacks lived in the South (mostly in rural areas), and by 1970, only half of African Americans lived in the south, of which less than 20% lived in rural areas.

The Civil Rights Act of 1964 abolished Jim Crow (Hall, 2014) but not the institutionalised racism that had become ubiquitous. Now, the African American struggle for freedom had morphed into a struggle for equality and first-class citizenship. While charismatic leaders were often the most visible, the movement was galvanised, for the most part, by everyday African Americans (Ezra, 2009). Claudette Colvin, Rosa Parks, Ruby Bridges, the Selma to Montgomery marches, the sit-in at the Woolworth's counter, and the civil rights movement soon drove social reform and associated efforts to replace racism with equality. Martin Luther King, Jr. became the most notable leader of the civil rights movement, with a focus on non-violence as the path to equality. While his assassination dealt a serious blow to the collective psyche of the civil rights movement, it also served to invigorate those seeking to address ongoing issues of housing, education, healthcare, employment, and Black power (Ezra, 2009). The Black Lives Matter movement, grounded in the civil rights movement, bears witness to the fact that while progress has been made, the promises of the Great Tradition, multiple civil rights acts, *Brown v. the Board of Education*, and the potential for equality remain unfulfilled (McKersie, 2021).

Tourism after the civil rights movement

The Civil Rights era led to greater social and economic mobility for African Americans. It allowed for equal educational opportunities, increased earning potential, and freedom of movement. Gordon (2015) highlights a series of travel industry advertisements published in *Ebony* magazine in the 1970s aimed at African American travellers. The ads featured attractions that celebrated the renewed black culture and historical sights of interest to African Americans, such as the jazz and blues music scene in Memphis, Tennessee, Dodge City, Kansas, home of the all-Black 10th US Cavalry, and San Francisco's Liedesdorff Street, named after "the first Black millionaire" William Alexander Liedesdorff (Gordon, 2015). These Black travel agencies partnered with Amtrak, Greyhound, and a number of airlines and expanded trips into Europe to celebrate European "Africanness". This era gave rise to pioneering Black entrepreneurs in the travel agency sector, including Fran Blackwell, who brought a United Nations delegation to Harlem, New York to experience African American art and culture, and Freddye and Jacob Henderson, who made the arrangements for Dr. Martin Luther King to travel to Norway to receive his Nobel Prize in 1964 (Travel Noire, 2021).

As African Americans gained mobility, they engaged in travel writing. Fish (2004) argues that travel writing in the 19th century perpetuated colonial stereotypes and "notions of identity, race, and class merge to influence the gaze and its narrativized forms within the travelogue" (Buzinde & Osagie, 2011, p. 406). By the 20th century, travel writing allowed for a forum to "voice their critiques of the US-American society and to speak with authority on public and private matters" (Kalous, 2021, p. 93). It allowed writers to compare and contrast experiences abroad with the discriminatory situation at home or to measure progress for racialised groups across the United States. Building on the early works of Matthew Henson (a Black arctic explorer) and Ida B. Wells (documenting her travels to Europe), authors, such as Langston Hughes and Era Bell Thompson, wrote about their travel experiences on the African continent. John A. Williams spent six years travelling across the United States for *Holiday Magazine* in the 1960s to document "the gauge of racial progress" (Winfield, 2013, p. 66), and Eddy L. Harris canoed the Mississippi River from Minnesota to New Orleans in the 1980s, using his travel experiences to "def[y] the practices of racialised exclusion and 'orientalist ideological work' that hinders access to travel for so many and 'continue[s] today as the underbelly of the tourist industry" (ibid., p. 164). As African American travel writers gained notoriety, a new world of travel possibilities became visible to everyday African Americans.

However, travel by African Americans was fraught with new challenges. Lee and Scott (2017) argue that segregation and institutional discrimination have had long-lasting effects on the desire to travel by many African Americans, and that "African Americans believe they would not be welcome in many leisure settings" (p. 382). While travel opportunities increased, as did wages for African Americans, Lee and Scott (2017) write, "brutality lingered in the social memory of the African American community and continued to negatively impact their travel patterns" (p. 382). Heritage interpretation was dominated by White narratives, and many African American attractions were located in predominantly White communities where they faced discrimination or outright violence (Benjamin et al., 2016). One could argue that African Americans were portrayed as victims of discrimination, repression, and violence by the travel and tourism industry in a time when they were looking for a celebration of their contributions to the economic, scientific, and political achievements of their country.

Black lives matter and tourism today

The Black Lives Matter movement (BLM) began in 2013 after a police officer was acquitted in the killing of Trayvon Martin and grew to become a world-wide social movement after the police killings of Michael Brown, Eric Garner, and George Floyd (Howard University School of Law, n.d.). The mission statement of the BLM Foundation is "to eradicate White supremacy and build local power to intervene in violence inflicted on Black communities by the state and vigilantes" (BLM Foundation, n.d.). As the hash tag #blacklivesmatter garnered support for the movement, so did push back from "racialized politics of solidarity" (Hooker, 2016, p. 449). As demonstrations exploded across the United States, different factions presented different narratives, some praising the "uprisings" and others criticising the "riots" (ibid.), showing a nation divided in its fight for social justice. Many institutions have had to rethink their policies and practices, including the travel and tourism industry. Moreover, the tourism academic literature remains silent on the subject of Black Lives Matter.

As America addresses its racist past, many contemporary tourist attractions must rethink their contribution to American heritage and history. Most notably, southern historic sites that have emphasised Confederate heroes and Civil War events have come under scrutiny. Rex and Watson (2021) remind us that tourism is an important avenue to shape collective understandings of heritage through memory making (remembering) and, more recently, memory re-making (un-forgetting). They write "public memory is different than history in that it accounts for more of the informal, unofficial, unsettled, or changeable ways in which communities create, maintain, and alter a sense of the past that is held in common" (p. 7). Tourism within the United States has actively silenced African American history, in part because it has catered to its current demographics which are mainly White Americans (Howard, 2021). The goal, now, is to repair "this flawed and freighted past we hold in common" (Watson, 2021, p. 154).

As African Americans find their place in modern society, the stories of their contributions are emerging through books, movies, music, and art. From the opening of the African American Museum of History and Culture, as part of the Smithsonian Institute in Washington, DC, to movies such as *Hidden Figures*, *Respect*, and *Harriet*, contemporary media is beginning to highlight the impact African Americans have made throughout history. Tourism in the United States is slowly changing, reassessing the role of African Americans in our society. The removal of Confederate monuments and the renaming of sites have finally begun. Even the National Park Service, which has long struggled to draw the diverse travellers (Weber & Sultana, 2013), now highlights the role of the Buffalo Soldiers as the first park rangers of Yosemite National Park (National Park Foundation, n.d.).

Yet, tourism still has a long way to go to undo institutionalised racism inherent in its history. The Castell Project (2021) found that at the end of 2020, only 1.6% of hospitality industry executives (director through CEO) were Black, which is 10.9 times lower than their 17.5% share of overall hospitality employment and substantially lower than Black leadership in S&P 500 companies (of which 4% are Black). These numbers are lower than in 2019, which implies "the hospitality industry let go a higher proportion of its Black workforce than other employees" (p. 5) during the COVID lockdown in 2021. Moreover, in an interview with Event Business Formula, Elliott Ferguson, the CEO of Destination DC, claims "in 2021, America is a nation with 600–700 DMOs, and less than ten of them are run by people of color and females" (Rozenberg, 2021, n.p.).

Where to from here?

Inclusivity requires a re-thinking of the way we do business, from formal policies that exclude certain populations to informal business practices that result in micro-aggressions towards people of colour. As the old adage reminds us, "build it and they will come"; if you build an inclusive organisation, diversity in patronage will follow. Attride (n.d.), an editor and Black traveller, challenges the travel and tourism industry to "make Black travelers feel heard, accepted, and genuinely welcome" (n.p.). Yet changing a structural environment is fraught with challenges, especially when there already exists a lack of diversity within policymaking bodies.

The first step must include an assessment of an organisation's internal work environment. Occupational segregation, whereby minority workers often end up in lower-paid jobs than White males (Penner, 2008), is rife in the tourism industry (Benjamin, & Dillette, 2021). It is not a matter of *how many* African Americans are employed but rather *in which positions* they are employed and whether these jobs allow for equal career advancement. In particular, low-profile positions in maintenance, housekeeping, or landscape management hide a company's diversity and may not offer the skill development needed for promotion. Benefit packages that include university tuition, workforce training, or other avenues to learn management skills must be available and visible to employees at all levels. Moreover, finding avenues to advertise open positions should include outlets that specialise in diversity, such as blackjobs.com or blackcareernetwork.com. Ken Frazier, CEO of Merck, urges companies "to take a skills-first approach rather than a credentials approach, which will eliminate some of the systemic barriers African Americans have faced" (Adams, 2020, n.p.). The implementation of diversity apprenticeship programmes can also support the recruitment (and advancement) of people of colour.

To ensure informed decision-making regarding racial inclusion, it is vital to have people of colour not only in leadership roles but within the groups that advise on policies and strategies. Al Hutchinson, president and CEO of Visit Baltimore, emphasises that

> boards need to represent the communities they serve with special emphasis given to underserved communities. Additionally, organizations should review their strategic plans, mission statements and core values to make sure there is a commitment to social justice and the eradication of racism
> (Ruppenstein, 2020, n.p.).

Homogenous leadership is generally unable to recognise and correct policies that discriminate against minority groups. African American leadership should be actively involved in strategic developments as a way to mitigate unconscious bias throughout the process.

Benjamin and Dillette (2021) argue that continued discrimination creates inhospitable experiences for African American travellers. However, Martinique

Lewis, a travel consultant, argues "if your team internally is diverse, all your messaging will be too" (Ruppenstein, 2020, n.p.). Once an organisation has begun addressing racism from within, it should begin to showcase its achievements, ensuring that African American visitors are welcome and that they feel akin to the organisation through visible commitments to diversity. For example, Attride (n.d.) prompts "including Black people in photos and video marketing – this simple act of representation lets us know that we are welcome" (n.p.). Inclusive messages must avoid stereotyping, such as using photos of White tourists taking pictures of impoverished Black children or a Black "subservient" employee catering to White visitors. However, simple pictures are not enough. Understanding the African American visitor requires a new way of doing marketing research.

Moreover, practice what you preach. If an organisation has promised an inclusive experience, ensure that your guests actually receive an inclusive experience. Carnival Chief Executive Arnold Donald believes "It is not about marketing slogans or campaigns in my view, but about the proactive actions each of us personally take and hold ourselves accountable for" (Goodwin, 2020, n.p.). It is a place where real-world learning can take place, and training that helps employees recognise and overcome their inherent, and often unconscious, bias is necessary. Providing avenues for tracking common discretionary practices, such as stereotyping, micro-aggressions, harassment, and negative visitor experiences, and using these example as constructive learning tools can enhance the Black visitor experience. Tracking online travel review sites allows organisations to see, and hopefully correct, lingering discriminatory practices noticed and communicated by travellers of colour.

The role of academe

It is important to note that further research into institutional bias, structural racism, and discrimination is warranted, and multiracial studies into travel experiences, motivations, and expectations are needed. Francis (n.d., n.p.) notes,

> We must find ways to address and stop conscious or unconscious racist behaviour towards travellers of colour. Part of this is proactively seeking to better understand the entire experience of travel for people of colour, from start to finish: from marketing brochures, through booking and travel, to arrivals and departures. There's still too little research around tourism and race.

For example, the lack of research into the impacts of Black Lives Matter on tourism is noticeable. As the COVID pandemic continues to rage, there is definitive evidence that our African American travel colleagues are facing the brunt of employment downsizing (Castell Project, 2021). Evidence also suggests that police brutality increases the risk for African Americans travelling by car (Lee & Scott, 2017), as do discriminatory practices with airport security (Benjamin & Dillette, 2021). Adding the African American voice to research is vital in understanding lingering issues of racism.

Lastly, we challenge our academic colleagues to critically examine their marketing, recruitment, and admission standards for potential students of colour. For African Americans to rise to the top of our industry, universities must be actively engaged in recruitment and retention. Visiting local high schools in underrepresented communities shows a university's interest in a diverse student body. As universities move toward the use of big data in recruiting potential students (Selingo, 2017), re-evaluating inherent discriminatory acceptance criteria is increasingly important. Moreover, many of the recommendations for industry listed earlier are applicable to academia to ensure an inclusive and welcoming environment that encourages the retention of Black talent.

The diversity of the travel and tourism industry begins with the young, nurtures and supports each employee throughout a career, and ensures fair and equitable advancement opportunities throughout. In turn, diverse perspectives begin to influence the policy and practices of organisations, building an industry that is innovative and responsive to the needs of all customers. This new perspective can influence the communities in which we operate and increase the involvement of our stakeholders. The result can be a celebration of all of our unique attributes and perspectives, a growth in our market share, and access for all the people to the world's largest (and most exciting) industry.

References

Adams, C. (2020, December 10). Several top companies vow to hire a total of 1 million Black people over 10 years. *NBC News*. Retrieved January 7, 2022, from www.nbcnews.com/news/nbcblk/several-top-companies-vow-hire-total-1-million-black-people-n1250776

Alderman, D. H., & Inwood, J. (2014). Toward a pedagogy of Jim Crow: A geographic reading of The Green Book. In L. Estaville, E. Montalvo, & F. Akiwumi (Eds.), *Teaching ethnic geography in the 21st century* (pp. 68–78). National Council for Geographic Education.

Attride, T (n.d.). Three first steps toward an anti-racist travel industry, as told by a black editor. *Here Magazine*. Retrieved December 30, 2021, from www.heremagazine.com/articles/anti-racism-travel-industry

Bailey, Z. D., Krieger, N., Agénor, M., Linos, N., & Bassett, M. T. (2017). Structural racism and health inequities in the USA: Evidence and interventions. *The Lancet, 389*(10077), 1453–1463. https://doi.org/10.1016/S0140-6736(17)30569-X

Benavides, J. (2014). *A summary of African American travel interests and behaviors*. University of Minnesota Tourism Center. Retrieved January 17, 2022, from https://conservancy.umn.edu/bitstream/handle/11299/169872/African-American%20Travel%20Market%20report – final.pdf;sequence=1

Benjamin, S., & Dillette, A. K. (2021). Black travel movement: Systemic racism informing tourism. *Annals of Tourism Research, 88*, 103169.

Benjamin, S., Kline, C., Alderman, D., & Hoggard, W. (2016). Heritage site visitation and attitudes toward African American heritage preservation: An investigation of North Carolina residents. *Journal of Travel Research, 55*(7), 919–933.

Black Lives Matter Foundation (n.d.). *About us*. Retrieved January 1, 2022, from https://blacklivesmatter.com/about/

Blackface! Minstrel Shows (n.d.). Retrieved December 2, 2021, from http://black-face.com/minstrel-shows.htm

Blackmon, D. A., & Boutsikaris, D. (2009). *Slavery by another name. The re-inslavement of black Americans from the Civil War to World War II*. Anchor.

Brennen Center for Justice. (2021, October 4). *Voting laws roundup: October 2021*. Retrieved January 8, 2022, from www.brennancenter.org/our-work/research-reports/voting-laws-roundup-october-2021

Buder, S. (2020). *New study reveals the spending power of Black U.S. travelers*. Retrieved January 19, 2022, from www.afar.com/magazine/new-study-reveals-the-spending-power-of-black-us-leisure-travelers

Burnside, T. (2022). *Homer Plessy, of Plessy v. Ferguson's "separate but equal" ruling, pardoned by Louisiana governor*. Retrieved January 17, 2022, from www.cnn.com/2022/01/05/us/plessy-pardon-signed-by-governor/index.html

Buzinde, C., & Osagie, I. (2011). William Wells Brown: Fugitive subjectivity, travel writing, and the gaze. *Cultural Studies, 25*(3), 405–425.

Catton, B. (2004). *The civil war*. Houghton Mifflin.

Chen, V. (2020). *MMGY Global partners with advocacy groups to fill the gap in Black travel research*. Retrieved January 19, 2022, from www.travelagewest.com/Industry-Insight/Opinion/Editorial-Travel-to-Mexico-Coronavirus-2022

Dunn, P. (2020). *Michigan's "Black Eden": A short history of Idlewild*. Second Wave. Retrieved December 13, 2021, from www.secondwavemedia.com/features/Idlewild-mnrtf-series-14.asp

Encyclopedia Staff. (n.d.). *Lincoln Hills*. Retrieved December 13, 2021, from https://coloradoencyclopedia.org/article/lincoln-hills

Ezra, M. (2009). Introduction. In M. Ezra & P. C. Mancell (Eds.), *Civil rights movement people and perspectives* (pp. xi–xvii). ABC-CLIO.

Feldstein, R. (2013). *How it feels to be free: Black women entertainers and the Civil Rights Movement*. Oxford University Press.

Fish, C. J. (2004). *Black and white women's travel narratives: Antebellum explorations*. University Press of Florida.

Folmsbee, S. J. (1949). The origin of the first "Jim Crow" law. *The Journal of Southern History, 15*(2), 235–247. https://doi.org/10.2307/2197999

Foner, E. (1987). Rights and the constitution in black life during the Civil War and reconstruction. *The Journal of American History, 74*(3), 863–883.

Foster, M. (1999). In the face of "Jim Crow": Prosperous blacks and vacations, travel and outdoor leisure. 1890–1945. *The Journal of Negro History, 84*(2), 130–149.

Francis, J. (n.d.). *We need to talk about race and tourism*. Responsible Travel. Retrieved January 8, 2022, from www.responsibletravel.com/copy/race-and-tourism

Goodwin, H. (2020). *Racism in tourism*. Responsible Tourism Partnership. Retrieved January 7, 2022, from https://responsibletourismpartnership.org/racism-in-tourism/

Gordon, T. S. (2015). "Take Amtrak to Black History": Marketing heritage tourism to African Americans in the 1970s. *Journal of Tourism History, 7*(1–2), 54–74.

Gunderson, G. (1974). The origin of the American Civil War. *The Journal of Economic History, 34*(10), 915–950.

Hall, M. R. (2014). The negro traveller's guide to a Jim Crow South: Negotiating racialized landscapes during a dark period in United States cultural history, 1936–1967. *Postcolonial Studies, 17*(3), 307–319. https://doi.org/10.1080/13688790.2014.987898

Higginbotham, A. L., Jr., & Smith, W. C. (1992). The Hughes Court and the beginning of the end of the separate, but equal doctrine. *Minnesota Law Review, 73*, 1099–1131. https://scholarship.law.umn.edu/mlr/793

Höhn, M. (2018, January 30). African-American GIs of WWII: Fighting for democracy abroad and at home. *The Military Times*. Retrieved December 20, 2021, from www.militarytimes.com/military-honor/black-military-history/2018/01/30/african-american-gis-of-wwii-fighting-for-democracy-abroad-and-at-home/

Hooker, J. (2016). Black Lives Matter and the paradoxes of US Black politics: From democratic sacrifice to democratic repair. *Political Theory*, *44*(4); 448–469.

Howard, E. (2021). Slavery in the big easy: Digital interventions in the tourist landscape of New Orleans. In C. Rex & S. Watson (Eds.), *Public memory, race, and Heritage Tourism of Early America* (pp. 86–103). Routledge.

Howard University School of Law. (n.d.). *Black lives matter movement*. Retrieved January 1, 2022, from https://library.law.howard.edu/civilrightshistory/BLM

Jones, N., Marks, R., Ramirez, R., & Ríos-Vargas, M. (2021). *2020 census illuminates racial and ethnic composition of the country*. Retrieved January 18, 2022, from www.census.gov/library/stories/2021/08/improved-race-ethnicity-measures-reveal-united-states-population-much-more-multiracial.html

Kalous, I. (2021). *Black travel writing: Contemporary narratives of travel to Africa by African American and Black British authors* (Vol. 35). Transcript Verlag.

Lee, K. J., & Scott, D. (2017). Racial discrimination and African Americans' travel behavior: The utility of habitus and vignette technique. *Journal of Travel Research*, *56*(3), 381–392.

Little, B. (2019). *Before the green book, these resorts offered hidden safe havens for Black Americans*. Retrieved December 12, 2021, from www.history.com/news/green-book-black-travel-resorts-jim-crow

McKersie, R. B. (2021). The 1960s civil rights movement and Black Lives Matter: Social protest from a negotiation perspective. *Negotiation Journal*, *37*(3), 301–323.

National Park Foundation. (n.d.). *6 powerful places to immerse yourself in African American Heritage*. Retrieved December 30, 2021, from www.nationalparks.org/connect/blog/6-powerful-places-immerse-yourself-african-american-heritage

Olzak, S. (1990). The political context of competition: Lynching and urban racial violence, 1882–1914. *Social Forces*, *69*(2), 395–421.

Penner, A. M. (2008). Race and gender differences in wages: The role of occupational sorting at the point of hire. *The Sociological Quarterly*, *49*(3), 597–614.

Pilgrim, D. (2000). What was Jim Crow. *Ferris State University*, *16*, 2007.

Powell, J. A. (2008). Structural racism: Building upon the insights of John Calmore. *NCL Review*, *86*, 791–816.

Reskin, B. (2012). The race discrimination system. *Annual Review of Sociology*, *38*, 17–35. https://doi.org/10.1146/annurev-soc-071811–145508

Rex, C., & Watson, S. E. (2021). *Public memory, race, and heritage tourism of early America*. Routledge.

Rozenberg, E. (Host) (2021). *The business of meeting* [Audio podcast]. www.eventbusinessformula.com/ep-52-elliott-ferguson/

Ruppenstein, A. (2020, June 25). *Let's talk about racism in the travel industry*. Travel Courier. Retrieved January 7, 2022, from https://travelcourier.ca/coverstory-jun-25-2020/

Schmid, W. T. (1996). The definition of racism. *Journal of Applied Psychology*, *13*(1), 31–40. https://doi.org/10.1111/j.1468-5930.1996.tb00147.x

Selingo, J. (2017, April 11). How colleges use big data to target the students they want. *The Atlantic*. Retrieved January 8, 2022, from www.theatlantic.com/education/archive/2017/04/how-colleges-find-their-students/522516/

Smedley, A., & Smedley, B. D. (2005). Race as biology is fiction, Racism as a social problem is real. *American Psychologist*, *60*(1), 16–26. https://doi.org/10.1037/0003-066X.60.1.16

The Castell Project. (2021). *Black representation in hospitality industry leadership*. Retrieved January 1, 2022, from https://static1.squarespace.com/static/5c886e36c2ff610 63923506b/t/60a3d426e2d1e010d15326d6/1621349414799/Black+representation+in+ hospitality+industry+leadership+final.pdf

The origins of Jim Crow. (n.d.). Retrieved December 3, 2021, from www.ferris.edu/htmls/ news/jimcrow/origins.htm

Thompson-Miller, R., & Feagin, J. R. (2007). The reality and impact of legal segregation in the United States. In H. Vera & J. R. Feagin (Eds.), *Handbook of the sociology of racial and ethnic relations* (pp. 455–465). Springer.

Thompson-Miller, R., & Feagin, J. R. (2014). Jim Crow: A total institution – navigating a gateless prison system. In S. W. Bowman (Ed.), *Color behind bars, racism in the U.S. prison system* (pp. 7–38). Praeger.

Thompson-Miller, R., Feagin, J. R., & Picca, L. H. (2015). *Jim Crow's legacy: The lasting impact of segregation*. Rowman & Littlefield.

Travel Noire. (2021). *Henderson travel service: The first and oldest black-owned travel agency in America*. Retrieved December 31, 2021, from https://travelnoire.com/ henderson-travel-first-black-owned-travel-agency-america

US Census. (2020). *2020 census illuminates racial and ethnic composition of the country*. Retrieved February 6, 2022, from www.census.gov/library/stories/2021/08/improved-race-ethnicity-measures-reveal-united-states-population-much-more-multiracial.html

Wang, H. L. (2022). *Trump officials interfered with the 2020 census beyond cutting it short, email shows*. Retrieved January 18, 2022, from www.npr.org/2022/01/15/ 1073338121/2020-census-interference-trump

Watson, S. (2021). Afterword: Memory and heritage in the "era of just redemption". In C. Rex & S. Watson (Eds.), *Public memory, race, and heritage tourism of early America* (pp. 153–158). Routledge.

Weber, J., & Sultana, S. (2013). Why do so few minority people visit National Parks? Visitation and the accessibility of "America's Best Idea". *Annals of the Association of American Geographers*, *103*(3), 437–464.

Winfield, G. (2013). *Dream of an elsewhere: Contemporary African American travel writing*. Nottingham Trent University.

Woodward, C. V. (2002). *The strange career of Jim Crow*. Oxford University Press.

6 Overcoming institutional discrimination in USDA programmes

Food and agricultural tourism

Kynda R. Curtis, Debra Tropp, and Amy D. Hagerman

Introduction

Over the last two decades, the United States Department of Agriculture (USDA) has implemented and updated its agriculture-based federal assistance programmes to ensure access to socially disadvantaged audiences, including women, people of colour, the LGBTQ community, and veterans. Depending on the programme, funding includes grants and loans focused on assisting individuals and groups to develop or expand agriculture- or food-based businesses. While some programmes specifically target socially disadvantaged groups, others require a certain percentage of programme funds be awarded to projects that serve the socially disadvantaged.

This new era of USDA programmes is a direct result of court cases involving Hispanic and women farmers (Garcia & Love; Vilsack, 2014), Native American farmers and ranchers (Keepseagle; Natural Resource Conservation Service [NRCS], 2011), and Black farmers (Pigford & Pigford II; [Redacted] & [Redacted], 2013) who faced discrimination in USDA programme access from 1980 until 2000. After settling ongoing court cases, Agriculture Secretary Tom Vilsack (2014) stated,

> With today's announcement, we are continuing work to build a new era for civil rights at USDA: correcting our past errors, learning from our mistakes, and outlining definitive action to ensure there will be no missteps in the future. The process has been long and often difficult, but my staff and I have been working hard every day to make USDA a model employer and premier service provider that treats every customer and employee fairly, with dignity and respect.
>
> (para. 3)

Many USDA programmes support tourism projects, including food and agricultural tourism. These programmes focus on land-based agricultural development, as well as direct marketing and local food systems. Agritourism projects are specifically mentioned in several calls for proposal. Other programmes seek to help agricultural producers access important culinary markets in tourism destinations. Tourism provides opportunities for minority groups, including income generation, local planning and development, revitalisation of local culture and practices, and improved transportation and communication (Ministry of Culture, Sports, and Tourism, 2008). Additionally, tax revenues generated often lead to improved community education and health services. For example, US Native American tribes have begun to offer cultural experiences for tourists in Native American cooking, crafts, games, and music, including Iroquois White Corn cooking classes, the Hopi Art Trail, and "Cherokee Experiences" (Taylor, 2016). Tourism on Native American reservations is growing: from 2007 until 2015, the number of visitors to US Indian reservations increased by 180%, and overseas visitation increased by 19% from 2014 until 2015 alone (Taylor, 2016).

This chapter discusses how USDA programmes strive to overcome institutional biases and discrimination by providing assistance to socially disadvantaged groups seeking to develop food- and agriculture-based tourism projects. A discussion of specific USDA programmes and how they ensure use and access among socially disadvantaged groups is provided as are examples of projects funded under those programmes. This discussion serves as a framework for overcoming inequalities in government-based programmes.

Background

The farm bill (formally, the Agriculture Improvement Act) is a multiyear US law that governs USDA programmes in terms of funding and policy. Farm bill programmes often begin with a small amount of funding set aside for a pilot programme. USDA administers programmes specific to farmers and ranchers that are historically underserved or socially disadvantaged, often referred to "Section 2501 Programs" because they were first established in Section 2501 of the Food, Agriculture, Conservation, and Trade Act of 1990 (P.L. 101–624). These programmes originally provided incentives for participation by socially disadvantaged farmers and ranchers, defined as a farmer or rancher who is a member of "a group whose members have been subjected to racial or ethnic prejudice because of their identity as members of a group without regard to their individual qualities" (Food, Agriculture, Conservation, and Trade Act of 1990, §2501e1). In 1990, this included Asian, Black, Hispanic, Native American, Alaska Natives, and Pacific Islander farmers and ranchers. Today, the definition has expanded to include refugees and immigrants belonging to any of the minority groups, where many USDA programmes require citizenship. Women and veterans were originally only eligible for Section 2501 programmes if they were also a member of one of the minority groups described earlier, but subsequent farm bills added them to the definition of socially disadvantaged farmers and ranchers for specific programmes.

Section 2501 programmes did not expand between 1990 and 2002 (National Sustainable Agriculture Coalition [NSAC], 2019a), but the Farm Security and Rural Investment Act of 2002 (P.L. 107–171) reauthorised Section 2501 programmes and expanded appropriations. Those funds were discretionary and did not exceed $6 million in appropriations per year (NSAC, 2019a). Starting with the Food, Conservation, and Energy Act of 2008 (PL 110–246), programmes – particularly conservation programmes – were further targeted on socially disadvantaged groups (Johnson, 2021). The 2008 farm bill was the first to have a subtitle (Title XIV, Subtitle A) specifically dedicated to limited resource, economically disadvantaged, and beginning farmers and ranchers (Novak et al., 2015). This included waiving certain requirements and additional crop insurance subsidies. Nickerson and Hand (2009) reported that almost 40% of farms were owned by producers meeting the definition for historically underserved at the time the 2008 farm bill was passed. In addition, the *Pigford v. Glickman* lawsuit had been settled, resulting in payments to individuals who had been discriminated against by the USDA.

The Agricultural Act of 2014 (P.L. 113–79) continued to expand USDA-administered programmes and incentives for socially disadvantaged, limited resource, and underserved groups. The subtitle associated with Section 2501 programmes expanded the availability of noninsured agricultural production coverage under the Noninsured Crop Disaster Assistance Program (NAP). This programme is critically important for small speciality crop producers since these crops are not normally covered by federally subsidised multiperil crop insurance (Risk Management Agency, 2015). The 2014 bill also formed two offices: the Office of Tribal Relations (§12303) and the Military Veterans Agricultural Liaison (§12303) (Novak et al., 2015).

The Agricultural Improvement Act of 2018 (P.L. 115–334) combined programmes for underserved groups with those for beginning farmers and ranchers under the Farming Opportunities Training and Outreach (FOTO) programme (Office of Partnerships and Public Engagements [OPPE], 2022). The act also required that

> to the maximum extent practicable, in carrying out the program, the Secretary and eligible partners shall conduct outreach to beginning farmers and ranchers, veteran farmers and ranchers, socially disadvantaged farmers and ranchers, and limited resource farmers and ranchers to encourage participation by those producers in a project subject to a partnership agreement or funding agreement
>
> (Agriculture Improvement Act of 2018, §2706).

USDA programmes specifically containing incentives for underserved producers exist under the following titles: commodities (Title I), conservation (Title II), research/extension/related matters (Title VII), crop insurance (Title XI), credit (Title V), and miscellaneous (Title XII). Some of the most detailed programmes are found under conservation, credit, and miscellaneous. Figure 6.1 reports funding allocations for selected programmes in the 2018 farm bill.

USDA uses several key terms to describe minority and underserved audiences, and these criteria differ by agency and programme. *Historically underserved farmers and ranchers*, refers to any farmer or rancher who identifies as African

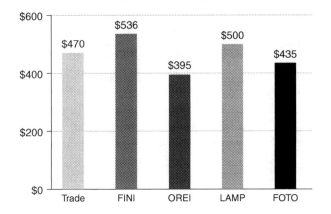

Figure 6.1 2018 farm bill funding for selected programmes (ten-year totals in millions $US).

Note. OREI, Organic Research and Extension Initiative; LAMP, Local Agriculture Market Programme; FOTO, Opportunities Training and Outreach Program.

Source: Adapted from the National Sustainable Agriculture Coalition (2018).

American, Alaska Native, American Indian, Hispanic, Asian, Native Hawaiian, Pacific Islander, or female. *Socially disadvantaged farmers and ranchers* are any individual or entity belonging to groups that have been subject to racial or ethnic prejudice (Economic Research Service [ERS], 2022). The first seven groups listed as historically underserved (listed earlier) are also designated as socially disadvantaged, but some programmes may not include women.

However, USDA programmes may also incentivise participation by *limited resource farmers and ranchers*: those who meet farm gross sales or household income limits, as defined by the USDA. The producer must have "direct or indirect gross farm sales not more than the current indexed value in each of the previous two years" (NRCS, 2021, n.p.). For 2020, this would have meant gross sales of less than $180,300 (ERS, 2022). In addition, the producer must have a total household income "at or below the national poverty level for a family of four, or less than 50 percent of a county median household income in each of the previous two years" (NRCS, 2021, n.p.).

Some of the most widely used USDA programmes for agritourism operations are associated with the *beginning farmers and rancher programmes*. A beginning farmer or rancher could be one who has worked outside of agriculture for many years before beginning an agricultural enterprise, so the designation has nothing to do with age. Rather, qualifications include having been an active farm or ranch operator for less than ten years. For a farmer or rancher to be "active", they must own a substantial portion of the business and actively participate in its operation. In addition, the farm or ranch cannot be more than 30% of the average farm size in their county, as determined by the Census of Agriculture. Additional experience requirements may also apply, depending on the programme. However, experience requirements can be partially offset by education, military service, or mentoring under another producer.

Veteran farmer and rancher programmes recognise the experience provided by military service members who are starting agricultural enterprises. As with beginning farmer and rancher programmes, veteran farmers and ranchers must have less than ten years as the primary operator of the business. However, they may also qualify if they achieved veteran status at any point in the last ten years. Qualifying veterans include those who were released in any manner other than "dishonourable" after having served in the "United States Army, Navy, Marine Corps, Air Force, or Coast Guard, including the reserve component thereof" (NRCS, 2021, n.p.).

Current programmes

As of 2021, some USDA programmes supporting the development and expansion of food and agritourism operations or related educational efforts specifically targeted underserved producers (e.g. Farm Service Agency, 2019) and others (e.g. National Institute of Food and Agriculture [NIFA], 2021), assisted all producers but required that a certain percentage of programme funds be awarded to projects serving socially disadvantaged groups – including those that meet USDA definitions for underserved, female, veteran, and beginning farmer and rancher and those with limited resources – or that members of these groups be awarded extra points in the review process. Points systems allow projects or applicants that meet multiple criteria to receive priority (e.g. Hispanic women or Native American veterans). USDA programmes targeting or encouraging applicants from socially disadvantaged groups include the following:

- Outreach and Assistance for Socially Disadvantaged and Veteran Farmers and Ranchers Program (the 2051 Program) (NIFA);
- Loans for Socially Disadvantaged Farmers and Ranchers (FSA);
- Beginning Farmer and Rancher Development Program (NIFA);
- Farmers Market Promotion Program and Local Food Promotion Program (AMS);
- Specialty Crop Block Grant Program (AMS); and
- Federally Recognized Tribal Extension Program (NIFA).

The USDA NIFA has two cornerstone programmes heavily focused on serving socially disadvantaged groups. The first is the Outreach and Assistance for Socially Disadvantaged and Veteran Farmers and Ranchers Program (The 2501 Program), which specifically mentions underserved audiences in its title. This programme is open to non-profits, educational institutions, tribes, etc., but all funding must serve socially disadvantaged and veteran farmers and ranchers. Projects focus on a broad range of small farm and agricultural activities, but projects related to food and agriculture tourism – especially the production of value-added foods – are common. A description of all projects funded under the programme can be found on the programme website (OPPE, 2021).

The second programme is the Beginning Farmer and Rancher Development Program (BFRDP) that is open to a broad variety of applicants and has encouraged projects serving socially disadvantaged audiences by awarding extra points in the review process for projects spending 25% or more of their budget on underserved audiences and by setting lower limits for overall programme funding. The current request for proposals states that

> At least 5 percent of the funds will support programs and services that address the needs of beginning farmers and ranchers with limited resources; socially disadvantaged beginning farmers or ranchers; and farm workers desiring to become farmers or ranchers. At least 5 percent of the funds will support programs and services that address the needs of veteran farmers and ranchers.
> (NIFA, 2021, n.p.)

This programme also funds a variety of agriculture-related projects, but direct-to-consumer marketing, including food and agritourism, is common.

These two programmes together provide $40 million in mandatory funding for fiscal year (FY) 2022 (a substantial increase over FY 2020) and increased funding to $50 million by FY 2023 (see FOTO funding in Figure 6.1). Annual funding is split equally between the BFRDP and the Section 2501 Program. Supplemental funds, in the amount of approximately $17 million, will also be awarded for FY 2022 under the Coronavirus Response and Relief Supplemental Appropriations Act, 2021 (P.L. 116–220) (OPPE, 2022). NIFA also funds the four Extension Risk Management Education Centers across the United States at a cost of $4.5 million annually (NIFA, 2022b). These centres provide grants to non-profits and educational providers, including universities, whose programming is focused on reducing risk for agricultural producers. Many of the grant projects include agritourism and similar market risk management techniques (e.g. "Expanding Direct Marketing Opportunities in the Intermountain West through Farm Shops", Curtis, 2014).

NIFA provides a publicly available search engine of projects funded under its programmes, called the Current Research Information System (NIFA, 2022a). Project descriptions provide the name of the applicant, dollar amount of funding, and project summary and objectives. This search tool serves several objectives, the primary one being transparency in government funding. A recent search on agritourism projects with socially disadvantaged applicants or audiences included

- Small Farm Agritourism as a Tool for Community Development in North Carolina;
- Teaching Choctaw Youth and Adults to Grow for and Access Local Markets;
- Development of a Veterans Incubator Small Farm for Specialty Food Enterprises Serving African American and Hispanic Veterans in the Treasure Coast and Central Florida Counties;

- Identifying Opportunities for Food and Fiber-Related Business Ventures: Addressing the Challenges of Business Ownership for Underserved Populations in Iowa's Small and Rural Communities;
- Agricultural Value-Added: Prospects for Small and Disadvantaged Farmers in North Carolina.

USDA AMS programmes case

A discussion of USDA's support of agritourism and its connected support to socially disadvantaged farmers, including BIPOC (Black, Indigenous, and People of Colour) farmers engaged in agritourism and related direct marketing activities, would be incomplete without acknowledging the sharp increase in targeted funding that Congress has appropriated to USDA's Agricultural Marketing Service (AMS). Since the late 2000s, support has targeted grants for producers and marketers of locally grown and speciality crops (e.g. fresh and dried fruit, vegetables, tree nuts, and nursery/horticultural products). AMS uses two primary vehicles to administer competitively awarded funds for agritourism: the Farmers Market Promotion Program (FMPP), which was first authorised in the 2002 farm bill and received funds appropriated by Congress for the first time in FY 2006; and the Specialty Crop Block Grant Program (SCBGP), first authorised in the Specialty Crops Competitiveness Act of 2004 (P.L. 108–465) and funded for the first time in FY 2006. In the case of the FMPP, the connection between the programme and support of agritourism is so explicit that the authorising legislation itself specifically indicates that the recipient of an FMPP grant may use the grant to support and promote agritourism (see Local Agriculture Market Program, 7 U.S.C. § 1627c, 2018).

As reported in Table 6.1, the amount of funding appropriated by Congress to AMS for the administration of FMPP and SCBGP has grown dramatically since FY 2008. The value of annual grant awards offered by the FMPP nearly quadrupled, from $3.4 million in FY 2008 to almost $13.5 million in FY 2020, while the value of annual SCBGP awards increased by more than 600%, from $9.4 million to $72.4 million over the same period, reaching a combined total of nearly $86 million in funding in the latest completed grant cycle (see LAMP funding in Figure 6.1).

Coupled with a steady expansion of eligible applicant categories on the FMPP side, oriented towards recruiting additional applicants with grassroots perspectives (e.g. producer networks/associations and food councils), the aggressive infusion of funding into the FMPP and the SCBGP by Congress in the past decade has enabled AMS to substantially raise its profile in terms of support for agritourism projects and direct agricultural marketing projects seeking to enhance the business capacity of BIPOC producers and food entrepreneurs. Within the FMPP portfolio specifically, the share of grants supporting agritourism rose from just over 1% in FY 2008 ($50,000 in value) to nearly 14% in FY 2020 (nearly $1.9 million in value), while the share of grants directly supporting BIPOC producers or direct food marketers increased from 19% in FY 2008 (around $660,000

Table 6.1 FMPP and SCBGP funding allocations, Fiscal Year (FY) 2008–2020.

Grant Programme/Activity	FY 2008	FY 2011	FY 2014	FY 2017	FY 2020
Farmers Market Promotion Program					
Total funding (millions $)	3.44	9.22	14.40	13.40	13.48
Value of funding to projects in Alaska, Hawaii, and eligible US commonwealths and territories (millions $)	0	.23	.42	.53	.64
Value of funding for projects that directly support BIPOC producers	.66	1.09	1.16	3.01	3.78
Value of funding for projects that directly support agritourism	.05	.05	.55	1.14	1.87
Value of funding for urban agriculture-related projects	0	.42	.38	1.31	1.18
Total number of funded projects	85	149	183	52	49
Number of projects funded in Alaska, Hawaii, and eligible US commonwealths and territories.	0	3	8	3	2
Number of funded projects that directly support BIPOC producers.	12	17	16	10	13
Number of funded projects that directly support agritourism	1	1	7	4	7
Number of funded projects that directly support urban agriculture	0	7	5	5	5
Specialty Crop Block Grant Program					
Total funding (millions $)	9.39	54.33	66.40	60.59	72.49
Value of funding to projects in Alaska, Hawaii, and eligible US commonwealths and territories (millions $)	0.65	1.55	1.94	2.01	2.28
Value of funding for projects that directly support BIPOC producers	N/A	N/A	N/A	N/A	6.04
Value of funding for projects that directly support agritourism	N/A	N/A	N/A	N/A	1.06
Value of funding for urban agriculture-related projects	N/A	N/A	N/A	N/A	.95
Total number of funded projects.	252	765	839	678	687
Number of projects funded in Alaska, Hawaii, and eligible US commonwealths and territories	17	36	36	40	33
Number of funded projects that explicitly support BIPOC producers	11	34	45	54	53
Number of funded projects that directly support agritourism	9	10	11	12	11
Number of funded projects that directly support urban agriculture	0	5	9	11	20

Note. Minimum and maximum award levels for individual FMPP grants were increased substantially in FY 2016 in view of overall increases in programme funding levels, resulting in fewer awards at higher dollar amounts (AMS, 2016). FY 2008 and FY 2011 FMPP awards were limited to entities within the 50 states and the District of Columbia. The Commonwealth of Puerto Rico, Guam, American Samoa, the US Virgin Islands, and the Commonwealth of the Northern Mariana Islands were added to the list of the FMPP's eligible locations in FY 2012. For this analysis, BIPOC (Black, Indigenous or People of Colour) projects are defined as projects that specifically serve a BIPOC grower or food maker audience (current or prospective) or producer-facing projects awarded to historically Black colleges and universities (HBCUs), Hispanic-serving institutions, tribal colleges/universities, or tribal governments. Projects that were primarily consumer focused (e.g. food access projects) were excluded from this tabulation. FY 2008, FY 2011, and FY 2014 data were obtained from AMS (2017). Public data related to SCBGP funding were not released on a project-by-project basis prior to FY 2020 but were simply aggregated at the applicant level (state/commonwealth/territory), making it impossible to aggregate the value of grants by thematic category.

in value) to 28% in FY 2020 (around $3.8 million in value). As a result of these substantial increases in appropriated funds, the combined investment of the FMPP and SCBGP now accounts (based on FY 2020 figures) for $2.9 million in annual support for agritourism-related grants (representing around 3% of combined programme funds) and nearly $10 million for BIPOC producers and/or aspiring producers (representing more than 11% of combined programme funds).

The recent shift towards greater use of FMPP funds for agritourism purposes may be explained by the fact that AMS began, in recent years, to insert language in the SCBGP solicitation for applications requesting that prospective applicants consider using the FMPP rather than the SCBGP to support agritourism and other direct-to-consumer farm marketing activities. Consequently, despite its much smaller financial footprint, the FMPP has emerged as a more significant funder of agritourism than the SCBGP as far as dollars are concerned, though it still ranks behind SCBGP in terms of the number of agritourism projects funded annually. While these two grant-funding mechanisms have distinct origins and intended purposes, they do share some common characteristics that help explain the profound combined influence they have had on supporting the development of agritourism activities across the United States, including broad eligibility of applicants and/or project participants; flexibility in project scope and design; and encouraging applications from smaller-scale, underserved producers and communities; commitment to stakeholder engagement and responsiveness.

Broad eligibility of applicants and/or project participants

Unlike other USDA research-oriented grant programmes, which have historically favoured applicants from academic institutions or state agencies, both the FMPP and the SCBGP provide extensive latitude to applicants regarding the composition of project team members and beneficiaries. In the case of the FMPP, for example, applicants eligible to apply for grant funds include a broad swath of entities across the private, public, and non-profit sectors:

- Agricultural businesses and cooperatives;
- Community-supported agriculture (CSA) networks and associations;
- Food councils (such as county and municipal local food policy councils);
- Economic development corporations;
- Local governments;
- Non-profit and public benefit corporations;
- Producer networks or associations;
- Regional farmers' market authorities; and
- Tribal governments.

These eligibility categories have been amended and expanded since the programme was originally implemented. Producer networks and associations were added to the FMPP's category of eligible applicants following the adoption of the 2008 farm bill while food councils were incorporated as part of the eligible applicant category in FY 2019, attesting to the increasingly broad grassroots reach of the programme. To further enhance the diversity pool of applicants and extend the reach of the FMPP, the Commonwealth of Puerto Rico, Guam, American Samoa, the US Virgin Islands, and the Commonwealth of the Northern Mariana Islands were added to the list of eligible applicant locations in FY 2012.

Under the SCBGP, eligible applicants are the primary agricultural agencies for the US state/commonwealth/territory themselves, and these agencies bear responsibility for determining the process by which prospective subgrantees may apply for funds. Most typically, they allocate their share of block grant funding to project managers using a competitive regranting process. Project partners have included (but are not limited to) state agencies, tribal governments, land grant or state universities or colleges, speciality crop producer organisations, non-profit organisations, and community-based organisations.

Flexibility in project scope and design

In accordance with authorising legislation, all FMPP-funded projects are expected to increase access to locally and regionally produced agricultural products by developing, coordinating, and expanding direct producer-to-consumer markets. Beyond that single requirement, however, the programme places few restrictions on the methods by which this goal should be achieved, other than prohibiting grants that are intended to benefit a single individual/organisation/institution. Moreover, the programme explicitly invites applications that address diverse aspects of direct producer-to-consumer transactions, from adopting relevant technology and strategies to reduce food waste to implementing food safety certification training and process improvements.

Similarly, in the case of the SCBGP, the only two uniform requirements connecting all funded grants are that they be explicitly designed to enhance the competitiveness of speciality crops and they generate measurable outcomes that have broad utility for the speciality crop industry (not just for a single organisation, institution, or individual.) As described by the NSAC (2019b), projects funded by the SCBGP have focused on a wide variety of outcomes, including:

- Increasing nutritional knowledge and speciality crop consumption;
- Improving efficiency within the distribution system;
- Promoting food safety and good agricultural, handling, and manufacturing practices while encouraging audit cost sharing for small farmers and processors;
- Supporting research, developing improved seed varieties, and controlling pests and diseases;
- Creating organic and sustainable production practices;
- Establishing local and regional food systems and "Buy Local" programmes;
- Developing school and community gardens and farm-to-school programmes;
- Expanding access to speciality crops in underserved communities; and
- Encouraging the development of value-added agricultural products.

Emphasis on inviting grant proposals that benefit underserved producers and communities

Although grant applications are technically welcomed from all eligible entities, regardless of scale, both FMPP and SCBGP specifically encourage the submission of grant proposals that seek to benefit socially disadvantaged and/or historically underrepresented populations. For example, in the most recent grant solicitation material for FMPP and SCBGP in FY 2021, AMS explicitly encouraged the development of grant proposals that benefit smaller farms and ranches, new and beginning farmers and ranchers, socially disadvantaged producers, veteran producers, and/or [other] underserved communities. Underscoring the agency's intention to better empower communities that have historically lacked equal access to federal assistance programmes and allow them to direct the use of available financial resources, AMS also explicitly encourages prospective applicants to involve members of these intended beneficiary groups when developing their grant proposals.

Responsiveness to stakeholder feedback

In July 2021, AMS announced updated performance measures for most of its grant programmes, including the FMPP and the SCBGP, which will apply to grants awarded during future grant cycles beginning in FY 2022. The new performance measures are intended to:

- Improve recipients' ease of data collection and outcome reporting;
- More accurately reflect grant recipients' accomplishments;
- Reduce burden on grant applicants and recipients;
- Improve AMS' ability to report on the impact of its grant programmes; and
- Standardise measures across programmes where appropriate.

The updated performance measures satisfy the 2018 farm bill directive for AMS to examine and develop new SCBGP performance measures in consultation with the National Association of State Departments of Agriculture and other speciality crop stakeholders. In a gesture of accommodation to stakeholder concerns, the agency took this congressional mandate as an opportunity to update performance measures across multiple grant programmes to make it easier for all grant recipients, regardless of capacity, to carry out their oversight and documentation responsibilities more successfully. Beginning with the FY 2022 requests for applications, AMS will provide specially tailored tools and resources to help grant applicants and recipients adopt the new measures and will make dedicated funding available so that grant recipients are better equipped to conduct their own project evaluations.

Another indication of AMS's commitment to stakeholder outreach and engagement is the fact that the agency regularly convenes current FMPP grant managers to learn about best practices and cutting-edge innovations in the direct farm marketing industry and creates an opportunity for grant recipients to develop professional networks with their industry peers. For example, taking advantage of the multidisciplinary and diverse expertise of agency personnel, AMS's Marketing Services Division and Grant Division partnered to host the first "National Direct Agricultural Marketing Summit" in 2018, designed to assist FMPP grant managers and other key industry leaders in better managing – and documenting the results of – their direct marketing activities by creating a series of interactive training workshops featuring some of the nation's leading researchers and technical service providers in the direct farm marketing field. To make this training as accessible as possible, travel stipends were offered in advance of the first summit to at least one representative of all organisations that were currently managing an FMPP grant. The first summit was a success, with 400 attendees from 44 states and Canada, including more than 150 farmers' market managers and programme operators. It is now an annual event. At present, given the current state of the COVID-19 pandemic, the summit is being offered in a hybrid virtual and in-person format.

Discussion and conclusions

While the USDA has made great strides in expanding diversity and inclusion in its programmes, issues remain. For example, in 2020, the USDA Farm Service Agency (FSA) approved farm loans for only 37% of Black applicants but 71% of White applicants (Bustillo, 2021). Since 2021, USDA has increased efforts to make amends for years of discrimination and racism in its programmes, often a result of local USDA office personnel and policies. Secretary of Agriculture Tom Vilsack provided $4 billion in direct debt relief payments to black farmers (authorised in the American Rescue Plan Act of 2021). However, these payments are currently delayed due to lawsuits. Additionally, a provision was included in the Build Back Better Act (2021) to provide $6 billion in debt forgiveness on direct loans to underserved farmers. It also provides farmers who have experienced past USDA discrimination additional assistance up to $500,000 (Held, 2021). In order to highlight the importance of increasing programme access for socially disadvantaged groups, USDA Press Secretary Kate Waters stated that:

> Under the Biden Administration, USDA is serious about our efforts to dismantle barriers that historically underserved communities have faced in accessing USDA programmes and services. For generations, entrenched disparities in our society and economy – at times facilitated by USDA – have made it harder for people of colour to have a fair shot at the American dream . . . USDA will continue to make investments to advance equity throughout the department to help rebuild our economy and our social safety net so all people can thrive
>
> (Quoted in Held, 2021, para. 13).

Despite USDA's ongoing efforts to expand diversity and inclusion in its programmes, lessons learned through current programme offerings, as well as the successes described in the USDA AMS case study, provide a framework for establishing best practices. These best practices, for expanding diversity and inclusion, that are likely to increase the probability of success in other government-based programmes include the following:

- Instate broad eligibility of applicants and/or project participants;
- Promote to and encourage applications from socially disadvantaged groups;
- Prioritise applications (funding percentage, points, etc.) from socially disadvantaged groups;
- Allow flexibility in proposed project scope and design;
- Provide tools and resources to ease project implementation and reporting; and
- Respond to stakeholder feedback in programme design, implementation, and adjustments.

While these best practices are – at best – practices and do not ensure success, audience-appropriate promotional efforts and language are key. Guion et al. (2010) outline several strategies for successful programme promotion to diverse audiences:

- Value the cultural uniqueness of your target group;
- Value cooperation and bridge building with community leaders and other organisations working within the community;
- Value the cultural beliefs, symbols, and practices of your target group;
- Value differences in languages, accents, practices, and social conduct; and
- Value word-of-mouth and interpersonal communication to spread your message.

In an effort to appreciate the culture and differences of targeted socially disadvantaged groups, USDA programme peer-review panels are themselves diverse and largely representative of the desired applicant pool. Additionally, grant managers are allowed to pay for travel scholarships/subsidies to socially disadvantaged farmers so that they can participate in training and technical assistance offered within the scope of the grant. USDA's continued commitment to this mission is reinforced by their recently published Equity Action Plan (announced April 14, 2022) as part of the US Executive Order 13985 Advancing Racial Equity and Support to Underserved Communities (USDA, 2022). The actions listed in its Equity Action Plan include the following:

- Partner with trusted technical assistance providers;
- Reduce barriers to USDA programmes and improve support to underserved farmers, ranchers, landowners, and farm workers;
- Expand equitable access to USDA nutrition assistance programmes;
- Increase USDA infrastructure investments that benefit underserved communities;
- Advance equity in federal procurement;

- Uphold Federal trust and treaty responsibilities to Indian Tribes; and
- Institutionalise an unwavering commitment to and actions towards ensuring civil rights.

Current USDA programmes strive to overcome institutional biases and discrimination by providing programmes to socially disadvantaged groups seeking to develop food- and agriculture-based tourism projects. Agritourism is considered a legitimate part of the agricultural marketing landscape by the USDA, and prospective applicants should not be discouraged from applying for support for their agritourism ventures, especially those that showcase geographically and culturally distinctive agricultural practices and products.

References

Agricultural Act of 2014, P.L. 113–79, 128 Stat. 649. (2014). www.congress.gov/113/plaws/publ79/PLAW-113publ79.pdf

Agricultural Improvement Act of 2018, P.L. 115–334, 132 Stat. 4490. (2018). www.congress.gov/115/plaws/publ334/PLAW-115publ334.pdf

Agricultural Marketing Service. (2016). *Farmers market promotion program: Fiscal year 2016 request for applications*. U.S. Department of Agriculture. www.ams.usda.gov/sites/default/files/media/FMPP RFA 2016.pdf

Agricultural Marketing Service. (2017). *Farmers market promotion program, 2016 report: Connecting rural and urban communities*. U.S. Department of Agriculture. www.ams.usda.gov/sites/default/files/media/FMPP2016Report.pdf

American Rescue Plan Act of 2021, P.L. 117–2, 135 Stat. 4. (2021). www.congress.gov/117/plaws/publ2/PLAW-117publ2.pdf

Build Back Better Act, H.R. 5376, 117th Cong. (2021). www.congress.gov/117/bills/hr5376/BILLS-117hr5376rh.pdf

Bustillo, X. (2021, July 5). "Rampant issues": Black farmers are still left out at USDA. *Politico*. www.politico.com/news/2021/07/05/black-farmers-left-out-usda-497876

Coronavirus Response and Relief Supplemental Appropriations Act, 2021, P.L. 116–220, 134 Stat. 1909. (2021). www.congress.gov/116/plaws/publ260/PLAW-116publ260.pdf

Curtis, K. (2014). *Expanding direct marketing opportunities in the Intermountain West through farm shops*. (Completed Project Report). Extension Risk Management Education (RME) Regional Centers. http://extensionrme.org/Projects/ProjectReport.aspx?ID=ee636c0f-417d-4f66-b129-5bc67521915e

Economic Research Service. (2022). *Socially disadvantaged, beginning, limited resource, and female farmers and ranchers*. U.S. Department of Agriculture. www.ers.usda.gov/topics/farm-economy/socially-disadvantaged-beginning-limited-resource-and-female-farmers-and-ranchers/

Farm Security and Rural Investment Act of 2002, P.L. 107–171, 116 Stat. 134. (2002). www.congress.gov/107/plaws/publ171/PLAW-107publ171.pdf

Farm Service Agency. (2019). *Loans for socially disadvantaged farmers and ranchers* (Fact Sheet). U.S. Department of Agriculture. www.fsa.usda.gov/Assets/USDA-FSA-Public/usdafiles/FactSheets/2019/sda_loans-fact_sheet-aug_2019.pdf

Food, Agriculture, Conservation, and Trade Act of 1990, P.L. 101–624, 104 Stat. 3359. (1990). www.congress.gov/101/statute/STATUTE-104/STATUTE-104-Pg3359.pdf

Food, Conservation, and Energy Act of 2008, P.L. 110–246, 122 Stat. 1651. (2008). www.congress.gov/110/plaws/publ246/PLAW-110publ246.pdf

Guion, L., Kent, H., & Diehl, D. (2010). *Ethnic marketing: A strategy for marketing programs to diverse audiences* (Rev. ed.). (Document No. FCS92233). University of Florida Extension.

Held, L. (2021, December 1). Black farmers still await dept relief as lawmakers resolve racist lawsuits. *Civil Eats*. https://civileats.com/2021/12/01/black-farmers-still-await-debt-relief-as-lawmakers-resolve-racist-lawsuits/

Johnson, R. (2021). *Defining a socially disadvantaged farmer or rancher (SDFR): In brief* (Report No. R46727). Congressional Research Service.

Local Agriculture Market Program, 7 USC 1627c, P.L. 115–334, § 10102(b), 132 Stat. 4888. (2018). www.congress.gov/115/plaws/publ334/PLAW-115publ334.pdf

Ministry of Culture, Sports, and Tourism. (2008). *Ethnic minorities development framework – Viet Nam: Sustainable tourism development project*. Asian Development Bank. www.adb.org/projects/documents/sustainable-tourism-development-project-ethnic-minorities-development-framework-v

National Institute of Food and Agriculture. (2021). *Beginning farmer and rancher development program*. U.S. Department of Agriculture. https://nifa.usda.gov/program/beginning-farmer-and-rancher-development-program-bfrdp

National Institute of Food and Agriculture. (2022a). *Current research information system (CRIS)*. U.S. Department of Agriculture. https://cris.nifa.usda.gov/search.html

National Institute of Food and Agriculture. (2022b). *Risk management education centers*. U.S. Department of Agriculture. https://nifa.usda.gov/risk-management-education-centers

National Sustainable Agriculture Coalition. (2018). *2018 farm bill by the numbers*. https://sustainableagriculture.net/blog/2018-farm-bill-by-the-numbers/

National Sustainable Agriculture Coalition. (2019a). *Outreach and assistance for socially disadvantaged and veteran farmers and ranchers (Section 2501)*. https://sustainableagriculture.net/publications/grassrootsguide/farming-opportunities/socially-disadvantaged-farmers-program/

National Sustainable Agriculture Coalition. (2019b). *Specialty crop block grants*. https://sustainableagriculture.net/publications/grassrootsguide/local-food-systems-rural-development/specialty-crop-grants/

Natural Resource Conservation Service. (2011). *Native American farmer and rancher class action settlement – Keepseagle v. Vilsack*. U.S. Department of Agriculture. www.nrcs.usda.gov/wps/portal/nrcs/detail/la/newsroom/?cid=nrcs141p2_015776

Natural Resource Conservation Service. (2021). *Historically underserved farmers and ranchers*. U.S. Department of Agriculture. www.nrcs.usda.gov/wps/portal/nrcs/detail/national/people/outreach/slbfr/?cid=nrcsdev11_001040

Nickerson, C., & Hand, M. (2009). *Participation in conservation programs by targeted farmers: Beginning limited-resource, and socially disadvantaged operators' enrollment trends* (Economic Information Bulletin EIB-62). U.S. Department of Agriculture Economist Research Service.

Novak, J., Pease, J., & Sanders, L. (2015). *Agricultural policy in the United States: Evolution and economics*. Routledge.

Office of Partnerships and Public Engagements. (2021). *Outreach and assistance for socially disadvantaged farmers and ranchers and veteran farmers and ranchers program (the 2501 program)*. U.S. Department of Agriculture. www.usda.gov/partnerships/socially-disadvantaged-farmers-and-ranchers

Office of Partnerships and Public Engagements. (2022). *Farming opportunities training and outreach grant program* (Fact Sheet). U.S. Department of Agriculture. www.usda.gov/sites/default/files/documents/2501-factsheet-2022.pdf

[Redacted] and [Redacted]. (2013). *The Pigford cases: USDA settlement of discrimination suits by Black farmers*. (Report No. RS20430). Congressional Research Service.

Risk Management Agency. (2015). *USDA proposes changes to expand crop insurance for underserved crops* (Press Release No. RMA-15–021). U.S. Department of Agriculture. https://rma.usda.gov/en/News-Room/Press/National-News-Archive/2015-News/2015-News/RMA-15–021-USDA-Proposed-Changes-to-Expand-Crop-Insurance-for-Underserved-Crops

Specialty Crops Competitiveness Act of 2004, P.L. 108–465, 118 Stat. 3882. (2004). www.congress.gov/108/plaws/publ465/PLAW-108publ465.pdf

Taylor, M. (2016, November 28). The latest in Native American tourism: Cultural experiences and educational opportunities. *The Street*. www.thestreet.com/lifestyle/travel/the-latest-in-native-american-tourism-cultural-experiences-and-educational-opportunities-13905349

U.S. Department of Agriculture. (2022, April 14). *USDA releases equity action plan*. www.usda.gov/media/press-releases/2022/04/14/usda-releases-equity-action-plan

Vilsack, T. (2014, March 12). *USDA announces claims process for Hispanic and women farmers*. U.S. Department of Agriculture. www.usda.gov/media/blog/2011/02/25/usda-announces-claims-process-hispanic-and-women-farmers

7 Decolonising our curriculum
Addressing the "miseducation" of tourism

Sally Everett

Introduction

The higher education sector has been reacting to seismic shifts in society and ongoing geo-political uncertainty and volatility. Some of the most recent challenges have included how universities continue to respond to the repercussions and implications of the Black Lives Matter movement, navigate a post pandemic world, and deconstructing a system that has invisibilised marginalised knowledge (Arday & Mirza, 2018). As concerns intensify about the continuing "miseducation" of our students (Nkomo, 2015), we increasingly find ourselves at a juncture where equality and diversity issues are beginning to inform significant structural changes (Liyanage, 2020). In tourism, the arguments for more inclusive approaches to education and research have progressively coalesced around the concept of "decolonisation" (Chambers & Buzinde, 2015), and, therefore, it is timely to undertake a reconsideration of the dominance of colonial knowledge in how we learn and teach.

The concept of decolonisation is a sensitive and contested one, with various definitions being offered to explain how we might look to redress forms of disadvantage associated with racism and colonialism. As Arshad (2021, n.p.) highlights, it is about how we "situate the histories and knowledge that do not originate from the West in the context of imperialism, colonialism, and power and to consider why these have been marginalised and decentred". By unlocking and critically unpacking the "hidden curriculum", it may be possible to reclaim teaching methodologies and knowledge that have been historically marginalised and overlooked (Margolis, 2001). In specifically responding to the call for epistemological decolonisation posed by Chambers and Buzinde (2015), this chapter considers what it might mean for tourism education. By thinking about decolonisation as more than diversification (i.e. adding more), this chapter reflects on how we might proactively challenge racism and dismantle the processes and pedagogies inherited from colonialism that have shaped the study of tourism. Despite the sector being slow to act (Batty, 2020), there is clear value in ensuring that knowledge and practices of indigenous and colonised peoples are properly recognised, valued, and represented in our higher education curricula. As Lee (2017, p. 96) argues in her paper on indigenous knowledge and black female bodies in tourism

DOI: 10.4324/9781003255413-8

research, "decolonisation is not simply a theoretical rebuttal of colonisation, but a space to actively demonstrate why our difference counts and why our methodologies are important".

Chambers and Buzinde (2015, p. 10) posit that "part of the epistemological project of decolonisation in tourism also needs to be a transformation of our educational systems such that native knowledge and practices become integral to the tourism curriculum rather than as part of optional or specialist courses". One response to this call is to ensure action happens in our classrooms, placing decolonised knowledge at the core of our curricula (see also Aquino's (2019) paper on decolonisation of tourism research in the Philippines). Such studies help evidence why the academy must revaluate understandings of tourism development and more consciously consider the social-cultural associations of colonialism rather than impose a Western model of tourism education. One further example is Lewis-Cameron's (2015, p. 82) chapter on rethinking Caribbean tourism education, where it is argued that tourism education has been framed by "Western models", and "the time has come to shift the debate to the creation of Caribbean-centric tourism knowledge". These studies raise some key questions about the decolonisation of the tourism curriculum: namely, what, why, who, and how? In other words, what do we mean by decolonising the tourism curriculum? Why should curriculum decolonisation be such an important priority for tourism education? Who needs to be involved in achieving meaningful change? How do we collectively do this?

The underpinning aim of this chapter is to prompt thinking about decolonisation of our education. It seeks to suggest how change might be enacted to "unsilence" the voices of the populations who find themselves the objects of tourism scholarship. Therefore, in setting the context for this chapter, it firstly summarises the evolution of tourism education and the associated scholarship of diversity and inclusion. The literature is then used to inform a simple framework for approaching the decolonising of curriculum mapped against Hiatt's (2006) simple model of change management. The ADKAR model of change happens by moving from awareness through desire, knowledge, ability, and reinforcement. The reflections are structured under the headings challenge, consciousness, conversations, co-conspirators, and construction and concludes with a repositioning of the tourism curriculum (i.e. the sixth stage, which reinforces and embeds the change). Of course, decolonisation and dismantling much of what we have known cannot be boiled down to a simple "tick list" or set of guidelines, so I offer a starting point to encourage reflection on how we might disrupt the educational scaffolding that has dominated our tourism curriculum.

The evolution of tourism education

Tourism scholars have increasingly noted that a more explicit focus on signature pedagogies (Shulman, 2005) and educational methods and approaches is necessary to ensure that tourism matures and develops as a subject (Hsu et al., 2017). These calls have been strengthened by the growth and success of organisations such as the "Association of Tourism in Higher Education" and the emergence of journals dedicated to tourism education (e.g. *Journal of Hospitality and Tourism Education* (formally known as *Hospitality & Tourism Educator* (1988–1996)), *Journal of Hospitality, Leisure, Sport and Tourism Education* (1992) and the *Journal of Teaching in Travel and Tourism* (the publication managed by the International Society of Travel and Tourism Educators (ISTTE)). Furthermore, the increasing focus on pedagogy received a significant boost with volumes such as the *Handbook on Tourism and Hospitality Education* (Dredge et al., 2014) and the *Tourism Education Futures Initiative* (Prebežac et al., 2016) which cover a wide range of issues, including how we approach and think about globalisation, the neo-liberal management of universities, and the inclusion of values into tourism curricula.

Despite the growing interest in the development and advancement of tourism education, literature reviews over the past 20 years have found limited work covering decolonisation, inclusive education, and curriculum diversification. Notably, Tribe's (2002) review of tourism education papers (up to 2001) found relatively few studies on student progression and achievement, quality, teaching, learning, and resources with little mention of diversity and equality issues. Amongst the six thematic "gaps" identified by Tribe, there was nothing resembling what would be identifiable as a decolonisation agenda for education, or any consideration of whether postcolonial and critical theoretical perspectives were deemed important for student learning. Rather, the gaps found tended to be in generic areas, such as developing skills, educational theories, and student attainment. It was only in a later review of tourism education publications by Sheldon et al. (2008) that an emerging, and much needed, focus on global and sociocultural challenges was identified.

Most recently, Hsu et al.'s (2017) synthesis of hospitality and tourism education papers between 2005 and 2014 also found no coherent theoretical framework guiding the development of tourism curricula. They also realised very few threshold concepts relating to equality and diversity (see also Airey et al., 2015). Hsu et al.'s (2017) findings reflect the apparent tension outlined by Tight (2015, p. 95) regarding whether tourism education should be about developing hard work-focused skills or producing "well-rounded, knowledgeable and thoughtful individuals". Although it is pleasing that the review found more engagement with active learning, digital technology, sustainability, employability issues, and ethical issues in tourism research, it also found very little work that problematised tourism education. It is also somewhat surprising to find papers focused on the topic of "ethics" tended to focus on cheating and poor academic practice (Hudson & Miller, 2006; Marnburg, 2006) rather than examine issues concerning the (unethical) dominance of Western-centred knowledge and pedagogies in our classrooms (virtual and physical).

In the calls for a reconceptualisation of the role of tourism, Lewis-Cameron (2015) advocates for a shift in strategic focus from an educational system, which is a passive recipient of tourism, to one managed and designed by locals and sensitive to regional and social justice needs. To offer an education strategy, which

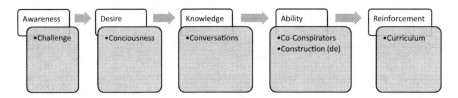

Figure 7.1 The 6C framework of decolonisation mapped against Hiatt's (2006) ADKAR model.

Source: Author

reflects national development plans and tourism development policies of the regions (Mayaka & Akama, 2007), a stakeholder-and regional-focused approach is necessary. In providing a response that actively embraces alternative decolonised knowledge, it must be specific to a region's needs and ambitions rather than simply cutting and pasting an imposed Western curriculum. Consequently, this chapter aims to encourage thinking on how we might respond to this call for action. It builds on the decolonisation sources, as well as draws on the conversations which emerged in the wake of anti-racist protests such as "Rhodes Must Fall" (see Kwoba et al., 2018) and the Black Lives Matters movement.

Hiatt's (2006) ADKAR change management model provides a useful roadmap for the delivery and management of significant far-reaching institutional transformation. Developed using an analysis of research data from over 900 organisations over a ten-year period, it has been adopted by some higher education providers to guide change processes in educational settings (e.g. Henningsmoen & Solis, 2018; Qadri et al., 2015). Although it is a simple model comprising five key building blocks, it offers a set of helpful stages that can be used to plan organisational change efforts. In brief, the model's ADKAR stages are awareness of the need to change; desire to participate and support the change; knowledge of how to change (and what the change looks like); ability to implement the change on a day-to-day basis; and reinforcement to keep the change in place (i.e. more permanent changes in place). In this chapter, the ADKAR model is mapped against six core "C words" (see Figure 7.1), moving from raising awareness (challenge) to reinforcement in what we embed into our programmes (i.e. curriculum). It is by no means an exhaustive list but is presented as a starting point for thinking about how to go about decolonising the tourism classroom.

Challenge

Singh (2019) argues that change does not happen without disruption and often outright insurgency, and this can only happen when people's awareness about an injustice or problem is raised (the first stage of Hiatt's 2006 ADKAR model). This is done through the first C word: challenge. Although many faculty and school missions purport to champion engagement with responsible tourism and seek to advance social justice in their scholarship and work, for this to happen, it is imperative that we make ourselves vulnerable and take a leap of faith (despite inevitable resistance) and reframe the conversation (Gopal, 2021; Tran, 2021). Work like Radcliffe and Radhuber's (2020) encourages us to engage in powerful questioning of the very foundations of our geographical knowledge and contradictory coloniality-modernity. In delving into the decolonisation debate, Bhambra et al. (2018) highlight the need to reflect on one's own practice and undertake a reassessment of the Western epistemologies and pedagogies, which have so often been accepted and adopted without question.

Hollinshead (2013, n.p.) has long argued for the decolonisation of tourism studies, perceiving it to be overly informed by the "cosmologies of the societies from which tourism scholars have traditionally hailed" (i.e. "western" ways of understanding the world). This echoes Nkomo's (1992) work in management studies, which contests Eurocentric non-inclusive universalisation and capitalistic ways of managing, leading, and doing business as superior. As Tran (2021) also argues, it is incumbent on us all to counter some commonly held views that suggest the world's history of colonialism, imperialism, and slavery is not relevant to contemporary knowledge and processes but rather highlights their origins. As Bhopal (2022) emphasises, we cannot claim our organisational practices are race neutral – they are not. It is this misleading sense of the neutrality of knowledge production that should be challenged. As we tackle our current global vortex of change with its intersecting challenges of COVID-19, racism, environmental degradation, economic inequality, and rising nationalism, we should look to transform the very places and practices upon which we have built our universities and schools; this needs to go further than removing statues and renaming buildings (Bannerjee et al., 2020).

The emergence of tourism's "Academy of Hope", under the guardianship of Pritchard et al. (2011) (see also Ateljevic et al., 2007), offered an important "critical turn" in tourism studies. It encouraged new ways of conceptualising tourism and questioned Eurocentric thinking and the dominance of Western ways of knowing. Their passion to privilege indigenous knowledge and traditionally marginalised ethnic groups inspired many to engage in a new form of critical pedagogy (e.g. Lee, 2017). Although this new "academy" attracted some criticism from scholars – such as Chambers (2007) who questioned the normative values inherent in their critical realist perspective, and its reliance on White Western theorists, and Bianchi (2009) who highlighted the need for more emancipatory structural analyses of power and inequality in tourism – it marked an important step change. Such debates were further advanced by Higgins-Desbiolles and Powys Whyte (2013) who drew attention to the problematic nature of researching marginalised (and often oppressed) communities when many tourism researchers come from positions of power and privilege. Such scholarship urges us to engage with a "radical project of epistemic de-linking from colonial ways of thinking" (Chambers & Buzinde, 2015, p. 3) and pursue a radical pedagogic project to raise awareness (Singh, 2019).

Consciousness

After raising awareness (according to Hiatt's ADKAR model) comes "desire". This is the genuine willingness to support the change required and this comes by placing one's own consciousness under scrutiny. Having previously engaged with postcolonial tourism research (e.g. Caton & Santos, 2008), Caton (2014) adopts the concept of "paideia" when considering its implications in tourism education. This Greek term encourages one to focus on what it means to be human, where a well-rounded education concerns the cultivation of self, "the ways you engage your own history, your own memories, your own mortality, your own sense of what it means to be alive as a critical, loving, aware human being" (Caton, 2014, p. 31). It is by working through some of the implications of first "decolonising the mind" (wa Thiong'o, 1981, p. 1) where we can see how vital self-reflection is and appreciate the value of pursuing our own internal journey in the evolution of tourism education. Moreover, scholars, such as Aquino (2019) and Grosfoguel (2007), stress that it is incumbent on us to engage with the possibility of finding alternative ways of understanding and being conscious of finding ways that do not privilege and prioritise male Western epistemologies and approaches (see also Lee, 2017).

It is perhaps only when we challenge ourselves that we begin to accept decolonisation as a centre of knowledge production (Tuck & Yang, 2012). In reflecting on our own positionality in our research (Everett, 2010) and teaching, we may see how our own practice might have been informed by accepted (and unquestioned) colonial ideologies. Thus, we must seek to create spaces for imagining a new university and a new tourism academy (Higgins-Desbiolles & Powys Whyte, 2013), taking time to reflect on the planning of teaching sessions, and question what knowledge we consider valuable and what means were used to produce it and make it "legitimate"? As Iwowo (2021, n.p.) asserted, "build your own consciousness which will in turn create new knowledge", and this will lead to the development and construction of new teaching content, methods, and pedagogy.

Conversations

Once awareness and a desire for change have been gained, developing the knowledge of how to change follows (according to Hiatt, 2006). This is done through the third C: conversations. Sharing stories is a powerful way of sharing knowledge and fostering understanding about the lived experiences of Others (Sonn et al., 2013); change comes when people are heard. Jammulamadaka et al. (2021, p. 718) argue that it is only by mainstreaming these issues that change will come, because it shifts us beyond "the periphery of debates about decolonising higher education". The conversations can happen at the local level, but the important aspect is that it happens. For example, faculty-run book clubs on critical race texts have been reported as high impact occasions for triggering important discussions and raising awareness (The University of Brighton, 2022). Another approach may be initiatives, such as "Conversations about Race" (Office for Students, 2022), that provide vehicles of social engagement, which bring students and staff together in safe spaces to share stories and lived experiences. These are the very events that Grewal (2021, n.p.) highlights as being less about "measuring" decolonisation and more about "the sharing and collaboration of ideas and practices, without epistemic appropriation".

Decolonisation aims to reverse gross epistemic injustice, so difficult conversations are inevitable. It is, however, difficult to overstate the psychological and emotional labour required. Given it is impossible to "un-do" what has been embedded without a consciousness, such as a conversation about "what exactly was done" and to whom (i.e. the rise of empire requiring ideological substitution and the global north travelling to exploit the cultural and natural resources of the global south), then, according to Tribe and Liburd (2016), we need to find ways of ensuring non-western ways of knowing are placed more centrally in our tourism educational systems. Although community organising techniques and external facilitation approaches can surface reflections and questions that have not been previously communicated, the academy should seek to create positions of authority and influence to ensure senior teams engage with these initiatives. Who are the leaders initiating the conversations? How are they using their power to include indigenous and under-represented voices, texts, and approaches? Securing the active engagement of colleagues and senior teams in this decolonisation work is a challenge that must be pursued by us all (Swain, 2019).

In their critique of business schools, Dar et al. (2020) stressed the need for collective action to dismantle racialised power structures. They highlight the need to find ways to foster openness, transparency, and visibility in our classrooms and faculties, in line with Bannerjee (2021) who calls for questioning the colonial basis of knowledge where only a Western knowing subject can produce histories and knowledge about the "Other". For such conversations to be effective, they must be direct, personal, and embedded throughout our work; they should be a core part of our classes, our modules, and our tourism programmes. This might include dedicating one week to critically reviewing the tourism literature in terms of the knowledge and texts we use or by designing an entire semester's module focused on the decolonisation of tourism, which allows our students to "journey beyond the existing frontiers of tourism knowledge" (Chambers & Buzinde, 2015, p. 14). This is where the curriculum has a key role to play. As Young et al. (2017) suggest, critically reflexive tourism educators have a key role to play in being able to improve outcomes for indigenous and non-indigenous students, and this should come via engagement with issues of distributive justice by drawing indigenous and non-Western knowledge into our teaching.

Construction (after deconstruction)

Next, we need to build the "ability" for change into our systems – the fourth stage. The industry and practice of tourism have been described as "the violence-rendering rhetorical instrument of imperialism" (Hollinshead, 2004, p. 31), and it is crucial that we explore whether the same might be said of tourism education.

Before we can construct a new curriculum, colleagues should be empowered with the knowledge of how to deconstruct systemic barriers and inequities and help challenge its "violence rendering" power and influence. We, then, reach a point from which we have the ability to rebuild and construct a more inclusive and equitable educational system (Tran, 2021). As outlined earlier, to truly embark upon a decolonisation agenda, we need to look beyond just the content (i.e. the places we study and the themes we address) and consider adopting new processes and ways of doing everything. As Fanon (1963, p. 36) argues:

> Decolonization, which sets out to change the order of the world, is, obviously, a program of complete disorder. But it cannot come as a result of magical practices, nor of a natural shock, nor of a friendly understanding. Decolonization, as we know, is a historical process: that is to say it cannot be understood, it cannot become intelligible nor clear to itself except in the exact measure that we can discern the movements which give it historical form and content.

Consequently, there is an urgency to remove and replace what has been embedded in the system for centuries (Kwoba et al., 2018) and a need to work with our students to deconstruct what we have known. After all, it was in the influential writing of bell hooks and particularly in *Teaching to transgress: Education as the practice of freedom* where she proposed "to educate as the practice of freedom is a way of teaching that anyone can learn . . . our work is not merely to share information but to share in the intellectual and spiritual growth of our students" (bell hooks, 1994, p. 13). Such a reformulation of education, combined with a shared endeavour to engage with different knowledge, which facilitate freedom should underpin efforts towards decolonising a curriculum.

In seeking to deconstruct and then to reconstruct, there is value in looking beyond the walls of tourism education practice and engaging with a multi-disciplinary range of resources and sources. For example, the BARC (2021) (Building the Anti-Racist Classroom) collective and the Decolonizing Alliance (2021, n.p.) encourage a broader rethink of education and foster a process of reflection "across scholarly communities about the importance of understanding the central features of decolonial thinking and praxis". The guidance these resources offer about reclaiming subject-hoods in the face of symbolic and material violence, and creating new spaces of liberation are powerful calls to action. In helping to disrupt White rationalities by centring the feelings and emotions in the room (BARC, 2021), it should be possible to identify and recognise the ideological violence done to the "Other" (Lee, 2017) and move beyond the epistemic blindness that invisibilises alternate ways of knowing and being (Bannerjee, 2021). This work, however, should be done together with "co-conspirators" for maximum impact.

Co-conspirators

The fifth C is co-conspirators (although this is placed under the fourth ADKAR element of "ability" together with "construction") given that the ability to make the change will only be realised through ally-ship. Activism should not lie solely with people of colour, women, and ethnic minority colleagues but be a shared endeavour across our community (Macfarlane & Burg, 2019). All too often the work to advance decolonisation and diversification of curricula has fallen on a small number of faculty champions or individuals directly affected by racism, bias, and oppression (Swain, 2019). Rather, Nkomo (2021) suggests a greater diversity of allies is warranted in this space and highlights a need for "co-conspirators" from across all communities and demographic sectors to properly advance this agenda. The recognition that everyone has a part to play echoes bell hooks:

> When liberal whites fail to understand how they can and/or do embody white-supremacist values and beliefs even though they may not embrace racism as prejudice or domination (especially domination that involves coercive control). They cannot recognise the ways their actions support and affirm the very structure of racist domination and oppression that they wish to see eradicated
>
> (bell hooks, 1989, p. 113)

Co-conspiracy offers a powerful and important step change, a change that will only come through committed collaboration and collective buy-in. Such a process is initiated through the meeting of people where they are and drawing them into this endeavour. However, as Mheta et al. (2018) note, community building around this issue in universities is not without its challenges. All too often the debates about colonialism/decolonisation can be difficult to tackle, with people thinking about "diversity" as opposed to having difficult conversations to help us move beyond historically imposed global frameworks.

Consequently, in looking for co-conspirators, we should be looking towards our students. Through partnership and co-creation, it may be possible to build classroom experiences where students and staff can research and make decisions together, thereby mutually benefitting from shared perspectives, experiences, and knowledge (Wilson et al., 2022). Increasingly, projects to decolonise the curriculum with students are gaining traction and impact (Arday & Mirza, 2018; Bhambra et al., 2018). It was, after all, students who fuelled the "decolonising the curriculum" agenda when the "Rhodes Must Fall" movement prompted widespread protest and demands for the removal of the Cecil Rhodes statue at the University of Cape Town in March 2015 and later at Oxford University in 2016. The power of student collaboration is also evidenced in initiatives such as Curriculum Advisers Schemes (Hall et al., 2021), Inclusive Curriculum Frameworks, and student campaigns such as "Why is my curriculum white"? (El Magd, 2016). As Felix and Friedberg (2019, n.p.) note "academics must be ready to learn from students too, rather than assume they know best". This student-staff collaboration can happen through honest conversations about our tourism education and about who (and what) is represented in our curricula.

To ensure this work is sustainable, we should also commit to funding and supporting a diverse pipeline of tourism academics who will continue to be conspirators in this endeavour (Williams et al., 2019). This can come through mentorship, scholarships, and ensuring all early career academics feel like they belong (Blockett et al., 2016). As Bhopal (2022, p. 1) highlights in her study of academics of colour in elite universities, we need to challenge what she calls the "unspoken system of exclusion" together. One simple way may be, as Singh (2021) suggests, not cloaking over issues and homogenising challenging areas that might alienate the very groups which we are looking to support. Despite the categorisation of "BAME" (Black, Asian, and Minority Ethic) becoming so prevalent in data sets in the United Kingdom, this homogenising acronym fails to reflect the experiences of different ethnic communities and thus hides the individual lived experience.

Curriculum

The last stage in the proposed framework embeds and "reinforces" the change. Having put the previous steps in place, it is possible to turn to the curriculum. It is the final "C" in this chapter. Our tourism curriculum remains stubbornly uniform despite attempts to engage with the kinds of critical debates that characterise other disciplines (Young & Maguire, 2017). There is an imperative to rewrite narratives, redefine knowledge, and challenge norms, which have been based on colonisation, imperialism, and radicalisation. For example, new teaching models might include indigenous practices as seen in New Zealand, where the Kaupapa Maori is adopted as a teaching model to reflect Maori life practices (see Smith, 2005). It could also be via the adoption of processes such as "deep listening" used by indigenous peoples in Australia (covered in Lee, 2017). These examples highlight that decolonisation is much more than adding an author from Africa, Asia, or from an indigenous population to a tourism module's reading list.

> [D]ecolonisation entails a fundamental re-evaluation of the existing forms of teaching, learning and pastoral support in higher education. It is about acknowledging the ways in which our institutions reproduce unequal social structures – so it is a larger project than simply the diversification of courses, for example. Therefore, meaningful engagement with decolonisation requires reassessing curricula, attainment and representation concurrently.
> (Liyanage, 2020, p. 14)

Increasingly, the word "decolonisation" has been mistakenly seen as the substitution of non-Western content, therefore posing a threat to established academic thinking and scholarship (Liyanage, 2020). Much of this confusion has come about because decolonisation and diversification are generally poorly managed in university and faculty communications. In *Decolonization is not a metaphor*, Tuck and Yang (2012) argue that the language of decolonisation is often superficially adopted, and the term, therefore, becomes distorted or a useful hashtag in a short-term communications plan. It needs to be deeper than this, and we need to not just think differently but proactively challenge and audit ourselves on what we teach. As one of Liyanage's (2020, p. 19) respondents suggest, "There isn't really a very articulate debate about it. You hear the term "decolonisation of the curriculum" without knowing necessarily exactly what that entails". Despite universities adopting the term, there is little engagement with what decolonisation actually means because it is so unsettling as a concept (Tuck & Yang, 2012). As Liyanage (2020, p. 9) states, decolonisation is often put under the umbrella of equality, diversity, and inclusion initiatives, which "can result in the conflation of decolonial practice with measures seeking to diversify universities and their courses", and it is different because it asks pedagogical questions that are "chronically under-addressed".

Given that the levels of intervention must be multiple and across the university, it is important our curriculum stretches beyond the formal classroom and reaches into "how" and "what" we teach. Meaningful change will require transformation of society and the breaking down of structural inequalities, and this work will then start to flow into our curricula. All too often, we approach this the wrong way (i.e. we seek to change the curriculum but ignore the structures and deep injustices behind their very creation). We need to create spaces that acknowledge the cultural, colonial, and race histories that have informed our tourism curriculum to date and capitalised on the multinational character of our multi-dimensional academy. Tourism students seek learning and knowledge to help them navigate complex global issues and problems, so we need to be seeking alternative models to engage our communities and (re)shape our pedagogies. Tick lists and audits may well be one short-term task necessary to kick off this change (but what do arbitrary metrics do apart from pressurise people?). Perhaps it is better we work with colleagues and students in a common and shared endeavour in a place of resistance and activism (Caton, 2014; Hooks, 1994) – ensuring we all have the resources, the recognition, the support, and the power to undertake the changes that need to be made in tourism education.

In moving beyond our spaces of epistemological "safety", we must all take critical and postcolonial tourism studies into our classrooms and into our teaching. As we build on this simple idea for radical change, I have suggested where we might start to tackle the decolonisation agenda. It was, after all, bell hooks (1994, p. 12), who argued, "The classroom remains the most radical space of possibility in the academy", so it is in the classroom where resistance should take place, as this is the space for change. Decolonisation of the tourism curriculum is more than placing a band-aid or sticky plaster on a bullet wound; it is a wholesale deconstruction and radical reconstruction. As has been reiterated here, decolonisation has no synonym (Tuck & Yang, 2012), and therefore, our engagement with it must be focused, deliberate, and action-led.

Conclusion

By framing this chapter within a framework of six "C words" mapped onto Hiatt's (2006) ADKAR change management model, it is hoped that readers are encouraged to think about the decolonisation of our tourism curriculum and seek to redress the "miseducation" in our courses. I could have added the need for a degree of "chaos" (disruption as we embark on this endeavour), or "cultural" change, or perhaps explicitly focus on what happens in the tourism "classroom", and, indeed, I would not want the list of "C" words to become some form of artificial framing that is merely a gimmick for this chapter. Above all, I hope it fuels a conversation (one very much ignited by work from scholars, such as Chambers and Buzinde (2015), Lee (2017), and Wijesinghe et al. (2019). Rather than threaten or dilute the quality and robustness of our tourism teaching, if we embrace decolonisation and accept the challenge to undertake a reassessment of courses and pedagogy, it will raise academic standards. Such a stance would help ensure our students are developing the global mindset and crucial cultural competencies a future world needs (Saito & Pham, 2019). Therefore, we need to ensure "decolonisation is central to a rounded, fulfilling and rigorous university education" (Liyanage, 2020, p. 32) and advance a commitment to equity in relation to race, ethnicity, and social justice (Young & Maguire, 2017).

Recently, Wijesinghe et al. (2019) argued that the processes and structures in academia nurture the permeation of Western and Eurocentric ideologies (also see Aquino, 2019). This dominance of Western thinking has translated into the pedagogies informing and shaping our educational systems. By acknowledging the social and cultural control of our academy by a minority of Western thinkers (Quijano, 2007) and ongoing domination of English-speaking scholarship through our textbooks and journals (Mura et al., 2017), the case for our decolonisation of the tourism curriculum is clear. Tourism scholarship is an important component of the intellectual economy that upholds the system; it is the "how exactly it does this" that we need address. Of course, it is difficult to entertain the "otherwise" and unlearn much of what we have learned, but if we cannot do this as an academic community, then what hope is there for other sectors and organisations? If we are to challenge systems in line with the position Audre Lorde (2018[1979]) takes in *The master's tools will never dismantle the master's house*, then our students must play a central role in shaping the future. It is through their questioning and critical analysis of our examples, theories, cases, and approaches that we might find new ways to give voice to previously silenced (non-Western) perspectives. This work should be facilitated through our teaching, so the responsibility remains squarely on us to challenge, communicate, and work with others in our tourism community to help facilitate this transformation.

References

Airey, D., Tribe, J., Benckendorff, P., & Xiao H. (2015). The managerial gaze: The long tail of tourism education and research. *Journal of Travel Research, 54*(2), 139–151.

Aquino, R. (2019). Towards decolonising tourism and hospitality research in the Philippines. *Tourism Management Perspectives, 31*(1), 72–84.

Arday, J., & Mirza, H. S. (Eds.). (2018). *Dismantling race in higher education: Racism, whiteness and decolonising the academy*. Palgrave Macmillan.

Arshad, R. (2021). Decolonising the curriculum – how do I get started? *Times Higher Education*. www.timeshighereducation.com/campus/decolonising-curriculum-how-do-i-get-started

Ateljevic, I., Pritchard, A., & Morgan, N. (Eds.). (2007). *The critical turn in tourism studies*. Routledge.

Bannerjee, B., Rodriguez, J., & Dar, S. (2020, July 13). Beyond name changes and pulling down statues – how to decolonise business schools. *The Conversation*. https://theconversation.com/beyond-name-changes-and-pulling-down-statues-how-to-decolonise-business-schools-142394

Bannerjee, S. B. (2021). Decolonizing management theory: A critical perspective. *Journal of Management Studies*. https://doi.org/10.1111/joms.12756

Batty, D. (2020, June 11). Only a fifth of UK universities say they are "decolonising" curriculum, *The Guardian*. www.theguardian.com/us-news/2020/jun/11/only-fifth-ofuk-universities-have-said-they-will-decolonise-curriculum

Bhambra, G. K., Gebrial, D., & Nişancıoğlu, K. (Eds.). (2018). *Decolonizing the university*. Pluto Press.

Bhopal, K. (2022). Academics of colour in elite universities in the UK and the USA: The unspoken system of exclusion. *Studies in Higher Education* (online). www.tandfonline.com/doi/full/10.1080/03075079.2021.2020746

Bianchi, R. (2009). The 'Critical Turn' in tourism studies: A radical critique. *Tourism Geographies*, *11*(4), 484–504.

Blockett, R. A., Felder, P. P., Parrish III, W., & Collier, J. (2016). Pathways to the professoriate: Exploring black doctoral student socialization and the pipeline to the academic profession. *Western Journal of Black Studies*, *40*(2), 95–110.

Building the Anti-Racist Classroom (BARC). (2021). *Workshop guide*. https://barcworkshop.org/workshop-guide/

Caton, K. (2014). Underdisciplinarity: Where are the humanities in tourism education? *Journal of Hospitality, Leisure, Sport and Tourism Education*, *15*(1), 24–33.

Caton, K., & Santos, C. A. (2008). Closing the hermeneutic circle? Photographic encounters with the other. *Annals of Tourism Research*, *35*(1), 7–26.

Chambers, D. (2007). Interrogating the "Critical" in critical approaches to tourism research. In I. Ateljevic, A. Pritchard, & N. Morgan (Eds.), *The critical turn in tourism studies: Innovative research methodologies* (pp. 105–119). Elsevier.

Chambers, D., & Buzinde, C. (2015). Tourism and decolonisation: Locating research and self. *Annals of Tourism Research*, *51*(1), 1–16.

Dar, S., Liu, H., Martinez Dy, A., & Brewis, D. N. (2020). The business school is racist: Act up! *Organization*, *28*(4), 695–706. https://doi.org/10.1177/1350508420928521

Decolonizing Alliance. (2021). *Decolonizing alliance*. https://decolonizingalliance.wordpress.com/2021/04/02/writing-orally-speaking-on-the-collective-praxis-of-writing-decolonially/

Dredge, D., Airey, D., & Gross, M. (Eds.). (2014). *The Routledge handbook of tourism and hospitality education* (1st ed.). Routledge. https://doi.org/10.4324/9780203763308

El Magd, N. (2016). *Why is my curriculum white? – Decolonising the academy*. NUS Connect. Retrieved February 9, 2016, from www.nusconnect.org.uk/articles/why-is-my-curriculum-white-decolonising-the-academy

Everett, S. (2010). Lessons from the field: Reflecting on a tourism research journey around the "celtic" periphery. *Currents Issues in Tourism*, *13*(2), 161–175.

Fanon, F. (1963). *The wretched of the earth*. Grove Press.

Felix, M., & Friedberg, J. (2019). *To decolonise the curriculum, we have to decolonise ourselves*. WONKHE 9/4/19. Retrieved January 6, 2022, from https://wonkhe.com/blogs/to-decolonise-the-curriculum-we-have-to-decolonise-ourselves

Gopal, P. (2021). On decolonisation and the university. *Textual Practice*, *35*(6), 873–899. https://doi.org/10.1080/0950236X.2021.1929561

Grewal, M. (2021, March 9). To "decolonise" education, we need to ask different questions. *Times Higher Education*. www.timeshighereducation.com/opinion/decolonise-education-we-need-ask-different-questions

Grosfoguel, R. (2007). The epistemic decolonial turn. *Cultural Studies, 21*(2–3), 211–223.

Hall, J., Velickovic, V., & Rajapillai, V. (2021). Students as partners in decolonising the curriculum. *The Journal of Educational Innovation, Partnership and Change, 7*(1), 1–9.

Henningsmoen, E., & Solis, A. (2018). Developing intercultural competence amongst higher education staff. *The Journal of Educational Thought (JET)/Revue de la Pensée Éducative, 51*(3), 239–260.

Hooks, B. (1989). *Talking back: Thinking feminist, thinking black* (Vol. 10). South End Press.

Hooks, B. (1994). *Teaching to transgress: Education as the practice of freedom*. Routledge.

Hiatt, J. (2006). *ADKAR: A model for change in business, government, and our community*. Prosci.

Higgins-Desbiolles, F., & Powys Whyte, K. (2013). No high hopes for hopeful tourism: A critical comment. *Annals of Tourism Research, 40*, 428–433.

Hollinshead, K. (2004). Tourism and new sense. In C. M. Hall & H. Tucker (Eds.), *Tourism and postcolonialism: Contested discourses, identities and representations* (pp. 25–42). Routledge.

Hollinshead, K. (2013). *Speaking of tourism Part II: The ongoing development of a conceptual glossary on fantasmatics*. Conference presentation at the Welcoming Encounters: Tourism in a post-disciplinary era conference, Neutchatel, Switzerland, June 19–22.

Hsu, C. H., Xiao, H., & Chen, N. (2017). Hospitality and tourism education research from 2005 to 2014: Is the past a prologue to the future? *International Journal of Contemporary Hospitality Management, 29*(1), 141–160.

Hudson, S., & Miller, G. (2006). Knowing the difference between right and wrong: The response of tourism students to ethical dilemmas. *Journal of Teaching in Travel & Tourism, 6*(2), 41–59.

Iwowo, V. (2021). *Decolonisation of the business curriculum*. Panel keynote for Chartered Association of Business Schools, Decolonising the Curriculum Workshop, 8 September 2021, online.

Jammulamadaka, N., Faria, A., Jack, G., & Ruggunan, S. (2021). Decolonising management and organisational knowledge (MOK): Praxistical theorising for potential worlds. *Organization, 28*(5), 717–740. https://doi.org/10.1177/13505084211020463

Kwoba, B., Chantiluke, R., & Nkopo, A. (Eds.). (2018). *Rhodes must fall: The struggle to decolonise the racist heart of empire*. Zed Books Ltd.

Lee, E. (2017). Performing colonisation: The manufacture of Black female bodies in tourism research. *Annals of Tourism Research, 66*, 95–104.

Lewis-Cameron, A. (2015). Rethinking Caribbean tourism education. In P. J. Sheldon & C. H. C. Hsu (Eds.), T*ourism education: Global issues and trends (Tourism Social Science Series, Vol. 21)* (pp. 81–97). Emerald Group Publishing Limited. https://doi.org/10.1108/S1571-504

Liyanage, M. (2020). *Miseducation: Decolonising curricula, culture and pedagogy in UK universities*. www.hepi.ac.uk/wp-content/uploads/2020/07/HEPI_Miseducation_Debate-Paper-23_FINAL.pdf

Lorde, A. (2018). *The master's tools will never dismantle the master's house*. Penguin UK. [This is reproduced from earlier comments at "The Personal and the Political" Panel (Second Sex Conference, October 29, 1979)].

Macfarlane, B., & Burg, D. (2019). Women professors and the academic housework trap. *Journal of Higher Education Policy and Management, 41*(3), 262–274. https://doi.org/10.1080/1360080X.2019.1589682

Margolis, E. (Ed.). (2001). *The hidden curriculum in higher education*. Routledge.

Marnburg, E. (2006). "I hope it won't happen to me!" Hospitality and tourism students' fear of difficult moral situations as managers. *Tourism Management, 27*(4), 561–575.

Mayaka, M., & Akama, J. S. (2007). Systems approach to tourism training and education: The Kenyan case study. *Tourism Management, 28*(1), 298–306.

Mheta, G., Lungu, B. N., & Govender, T. (2018). Decolonisation of the curriculum: A case study of the Durban University of Technology in South Africa. *South African Journal of Education, 38*(4). https://doi.org/10.15700/saje.v38n4a1635

Mura, P., Mognard, E., & Sharif, S. P. (2017). Tourism research in non-English-speaking academic systems. *Tourism Recreation Research, 42*(4), 436–445.

Nkomo, S. M. (1992). The emperor has no clothes: Rewriting race in organizations. *Academy of Management Review, 17*(3), 487–513.

Nkomo, S. M. (2015). Challenges for management and business education in a "developmental" state: The case of South Africa. *Academy of Management Learning and Education, 14*(2), 242–258. https://doi.org/10.5465/amle.2014.0323

Nkomo, S. M. (2021). *The mis-education of business education*. Panel keynote for Chartered Association of Business Schools, Decolonising the Curriculum Workshop, 8 September 2021, online.

Office for Students. (2022). *Conversations about race*. www.officeforstudents.org.uk/advice-and-guidance/promoting-equal-opportunities/effective-practice/conversations-about-race/

Prebežac, D., Schott, C., & Sheldon, P. (Eds.). (2016). *The tourism education futures initiative: Activating change in tourism education*. Routledge.

Pritchard, A., Morgan, N., & Ateljevic, I. (2011). Hopeful tourism: A new transformative perspective. *Annals of Tourism Research, 38*(3), 941–963.

Qadri, M., Hussain, M. K., & Bin Ahmad Dahlan, A. R. (2015). Role of change management in the successful roll-out of IT projects: A case study of higher learning institutes in Malaysia. *International Journal of Management and Commerce Innovations, 3*(2), 275–281.

Quijano, A. (2007). Coloniality and modernity/rationality. *Cultural Studies, 21*(2–3), 168–178.

Radcliffe, S. A., & Radhuber, I. M. (2020). The political geographies of decolonization: Variegation and decolonial challenges of/in geography. *Political Geography, 78*, 102128. https://doi.org/10.1016/j.polgeo.2019.102128

Saito, E., & Pham, T. (2019). A comparative institutional analysis on strategies that graduates use to show they are "employable": A critical discussion on the cases of Australia, Japan, and Vietnam, *Higher Education Research & Development, 38*(2), 369–382.

Sheldon, P., Fesenmaier, D., Woeber, K., Cooper, C., & Antonioli, M. (2008). Tourism education futures, 2010–2030: Building the capacity to lead. *Journal of Teaching in Travel & Tourism, 7*(3), 61–68.

Shulman, L.S. (2005). Signature pedagogies in the professions. *Daedalus, 134*(3), 52–59.

Singh, G. (2019, September 19). *Decolonisation the university and radical insurgent pedagogy*. Presentation at the Radical Pedagogies Macpherson 20 years Conference, The Stephen Lawrence Research Centre, De Montfort University, Leicester, UK. singh-g-2019-radical-insurgent-pedagogy.-leicester-dmu-19.9.19.pdf.

Singh, G. (2021). *Stimulus paper: Beyond BAME: Rethinking the politics, construction, application, and efficacy of ethnic categorisation*. https://pureportal.coventry.ac.uk/en/publications/beyond-bame-rethinking-the-politics-construction-application-and-April

Smith, L. T. (2005). On tricky ground: Researching the native in the age of uncertainty. In N. K. Denzin & Y. S. Lincoln (Eds.), *The SAGE handbook of qualitative research* (3rd ed., pp. 85–108). Sage.

Sonn, C. C., Stevens, G., & Duncan, N. (2013). Decolonisation, critical methodologies and why stories matter. In G. Stevens, N. Duncan, & D. Hook (Eds.), *Race, memory and the Apartheid archive* (pp. 295–314). Palgrave Macmillan.

Swain, H. (2019). Black academics "can't fight race inequality alone". *The Guardian*. www.theguardian.com/education/2019/jul/02/black-academics-bear-brunt-of-university-work-on-race-equality

The University of Brighton. (2022). *DeCol – Decolonising the curriculum student-staff collective Brighton University*. https://blogs.brighton.ac.uk/decolonisingatfalmer/

Tight, M. (2015). Theory development and application in higher education research. *Journal of Educational Administration and History*, *47*(1), 84–99.

Tran, D. (2021). *Decolonizing university teaching and learning*. Bloomsbury.

Tribe, J. (2002). Research trends and imperatives in tourism education. *ActaTuristica*, *14*(1), 61–81.

Tribe, J., & Liburd, J. J. (2016). The tourism knowledge system. *Annals of Tourism Research*, *57*(1), 44–61.

Tuck, E., & Yang, K. (2012). Decolonization is not a metaphor. *Decolonization: Indigeneity, Education & Society*, *1*(1), 1–40.

wa Thiong'o, N. (1981). *Decolonising the mind: The politics of language in African literature*. James Currey.

Wijesinghe, S., Mura, P., & Culala, H. (2019). Eurocentrism, capitalism and tourism knowledge. *Tourism Management*, *70*(1), 178–187.

Williams, P., Bath, S., Arday, J., & Lewis, C. (2019). *The broken pipeline: Barriers to Black PhD students accessing research council funding*. U.K., Leading Routes. https://leadingroutes.org/mdocs-posts/the-broken-pipeline-barriers-to-black-students-accessing-research-council-funding

Wilson, C., Broughan, C., & Daly, G. (2022). Case study: Decolonising the curriculum – An exemplification. *Social Policy and Society*, *21*(1), 142–150.

Young, T., & Maguire, A. (2017). Indigenisation of curriculum: Trends and issues in tourism Education. In P. Benckendorff & A. Zehrer (Eds.), *International handbook of teaching and learning in tourism* (pp. 455–466). Edward Elgar Publishers.

Young, T., Sibson, R., & Maguire, A. (2017). Educating managers for equity and social justice: Integrating Indigenous knowledges and perspectives in Australian sport, recreation and event management curricula. *Journal of Hospitality, Leisure, Sport & Tourism Education*, *21*, 135–143. https://doi.org/10.1016/j.jhlste.2017.08.005

Part II
The experiences of the "Other" in tourism

8 Othering in accessible tourism

Selin Altun, Gürel Çetin, and İsmail Kizilirmak

Introduction

People have been travelling for various reasons and benefitting from transportation, accommodation, food and beverage, and similar tourism activities. Due to the fact that tourism has a structure that affects other economic sectors, researchers have different definitions related to tourism. In this chapter, we consider tourism to be a set of events arising from people's requests for temporary stays and includes their expenses for goods and services provided by tourism enterprises, where they meet their usual daily needs, but travel outside their places of residence (Kozak et al., 2010). With the increase of fast, cheap, and comfortable transportation services and convenience in the provision of tourism services, travel is on the rise.

People's motivations to discover and learn about new places have led to the development of the tourism and travel sector. As these developments have occurred, alternative types of tourism have emerged; however, people with disabilities do not equally participate in tourism activities due to the difficulties they face during travel. That is why recent work has argued that people with disabilities should be allowed to participate in travel and that services should be accessible. Accessibility means that people can easily and smoothly access outdoor areas, architectural places, universal designs, and tourism activities (Darcy et al., 2010; Darcy & Dickson, 2009). The definition of accessible tourism is the ongoing endeavour to ensure tourist destinations, products, and services are accessible to all people, regardless of their physical limitations, disabilities, or age (United Nations, 2013, n.p.). Various concepts are used interchangeably to address accessible tourism: unhindered tourism (Edgell, 1995); disabled tourism (Allan, 2013); inclusive tourism (Scheyvens & Biddulph, 2017); responsible tourism (Tecau et al., 2019); and tourism for all (Belanger & Jolin, 2011; Frances, 1991). While the most common concepts used to refer to tourists with disabilities are accessible tourism (Luiza, 2010; Zsarnoczky, 2017) and disabled tourism (Tüfecki & Öndül, 2016), there is a difference between these two concepts in terms of the people they cover. Disabled tourism includes only persons with disabilities, while accessible tourism refers to all disadvantaged groups (disabled, elderly, pregnant women, the elderly, and so on) (Darcy et al., 2010; Darcy & Dickson, 2009). On the other hand, although there are differences between these two concepts, they both attempt to eliminate obstacles that prevent people from participating in tourism.

Accessibility is a major factor in the decision-making process of persons with disabilities. Accessibility can be measured in terms of the distance travelled, the elapsed time, or the associated opportunity costs (Toth & David, 2010), as accessibility in tourism is a function of the distance from a population centre and the desired attractions that make up the tourism markets. Stakeholders serving the tourism and travel sector should consider the visual, hearing, and cognitive needs of people with disabilities, as well as physical access. Another important point in accessible travel is ensuring the awareness of tourism employees about the needs of people with disabilities. In this context, the inclusion of trainings for accessible tourism in the curricula of tourism-related educational institutions may support the ease of travel for potential tourists with disabilities (Devile & Kastenholz, 2018).

Initial disability models were explored from medical perspectives during the 1960s (Deniz, 2018), which viewed people with disabilities within the scope of accessible tourism as incomplete, defective, and in need of assistance by society. However, advocates for persons with disabilities have challenged this understanding on the grounds that these models do not fully explain disability nor the challenges they face. These theorists state that factors, such as poverty and lack of education, that make persons with disabilities in need of assistance and dependent on others are caused not by physical limitations but by the systematic alienation of these people from full social participation (Prilleltensky, 2012, p. 333). On the other hand, along with developing technology that supports accessibility, research has been carried out within the medical model framework in an attempt to better understand the lives of persons with disabilities. Since the 1970s, persons with disabilities have been evaluated within the framework of social models and sociocultural perspectives. In the late 1980s, research on persons with disabilities in the tourism sector began to focus on the lack of physical access in tourism and hospitality (Burnett & Baker, 2001).

The aim of this research is to create a Participation Cycle of Persons with Disabilities in Tourism Activities model that will serve as a framework for determining the *othering* factors in accessible tourism and support the elimination of obstacles in the decision-making processes to enhance the participation of persons with disabilities in tourism activities. In this context, the concepts of "otherness" and disability are examined in the first three sections of the chapter. The next sections apply these theoretical concepts to travel and tourism in an attempt to better understand the role disability plays in travel decision-making. Lastly, the Participation Cycle of Persons with Disabilities in Tourism Activities model is presented.

The concept of othering

In order to understand the *othering* process in accessible tourism, one should study the concept of "othering" in sociology. The "me", which is the basic concept of *othering*, is an important criterion of difference in defining both oneself and those different than oneself. In other words, the "Other" is that which is "different from what is known, distant in importance and position from two other or similar objects. *Otherness* is the state in which the 'Other' is located" (Nazlı, 2012, pp. 16–17). Although race, gender, age, and similar criteria of difference are at the forefront of the content of *otherness*, people with disabilities can also be included in the criteria of physical and psychological *othering*.

Beauvoir (1993, p. 17) in *Le Deuxiem Sexe*, one of the most influential works of its era, mentioned the decoupling between men and women with the words "man is the subject and the absolute and woman is the Other". In this context, the sentence in question has been used as a reference in many studies in which the *othering* concept is investigated. While Bauman (2003) drew attention to the concept of *otherness* in a similar way in his study, he emphasised that *othering* can occur in general situations of opposition, such as human-animal, diseased-healthy, disabled-non-disabled, or alien-native relationships. The process of excluding and branding people, animals, cultures, and beliefs, which are different, can result in their exclusion from mainstream society (Coleman, 2006).

In Figure 8.1, the perceptions of *othering* are displayed. An individual is the initial point of consideration for *othering*, where the ME-US and ME-OTHERS connections occur. When commonalities exist, the individual will move to the US-OTHERS to form OUR GROUP relationships. The resulting individuals excluded from OUR GROUP are considered the OTHER GROUP and may be prone to *othering* by the OUR GROUP members. People usually communicate easier with people who are like-minded and form bonds with the people perceived as part of the OUR GROUP category. In other words, similarities strengthen communication and relationships, while differences limit communication, resulting in discrimination, social exclusion, and *othering* (McPherson et al., 2001). For

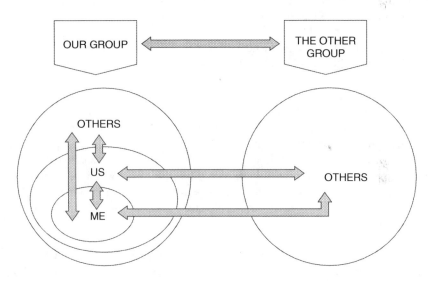

Figure 8.1 The process model of othering.

people in the OTHER GROUP, *othering* may trigger feelings of unwantedness, weakness, and inadequacy (Polat & Kaya, 2017).

Othering puts oneself in the centre of a group with which an individual identifies, pushing people who are not like them out of the group based on preconceptions. More than one "Other" can be created within a group (Staszak, 2009), resulting in two types of *otherness*. The first is the attitude of *otherness* as applied to the OTHER GROUP, and the second is the attitude of *otherness* based on internal differences within the OUR GROUP.

The concept of disability

With some exceptions, persons with disabilities have been subject to various forms of discrimination, exclusion, and *othering* behaviours. Society has defined appropriate physical characteristics, and people who exhibit abnormal differences have been determined by society as the "Other" (Nazlı, 2012). In other words, by questioning normality among people, society is searching for answers to determine "who is normal?" and "who are the Others?" Often people from disadvantaged groups, including people with disabilities, are *othered*.

There are many definitions related to the concept of disability. The Turkish Language Institution defines a person with disabilities as "one that is missing or defective in its body" (Türk Dil Kurumu, 2021, n.p.). It can also be considered as "an individual affected by attitudes and environmental conditions that restrict full and effective participation in society on an equal footing with other individuals due to various levels of loss of physical, mental, spiritual, and sensory abilities" (Law on the Disabled of Turkey, 2005, p. 9463). In other words, disability is a temporary or permanent disorder in the physiological, psychological, and anatomical characteristics of an individual (Baş, 2016). People with disabilities are generally segmented into four groups:

- Hearing impaired: people who have different degrees of hearing loss, including those with complete or partial hearing loss and those who use a hearing aid (Baş, 2016).
- Intellectual disability: people who have limitations in their intellectual functions and/or adaptive behaviour that are categorised according to their occurrence before, during, and after childbirth and can affect a person's ability to function in society (Çağlayan, 2014).
- Physical disability: people who experience health-related challenges in the shape and structure of their bones and joints and those who have a coordination disorder or uncontrolled muscle development (Çivici & Gönen, 2015).
- Visually impaired: people with complete or partial loss of vision (Kaçmaz, 2014).

The number of people with disabilities is more than a billion worldwide, and the disabled population in Europe and America is estimated at over 100 million (Burnett & Baker, 2001). Hence, the market for accessible tourism is expected to grow. In addition, people with disabilities have the potential for high purchasing power (Ray & Ellen, 2003) with enhanced social support and inclusion strategies. Therefore, enhancing accessibility for people with disabilities to participate in tourism activities is significant for destinations.

Othering on the basis of disability

Disability is more than a physical condition, as people with disabilities face social pressures caused by alienation due to their physical and biological characteristics (Burcu, 2015). Literature has acknowledged that people with disabilities are socially excluded, subject to violence, and under psychological pressure. Multinational organisations are attempting to remedy this. One example is the United Nations Convention on the Rights of Persons with Disabilities (2008), which obliges the signatories of the United Nations Convention on the Rights of Persons with Disabilities to eliminate discrimination towards people with disabilities. The eighth article of the Convention (awareness raising) states the following (p. 8):

- To raise awareness throughout society, including at the family level, regarding persons with disabilities and to foster respect for the rights and dignity of persons with disabilities;
- To combat stereotypes, prejudices, and harmful practices relating to persons with disabilities, including those based on sex and age, in all areas of life; and
- To promote awareness of the capabilities and contributions of persons with disabilities.

In addition, this agreement includes purposeful measures for the contributions of people with disabilities in society, such as maintaining effective public awareness campaigns, recognising the skills, merits, and abilities of people with disabilities, fostering an equitable education system for all children, and encouraging the media to portray persons with disabilities in a manner "consistent with the purpose of the present Convention" (p. 8).

Many of the challenges facing persons with disabilities are addressed in the literature. Accessibility of the physical environment comes to the fore when persons with disabilities are to be included in society. Based on a research conducted by ÖZİDA (2010), 7% of people with disabilities had difficulties in accessing public places, such as roads, sidewalks, and parks, due to a lack of necessary regulations and accommodations, and 70% of people with disabilities have experienced various difficulties in buildings where public services are provided. Overall, 58% of the study participants think that they have been subjected to discrimination (ÖZİDA, 2010). The Platform for Preventing and Combating Disability Discrimination (2012) conducted a study where almost half of the respondents believed that society pities them; specifically, 8% felt despised, 11% felt they were a burden, and 25% felt that society was indifferent to the needs of persons with disabilities.

However, despite the laws adopted by various countries and the increased awareness of the needs of persons with disabilities, it seems that people's psychological and behavioural *othering* attitudes remain (Deal, 2007). Aslan and Şeker (2011) present evidence of exclusion and marginalisation by persons with disabilities, surmising that people and their families are seen as "Others" because of their differences. It is recognised that even among groups of persons with disabilities, *othering* is possible, where the most negative attitudes are directed at the intellectually challenged and the physically challenged (Nowicki & Sandieson, 2002; Tasa & Mamatoğlu, 2018). Within tourism studies, current literature has focused on disabled tourism, accessible tourism, social exclusion in disabled tourism, discrimination, and the travel motivations of tourists with disabilities (Burnett & Baker, 2001; Darcy et al., 2010; Shaw & Coles, 2004; etc.). Limited literature exists on the *othering* factor of persons with disabilities, specifically in relation to participation within the scope of accessible tourism.

Tourism and persons with disabilities

Tourism is created by people's intention to buy tourist products or services and have unique experiences in places away from their everyday lives (Kozak et al., 2010). Franklin (2003) considers that general tourism theories are inadequate to describe the complexity of tourism as a social and cultural event. One important element in the definition of a tourism experience is the concept of "travel". For this reason, travel within the tourism sector is an integral activity.

Tourism is constantly developing and accelerating its involvement with new market opportunities. One of these markets is accessible tourism, which offers considerable growth potential. The accessible tourism market is important in terms of both size and spending power (Buhalis et al., 2012). Nonetheless, most tourism destinations and suppliers see the application of accessible tourism for persons with disabilities as an unnecessary burden (Shaw & Coles, 2004).

All people have the right to fully participate in social life (United Nations, n.d.). Kozak et al. (2010) emphasise the need to ensure that persons with disabilities are also included in social life. For this purpose, travel and tourism activities should facilitate the participation of all people regardless of race, gender, age, disability, and economic situation (Kenzhebayeva & Boylu, 2018). It is important for persons with disabilities to participate in tourism and travel activities in order to be involved in social life, integrate within society, and be able to experience different environments and cultures (Freeman & Selmi, 2010).

Freedom of movement is one of the major rights discussed under the Universal Declaration of Human Rights (United Nations, n.d.). For this reason, efforts are being made to develop accessible tourism for disadvantaged groups that cannot or do not usually participate in tourism. However, extant literature focuses on problems faced by persons with disabilities in their usual environment while overlooking the challenges they face during their travels (Baş & Ulama, 2014; Ercan, 2020; Neumann & Reuber, 2004; Packer et al., 2007; Yau et al., 2004). The Platform for Preventing and Combating Disability Discrimination (2012) found that more than half of the persons with disabilities participating in the study did not go on vacation at all, and 58% of those who did go on vacation travelled with their family. Moreover, it was found that people with visual impairment participated more in recreation activities (such as outdoor activities) than persons with other disabilities (Özgül et al., 2012).

People with disabilities are limited in their daily activities, and the level of participation in tourism varies according to the state of their disability (Pagan, 2012). Carlsson (2009) states that tourists with disabilities face many challenges, beginning with the moment they leave their home. Cavinato and Cuckovich (1992) examined two factors affecting travel participation of persons with disabilities. The first of these factors is whether tourism enterprises and destinations have facilities to assist persons with disabilities, and the second is based on the severity of the disability.

In this context, Packer et al. (2007) explain six stages of the travel process for tourists with disabilities in order to reveal the relationships between tourism and disability. These stages include travel as an impossibility; travel as an abstract idea; risk and reward; planning the trip; managing the trip; and the post-trip experience. The most important of these stages is the evaluation of all services in terms of accessibility, specifically certain micro-level travel elements (e.g. accommodation, transportation, and food and drink activities), which are often critical in making a travel decision (Cavinato & Cuckovich, 1992). According to Packer et al. (2007), VisitBritain has launched a qualitative investigation to raise awareness of persons with disabilities, which has revealed important factors that would enable persons with disabilities to participate in travel. Six factors were discussed as a result of the research: infrastructure facilities needed for accessible accommodation (ramp, elevator, wheelchair, and evacuation procedure in case of emergency); accessibility; internal and external security; loud music and lack of entertainment (especially for the hearing impaired); attitudes and behaviours of hotel employees towards people with disabilities; and the ease of travel to and from a tourist destination (VisitBritain, 2008). Moreover, persons with disabilities make travel decisions based on the positive or negative experiences of other persons with disabilities who have participated in travel activities (Neumann & Reuber, 2004).

Therefore, tourists with disabilities tend to choose places with easy access to local amenities and attractions or places that can accommodate their physical or intellectual challenges. In the initial decision-making processes, persons with disabilities will consider destinations that offer accessible accommodations and then will compare and contrast destinations according to their accessibility (Toth & David, 2010). In this regard, accessibility, especially in relation to lodging, plays a primary role in the choice of potential vacation destinations. Hence, Çizel and Çizel (2014) state that the tourism restrictions perceived by persons with disabilities negatively affect the desire to participate in tourism.

In order to increase the participation of persons with disabilities in travel, Devile and Kastenholz (2018) examined the factors that should be considered when designing accessible tourism applications, specifically: personal effects (e.g. personality, previous travel experience, curiosity, an admission of the disabled); interpersonal effects (e.g. travel companions and disability awareness of tourism staff); and structural effects (e.g. accessible information, applications, and tourism activities). Smith (1987) investigated three dimensions affecting the participation of persons with disabilities in travel, including internal, environmental, and interactive. Internal factors are caused by the type of disability the person has and the degree to which they accept the disability (e.g. parents or caregivers overprotectiveness and inadequate education). Environmental barriers include the accessibility of the physical space (architecture, ecology, transport, law, and regulations). Interactive barriers include communication barriers (accessing medication, communication, problem solving, and insurance). On the other hand, Veitch and Shaw (2011) listed the four factors that made people with disabilities feel anxious, including the choice of a vacation spot, logistical planning, finding information about accommodations, and finding information about accessible travel agencies.

When different studies conducted on disabilities are examined, some common factors that prevent persons with disabilities from travelling emerge. Table 8.1 consolidates the aforementioned studies and highlights factors influencing the ability of persons with disabilities to travel.

On the other hand, within the scope of accessible tourism, a number of innovations have reduced the barrier for participation by travellers with disabilities. For example, the application of recorded voice descriptions is used in museums and important historical sites for the visually impaired (Erbay, 2017). The United Nations (2013) also encourages the introduction of accessibility standards

Table 8.1 Factors affecting the travel participation of persons with disabilities.

Internal Factors		*External Factors*	
Personal Barriers	*Economic Barriers*	*Interpersonal Barriers*	*Structural Barriers*
Physical barriers	Income differences	Disability awareness of tourism staff	Transportation
Psychological-related barriers	Health costs	Negative references	Accessibility to tourism enterprises
Previous travel experience	Travel companionship	Negative behaviours	Accessibility to tourism activities
Personality		Motivation for participation in travel	Information that is not accessible
Acceptance of disability		Communication difficulties	Destination accessibility
The impossibility of travel			Applications
Health-related barriers			Safety
Curiosity			Infrastructure

Source: Adapted from Devile and Kastenholz (2018), McKercher et al. (2003), Smith (1987), and Veitch and Shaw (2011).

Table 8.2 Groups that benefit from accessible tourism.

Persons with disabilities	Young persons with disabilities	Hearing impaired people
		Visually impaired people
	Adult persons with disabilities	Physically challenged people
		Intellectually challenged people
Persons without disabilities	Groups that benefit from social tourism	Workers
		Officers
		Teens
		Farmer
		Retirees
	Groups that benefit from health tourism	Persons travelling for the purpose of treatment
		Persons with temporary disabilities
		Companions
	Groups that benefit from senior tourism	Elders
	Others groups	Pregnant women
		Obese, tall or short people
		Persons with strollers
		Foreigners
		Local people
		Persons carrying heavy loads

Source: Adapted from Baş (2016), Darcy et al. (2010), Ercan (2020), and Kozak et al. (2010).

for elevators, stairs, vehicles, parks, tourism services, theatres, and beaches as a means to promote accessible tourism and create social awareness around disability. In addition, the European Union has shown its support for the participation of persons with disabilities in tourism activities through the provision of travel agencies that provide specialised services, transport vehicles designed to suit special needs, and holiday itineraries suitable for persons with disabilities (Zsarnoczky, 2017). For example, Accessible Italy, a tour operator, designs tours offering accessible services. In addition, facilities, such as touch and feel exhibits, specially prepared tour routes, and guided museums, are offered for visually impaired people (Accessibleitaly, n.d.). Other regulations have included allowing disabled people to enter public places with their dogs and the creation of a national sign language (Akdu & Akdu, 2018). Table 8.2 displays groups that will benefit from increases in accessible tourism infrastructure.

Othering in tourism

Obstacles limit freedom, personal behaviours, and a sense of competence. Persons with disabilities sometimes consider internal and external factors as personal defeats. In turn, people with disabilities may experience negative emotions when deciding to travel. Tourism is the best way to escape from everyday life and its problems. However, factors affecting travel participation can also be forms of *othering*, which in turn increase barriers to tourism (Kaganek et al., 2017).

Otherness is among the pioneer factors that discourage persons with disabilities from travelling and experiencing a destination (Tüfecki & Öndül, 2016). According to Figure 8.2, *othering* for tourists with disabilities begins with the person himself and ends with social exclusion and inaccessible opportunities, services, and experiences. In tourism, the process of *othering* occurs through staff interactions, the host community, the physical set-up of tourism sites, as well as the disability itself. In this context, it is not enough for tourism and travel enterprises to provide an accessible service, interactions between stakeholder groups is an important part of accessibility and inclusion. In this case, training relating to communication strategies and appropriate behaviour should be considered, taking into account *othering* factors. Staff should be trained to be empathetic and accommodating towards persons with disabilities, especially in relation to communication. Every word, eye contact, behaviour, or inappropriate social attitudes might affect *othering* perceptions for persons with disabilities. Moreover, creating awareness about accessible tourism might assist in minimising *otherness*.

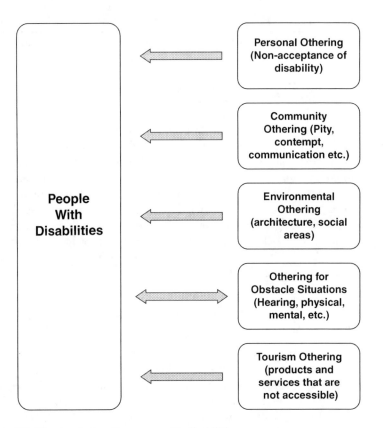

Figure 8.2 Othering factors in persons with disabilities.

The Participation Cycle of Persons with Disabilities in Tourism Activities model

The Participation Cycle of Persons with Disabilities in Tourism Activities model represents the travel decision-making process and avenues for active participation in tourism for persons with disabilities. As shown in Figure 8.3, the travel process begins with accessible booking communication, and the process continues with other accessible services. The inner circle represents the internal perceptions of potential tourists with disabilities, and in order for a positive perception of travel, *othering* factors and negative experiences should be eliminated. The elimination of *othering* factors and negative experiences also supports the intention to revisit and recommend destinations to other persons with disabilities. Therefore, the cycle of travel participation is reinforced by positive experiences. The smaller circles in

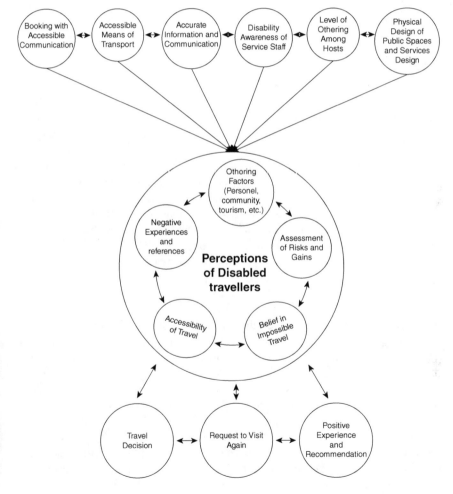

Figure 8.3 Participation Cycle of Persons with Disabilities in Tourism Activities model.

Figure 8.3 represent peoples with disabilities' general perceptions towards travel, while the larger circle represents destination characteristics and experiences at the destination, including pre-, during, and post-travel.

Prior to making a decision to travel, a person with disabilities will make an internal inquiry, asking, "can I easily access tourism activities?" at a certain destination. The answer to this question lies in their perceptions of themselves and the accommodations provided by service providers. Research into disability travel barriers shows that many people with disabilities see travel as an impractical event (Packer et al., 2007), because they may believe that the services offered are not readily accessible or designed for the accessibility market. Each service that is not accessible can make persons with disabilities feel "othered" or ignored, as if they are invisible to tourism providers. Perception of *othering* can be part of the risk factors evaluated prior to travel. In turn, online reviews that highlight *othering* experiences can create a negative connotation towards travel. Proactive marketing by destinations, highlighting accessibility, and encouraging travel by persons with disabilities can prevent the belief that travel is impossible.

Conclusion

In summary, disabled people face various *othering* factors that discourage them from travelling (Ray & Ellen, 2003; Tüfecki & Öndül, 2016). This chapter identified the *othering* factors, their implications, and possible influence on persons with disabilities in tourism. Using the findings and results of previous studies on the concept of travel barriers and *othering* towards persons with disabilities, the factors that create the "Other" feelings have been explored. A Participation Cycle of Persons with Disabilities in Tourism Activities model has been developed that lists the factors needed to enhance positive travel experiences, which create the desire to travel to, return to, and recommend destinations. Destinations and tourism service providers trying to attract tourists with disabilities should consider these factors and adjust their strategies to minimise *othering* in tourism.

That being said, by providing education, transportation, and infrastructure facilities, persons with disabilities can participate in tourism activities and play an active role in social life. The education of persons with disabilities will strengthen interpersonal communication and enable greater participation in social life. On the other hand, persons without disabilities should also be trained in communication and appropriate behaviour towards persons with disabilities. Education offers opportunities to reduce the *othering* factors. As a matter of fact, persons with disabilities usually hesitate to participate in travel and tourism activities due to inadequate practices. Therefore, it is necessary that tourism stakeholders, destination policymakers, law enforcement officers, and tourism personnel have more information about accessible tourism.

COVID-19 has shown the need for diversification in tourism markets. In this context, it is important to identify and facilitate accessible tourism, which is a growing potential market. Important duties fall on public and private stakeholders who want to access this market or play an active role in accessible travel and tourism activities. In the creation of travel and tourism activities, the determination of accessibility criteria and prevention strategies for factors that prevent participation in travel are important for the positive experiences of persons with disabilities.

References

Accessibleitaly. (n.d.). *Individual and group travelers with disabilities*. Retrieved January 12, 2021, from www.accessibleitaly.com/home_standard.htm

Akdu, U., & Akdu, S. (2018). Engelli turizmi: Yasal düzenlemeler ve uygulamalar. *Gümüşhane Üniversity, Institude of Social Sciences, 9*(23), 99–123.

Allan, M. (2013). Disability tourism: Why do disabled people engaging in tourism activities. European *Journal of Social Sciences, 39*(3), 480–486.

Aslan, M., & Şeker, S. (2011). Engellilere yönelik toplumsal algı ve dışlanmışlık (Siirt Örneği). In *Sosyal Haklar Uluslararası Sempozyumu* (pp. 449–463). Siirt Üniversitesi. Retrieved November 23, 2021, from https://acikerisim.siirt.edu.tr/xmlui/bitstream/handle/20.500.12604/699/aslanseker.pdf?sequence=1&isAllowed=

Baş, M. (2016). *Engelli Turizmi*. Nobel Akademik Yayıncılık.

Baş, M., & Ulama, Ş. (2014, Kasım 13–16). Türkiye'de engelli turizm pazarındaki farklı talep özelliklerinin analizi. In *Gazi Üniversitesi Turizm Fakültesi, 15. Ulusal Turizm Kongresi* (pp. 1532–1547). Nobel Akademik Yayıncılık.

Bauman, Z. (2003). *Modernlik ve müphemlik*. Ayrıntı Yayınları.

Beauvoir, S. (1993). *Le deuxiem sexe* (B. Onaran, Trans.). Payel Yayınları.

Belanger, C. E., & Jolin, L. (2011). The International Organisation of Social Tourism (ISTO) working towards a right to holiday and tourism for all. *Current Issues in Tourism, 14*(5), 475–482. https://doi.org/10.1080/13683500.2011.568056

Buhalis, D., Darcy, S., & Ambrose, İ. (2012). *Accessible tourism issues: Inclusion, disability, ageing population and tourism*. Channel View Publication.

Burcu, E. (2015). Türkiye'de yeni bir alan: "Engellilik Sosyolojisi" ve gelişimi. Sosyoloji Konferansları. *Journal of Sociological Studies/Sosyoloji Konferansları, 52*, 319–341.

Burnett, J. J., & Baker, H. B. (2001). Assessing the travel-related behaviors of the mobility disabled consumer. *Journal of Travel Research, 40*(4), 4–11.

Çağlayan, N. (2014). Zihinsel engelli bireylerin eğitiminde görsel sanatlarlar dersinin yeri ve önemi. *Sosyal Bilimler Enstitüsü Dergisi, 4*(1), 91–101.

Carlsson, G. (2009). Travelling by urban public transport: Exploration of usability problems in a travel chain perspective. *Scandinavian Journal of Occupational Therapy, 11*(2), 78–89.

Cavinato, J. L., & Cuckovich, M. L. (1992). Transportation and tourism for the disabled: An assessment. *Transportation Journal, 3*(31), 46–53.

Çivici, T., & Gönen, D. (2015). Balıkesir Üniversitesi çağış yerleşkesinin bedensel engelli öğrencilerin sosyal alanlara ulaşabilirliğinin değerlendirilmesi. *Süleyman Demirel Üniversitesi Mühendislik Bilimleri ve Tasarım Dergisi, 3*(3), 639–646.

Çizel, B., & Çizel, R. (2014). Engellilerin turizm kısıtları ve turist olma niyeti İlişkisinde aracı değişkenler: Motivasyon gücü ve öğrenilmiş çaresizlik. *Anatolia: Turizm Araştırmaları Dergisi, 25*(2), 176–189. https://doi.org/10.17123/atad.vol25iss280747.

Coleman, L. M. (2006). Stigma: An enigma demystified. In L. J. Davis (Ed.), *The disability studies reader* (2nd ed., pp. 141–153). Taylor & Francis Group.

Darcy, S., Comeran, B., & Pegg, S. (2010). Accessible tourism and sustainability: A discussion and business case study. *Journal of Sustainable Tourism, 18*(4), 515–537.

Darcy, S., & Dickson, T. J. (2009). A whole-of-life approach to tourism: The case for accessible tourism. *Journal of Hospitality and Tourism Management*, *16*(1), 32–44.

Deal, M. (2007). Aversive disablism: Subtle prejudice toward disabled people. *Disability & Society*, *22*(1), 93–107. https://doi.org/10.1080/09687590601056667

Deniz, P. (2018). Psikoloji ppenceresinden engel ve engellilik kavramlarına bakış. *PİVOLKA*, *8*(29), 6–10.

Devile, E., & Kastenholz, E. (2018). Accessible tourism experience: The voice of people with visual disabilities. *Journal of Policy Research in Tourism, Leisure and Events*, *10*(3), 265–285.

Edgell, D. L. (1995). A barrier-free future for tourism? *Tourism Management*, *16*(2), 107–110.

Erbay, N. Ö. (2017). Müzeler ve engelli ziyaretçilere yönelik eğitim projeleri. *Milli Eğitim Dergisi*, *46*(214), 345–358.

Ercan, F. (2020). *Erişilebilir turizm ve yardımcı teknolojiler*. Nobel Akademik Yayınları.

Frances, B. (1991). Tourism for all. *Tourism Management*, *12*(3), 258–260.

Franklin, A. (2003). *Tourism an introduction*. SAGE Publications Ltd.

Freeman, I., & Selmi, N. (2010). French versus Canadian tourism: Response to the disabled. *Journal of Travel Research*, *49*(4), 471–485.

Kaçmaz, Y. Y. (2014). *Engelli bireylerin turizm deneyimlerine yönelik bir araştırma: Alanya örneği*. Akdeniz Üniversitesi, Sosyal Bilimler Enstitüsü, Yayımlanmamış Yüksek Lisans Tezi.

Kaganek, K., Ambrozy, T., Mucha, D., Jurczak, A., Bornikowska, A., Janiszewska, R., & Mucha, T. (2017). Barriers to participation in tourism in the disabled. *Polish Journal of Sport and Tourism*, *24*(2), 121–129.

Kenzhebayeva, A., & Boylu, Y. (2018). Engelli bireylerin seyahat engellerinden etkilenmesinde psikolojik faktörlerin önemi. *Yönetim, Ekonomi ve Pazarlama Araştırmaları Dergisi*, *2*(4), 1–11.

Kozak, N., Kozak, M. A., & Kozak, M. (2010). *Genel turizm: İlkeler-kavramlar*. Ankara, Turkey, 9. Basım, Detay Yayıncılık.

Law on the Disabled of Turkey: 9463. (2005, July 1). *Türkiye 5378 sayılı Engelliler Hakkında Kanun*. Erişim Tarihi. Retrieved November 22, 2021, from www.mevzuat.gov.tr/MevzuatMetin/1.5.5378.pdf

Luiza, S. M. (2010). Accessible tourism: The ignored opportunity. *Annals of Faculty of Economics*, *1*(2), 1154–1157.

McKercher, B., Packer, T., Yau, M. K., & Lam, P. (2003). Travel agents as facilitators or inhibitors of travel: Perceptions of people with disabilities. *Tourism Management*, *54*(4), 465–474.

McPherson, M., Smith-Lovin, L., & Cook, J. M. (2001). Birds of a feather: Homophily in social networks. *Annual Review of Sociology*, *27*, 415–444. https://doi.org/10.1146/annurev.soc.27.1.415

Nazlı, A. (2012). 'Öteki beden'bir ötekilik biçimi olarak engelli beden ve engellilik. *Sosyoloji Dergisi*, *27*, 17–32.

Neumann, P., & Reuber, P. (2004). *Economic impulses of accessible tourism for all*. Berlin Study commissioned by the Federal Ministry of Economics and Technology and the Federal Ministry of Economic and Labour (BMWA) Vol. 526. www.ferdamalastofa.is/static/files/upload/files/peter_n.pdf

Nowicki, E. A., & Sandieson, R. (2002). A meta-analysis of school-age children's attitudes towards persons with physical or intellectual disabilities. *International Journal of Disability, Development and Education*, *49*(3), 243–265. https://doi.org/10.1080/1034912022000007270

Özgül, H., Polat, G., & Akbulut, S. (2012). *Engelli ayrımcılığı araştırması ve engelli ayrımcılığına karşı çözüm önerileri raporu.* Görme Özürlüler Derneği; Engelli Ayrımcılığını Önleme ve Mücadele Platformu (The Platform for Preventing and Combating Disability Discrimination). www.sabancivakfi.org/i/content/4854_2_Engelli_Ayrimciligi_ Arastirmasi_ve_Engelli_Ayrimciligina_Karsi

ÖZİDA. (2010). *Özürlülüğe dayalı ayrımcılığın ölçülmesi araştırması.* Başbakanlık Özürlüler İdaresi Başkanlığı.

Packer, T. L., Packer, T. L., McKercher, B., & Yau, M. K. (2007). Understanding the complex interplay between tourism, disability and environmental contexts. *Disability and Rehabilitation, 29*(4), 281–292.

Pagan, R. (2012). Time allocation in tourism for people with disabilities. *Annals of Tourism Research, 39*(3), 1514–1537.

Polat, F. Ç., & Kaya, E. (2017). An othering practice: Attitudes to Syrian refugees in Turkey. *Mersin Üniversitesi Sosyal Bilimler Enstitüsü e-dergi, 1*(1), 38–48.

Prilleltensky, I. (2012). Eleştirel psikoloji ve engelli çalışmaları: Anaakımı eleştirmek, eleştiriyi eleştirmek. In P. V. Fox (Ed.), *Eleştirel Psikoloji* (pp. 329–349). Ayrıntı Yayınları.

Ray, N. M., & Ellen, R. (2003). Abilities tourism: An exploratory discussion of the travel needs and motivations of the mobility-disabled. *Tourism Management, 24*(1), 57–72.

Scheyvens, R., & Biddulph, R. (2017). Inclusive tourism development. *Tourism Geographies: An International Journal of Tourism Space, Place and Environment, 20*(4), 589–609. https://doi.org/10.1080/14616688.2017.1381985

Shaw, G., & Coles, T. (2004). Disability, holiday making and tourism industry in the UK: A preliminary survey. *Tourism Management, 25*(3), 397–403.

Smith, R. W. (1987). Leisure of disabled tourists: Barriers to travel. *Annals of Tourism Research, 14*(3), 376–389.

Staszak, J. F. (2009). Other/otherness. In R. Kitchin & N. Thrift (Eds.), *International encyclopedia of human geography* (pp. 43–47). Elsevier.

Tasa, H., & Mamatoğlu, N. (2018). Attitude change towards disabled persons and sensitivity trainings. *Türkiye Klinikleri, Psychol-Special Topics, 3*(1), 11–21.

Tecau, A. S., Bratucu, G., Tescaşiu, B., Chitu, L. B., Constantin, C. P., & Foris, D. (2019). Responsible tourism – Integrating families with disabled children in tourist destinations. *Sustainability, 11*(16), 4420. https://doi.org/10.3390/su11164420

Toth, G., & David, L. (2010). Tourism and accessibility: An integrated approach. *Applied Geography, 30*, 666–677.

Tüfecki, Ö. K., & Öndül, G. (2016). Disabled tourism and suggestions for disabled tourism market: Antalya case. *Journal of Current Researches on Health Sector, 6*(1), 73–88.

Türk Dil Kurumu (TDK). (2021). *Türk dil kurumu, sözlükler.* Retrieved June 15, 2021, from www.tdk.gov.tr/, https://sozluk.gov.tr/

United Nations. (2008). *United Nations convention on the rights of persons with disabilities.* Retrieved February 1, 2022, from www.un.org/disabilities/documents/convention/convoptprot-e.pdf

United Nations. (2013). *Promoting accessible tourism for all.* Retrieved February 1, 2022, from www.un.org/development/desa/disabilities/issues/promoting-accessible-tourism-for-all.html

United Nations. (n.d.). *Universal declaration of human rights.* Retrieved December 5, 2021, from www.un.org/en/about-us/universal-declaration-of-human-rights

Veitch, C., & Shaw, G. (2011). Disability legislation and empowerment of tourist with disability. In D. Buhalis & S. Darcy (Eds.), *Accessible tourism: Concepts and issues* (pp. 62–72). Channel View Publications.

VisitBritain. (2008). *Access consumer research*. Retrieved November 14, 2021, from www.visitbritain.org/sites/default/files/vb-corporate/Documents-Library/documents/England-documents/national_accessible_scheme_consumer.pdf. Erişim Tarihi

Yau, M. K., McKercher, B., & Packer, T. L. (2004). Travelling with a disability: More than an access issue. *Annals of Tourism Research, 31*(4), 946–960.

Zsarnoczky, M. (2017, September). Accessible tourism in the European Union. In *6th central European conference in regional science conference proceedings: Engines of urban and regional development* (pp. 30–39). Faculty of Economics, Metej Bel University.

9 Gay men's experiences of prejudiced attitudes and discrimination in tourism

Carlos Monterrubio and César Caselin

Introduction

Gay men have been identified as a growing lucrative market in the tourism industry due to their alleged high economic power (United Nations World Tourism Organization (UNWTO), 2017). Travel and tourism hold special value, particularly for gay men. Existing research has found that, due to the social constraints experienced by gay men in a heteronormative society, many of them need to travel away from home in search of places in which to be gay (Cox, 2002; Hughes, 1997; Monterrubio, 2019; Pritchard et al., 2002; Vorobjovas-Pinta, 2018). Therefore, tourism is significant to gay men, not only in terms of rest and relaxation and other conventional tourist motivations but also in terms of their own sexual identity.

Even though, over the past five decades, the visibility and social acceptance of sexual and gender-diverse people has increased in the world (European Travel Commission (ETC), 2018; Ong et al., 2020), gay populations continue to be affected negatively by legislative, religious, and social prejudice, making them victims of structural and linked social discriminatory acts (Human Rights Watch (HRW), 2013). Discrimination can be understood as the behavioural expression of unfavourable attitudes towards a social group and its members (Hogg & Vaughan, 2008). It is commonly conceptualised in two forms: blatant discrimination, which is overt, intentional, and relatively easy to recognise, and subtle discrimination, which pervades societies, is less perceptible and ambiguous and is not easily recognised as discrimination (Van Laer & Janssens, 2011).

Discrimination, both overt and subtle, can have serious implications for gay men's lives, as it can cause them to feel isolated and to become targets of violence (Poria & Tailor, 2001). Due to its negative implications for the consumption of tourism, discrimination needs to be considered within the tourism market sphere (Andrade et al., 2021). In this vein, discrimination and negative attitudes towards homosexuality can be experienced during recreational travel leading to physical and mental stress (Ong et al., 2020) and, as revealed by this chapter, negative tourism experiences. Despite the significance that discriminatory acts can have in gay travel, however, empirical research into discrimination by gay men in travel and tourism outside the United States and Western Europe is practically non-existent (Rosenbaum et al., 2020).

DOI: 10.4324/9781003255413-11

This chapter contributes to fill this gap by exploring prejudiced attitudes and discrimination as experienced by gay men during holidays in Mexico. Mexico is a popular destination among gay tourists but at the same time, a sociopolitical and cultural context in which structural and social environments still remain largely repressive, discriminatory, and violent towards homosexual people (Monterrubio, 2021). As a result, Mexico provides an ideal setting for investigating how structural and interpersonal discrimination shape the travel experiences of gay men.

Literature review

Gay tourism

For decades, lesbian, gay, bisexual, and transgender (LGBT) tourism has been widely recognised as a growing and highly lucrative market segment (Korflür et al., 2006; Ram et al., 2019). It is estimated that in 2016, approximately 36 million overnight visitors who travelled to international destinations around the world were part of the LGBT community (UNWTO, 2017). Based on a survey conducted with members of the LGBT population in the United States in 2019, Community Marketing & Insights (CMI) (2019), a market research firm, revealed that LGBT people are frequent travellers, as they take, on average, 3.1 holiday or leisure trips and 1.5 business trips a year. Even during times of crisis, such as the COVID-19 pandemic, LGBT travellers, particularly white gay men, have shown the greatest propensity to travel (Markwell, 2021).

It has been reported that the LGBT population is a segment with high purchasing power and characterised by being DINK (double income, no kids), which partly explains its high tourism consumption (Hattingh et al., 2011). However, any generalisation regarding the high purchasing power of the LGBT population is misleading, since the available evidence is on limited coverage, incomplete, and unrepresentative surveys (Hughes, 2005). Furthermore, as Monterrubio et al. (2020) observe, because studies on LGBT tourism motivations and experiences have been largely based on male gay samples, they represent, at most, the motivations and experiences of gay and lesbian (GL) men rather than those of transgender and queer individuals (TQ). Even so, LGBT tourism, particularly male gay tourism, is a segment that has a presence in the economy of both developed and developing countries. Gay tourism activities are so diverse and range from surfing in Brazil, hiking in Peru, guided tours in Israel, to yoga workshops in Thailand (UNWTO, 2017). While major tourist cities and beach destinations in Europe remain popular among gay travellers, recent research revealed that destinations popular among gay tourists are experiencing a rapid diversification as compared with other forms of tourism (Dahl & Barreto, 2021; ETC, 2018). This implies that gay travellers intersect with mainstream tourists in spaces that are not necessarily gay friendly.

The motivations of gay tourism have been one of the most studied topics in gay tourism studies, though most of the evidence has been drawn from scholarly and marketing research in Western contexts (Hattingh, 2021). Existing studies have revealed that the motivations that drive gay people to travel are diverse, similar to those of other travellers (Waitt & Markwell, 2006), and vary on the basis of factors such as age, sexual identity, and relationship status (Hattingh, 2021). As in mainstream tourism, gay holiday motivations include rest and relaxation, getting away from ordinary life, exploration of new places, learning about other cultures, seeking adventure, enhancement of kinship relationships, and self-fulfilment (CMI, 2019; Hattingh, 2021; Hughes, 2006; Pritchard et al., 2000). As a matter of fact, recent research has found that popular gay-friendly destinations are not always a primary motivator for gay tourists; instead, gay tourists search for places with historical and natural scenery, relaxing atmospheres, good food, and nightlife (CMI, 2019; Hattingh, 2021).

However, as a specific market segment, gay tourism has its own motivational characteristics. For many male gay individuals, there is a need to escape heteronormativity (Hatting et al., 2011) and socialise with other gay people during travel (Hughes, 2002). Having fun; clearing oneself; connecting with a partner, friend, or relative; and sexually connecting with locals or other tourists at the destination have been reported as other relevant motivations for gay travellers (Clift & Forrest, 1999; CMI, 2019). Sexuality, it has been concluded, influences tourism consumption patterns for gay tourists (Poria & Tailor, 2001; Pritchard et al., 2000).

In this vein, travel and tourism hold special value, particularly for gay men. Existing research has found that, due to the social constraints experienced by gay men and lesbians in a heteronormative society, many of them need to travel away from home in search of safe places in which to be gay (Cox, 2002; Hughes, 1997; Monterrubio, 2019, 2021; Pritchard et al., 2002). Therefore, assuming tourism provides safe spaces in which to be gay, it is significant to gay men not only in terms of rest and relaxation and other conventional motivations but also in terms of their own sexual identity. As Vorobjovas-Pinta (2018) claims, "[g]ay travel is often presented as an idealised escape from the heteronormative strictures of everyday life, and an opportunity to embrace and express one's identity" (p. 3). Furthermore, Herrera and Scott (2005) argue that "[t]he gay identity, thus, fuels gay men's need to travel, and the act of travelling provides them new insights about themselves and paves the way for perhaps a new and certainly more positive conception of self" (p. 260). Tourism by gay men also has collective benefits as it contributes to enhancing the visibility, role, and recognition of the LGBT community and benefits destinations due to the association of their brand image with acceptance, inclusiveness, and diversity (UNWTO, 2017).

For gay leisure and tourism, gay space is quite significant. Gay space can be understood as physical and symbolic manifestations of gay communities in concentrations of pubs, clubs, cafés, shops, residences, and other public areas (Hughes, 1997). Gay spaces provide gay men with security, acceptance, tolerance, and – albeit temporarily – escape from heteronormativity (Waitt & Markwell, 2006). In gay spaces, sexuality is celebrated, and gay tourists are invited to be gay (Bailey, 2021). Unlike heteronormed spaces – in which gay manifestations are often disapproved and condemned – gay spaces allow gay tourists and locals to express themselves freely and to build and exercise their sexual identities (Herrera & Scott, 2005; Monterrubio, 2021). Identity is socially constructed and must be understood as collectively produced through social interactions (Lawler, 2008); thus gay spaces provide opportunities for such interactions between like-minded people and, therefore, to be oneself.

Attitudes towards homosexuality and gay tourism

While public support of the rights of LGBT people has increased considerably and quickly during the last decades in some nations (Flores, 2014), prejudiced attitudes and legal punishment towards homosexual people still prevail in many parts of the world (see the edited volume by Vorobjovas-Pinta, 2021). Recent research on public views towards homosexual men in the Caribbean, for example, has revealed that, at a social level, negative attitudes towards gay men are still present and constrain socialisation with homosexual people, and that these attitudes are strongly determined by heteronormativity and notions of hyper-masculinity (Beck et al., 2017). It has also been shown that men tend to have less positive attitudes towards feminine gay men in comparison with masculine gay men (Cohen et al., 2009); thus, effeminate, androgynous, or unmasculine gay men tend to suffer more from stigmatisation, discrimination, and hostility, not only from heterosexual society but also from other gay men (Taywaditep, 2002).

At a state level, while some countries have enforced constitutional protection, others have legalised the criminalisation of diverse sexual orientation. The International Lesbian, Gay, Bisexual, Trans, and Intersex Association's (ILGA's) report on homophobic global legislation concluded that by 2020 there were 67 United Nations Member States with provisions that criminalise same-sex sexual activity, including six countries in which the death penalty is the legal punishment for homosexual acts (ILGA, 2020). Both social prejudice and state constitutions on sexual orientation lead to discrimination and abuse, including "torture, killing and executions, arrests under unjust laws, unequal treatment, censorship, medical abuses, discrimination in health and jobs and housing, domestic violence, abuses against children, and denial of family rights and recognition" (HRW, 2013, n.p.), among others.

The manifestations of social prejudice towards homosexuality also take place in the travel and tourism arena. Research on local attitudes towards gay tourism in Mexico, for example, has reported that while the economic benefits of gay tourists are acknowledged, there are negative attitudes and a reluctance to support further flows of gay tourists – though such attitudes may be largely based on the overt sexual activity of gay men (Hughes et al., 2010). In other countries, such as Jamaica, largely negative attitudes towards homosexuality are deeply ingrained in the cultural, legal, and religious systems, and these attitudes have not only restrained the development of Jamaica as a gay-friendly destination but also served to marginalise its own gay population (Chambers, 2008). The recent overt reluctance of the Brazilian president to allow his country to become a gay destination (BBC News, 2019), the opposition of religious groups and death threats against tour companies for GL tourists in Ethiopia (Wilson, 2019), and the recent homophobic brutal attack with a hammer on a gay British tourist in a gay venue visiting Spain (Marr, 2021) show that homophobic acts against gay tourists are currently present in several parts of the world.

Context

Mexico ranked seventh in the list of top ten destinations by international tourist arrivals in 2019 (UNWTO, 2021) and is a popular international LGBT destination.

> Mexico is a true paradise for tourists and has beautiful beaches, impressive mountains, vast landscapes from the southern jungle to the desert in the north, a millennial history and a vibrant and colorful society that has emerged from the mix of three different cultures. Vibrant modern cities, fascinating small colonial villages and archaeological sites make the country a diverse holiday destination. The Mexican cuisine alone makes a visit to the country worthwhile.
>
> (Spartacus, 2021, n.p.)

Destinations, such as Puerto Vallarta, Cancun, and Mexico City, are top tourism destinations among US gay men (CMI, 2019). It is estimated that in 2017, 3.5 million travellers belonging to the LGBT community visited Mexico (Secretaría de Turismo, 2018). In the last few years, the Mexican federal government has made efforts to improve LGBT tourism supply, commercialisation, promotion, and training among the industry's providers to avoid discrimination (Monterrubio, 2021). Specifically, the government has made public declarations to recognise the economic value of, and to seek out, the LGBT market. It has started to attract the gay market based on the country's legal protections that defend tourists and citizens alike and laws allowing for equality in marriages and adoption in Mexico (Bailey, 2021).

In Mexico, there is also recognition of LGBT rights. The Mexican state has legislated in favour of the protection of the rights of LGBT people and the elimination of discrimination based on sexual orientation or gender identity. However, in practice, this has been applied differently in each of the states that make up the country. As a consequence, respect for LGBT rights in the country is the exception rather than the rule (López, 2017). In many parts of the country, the social and religious environment against gay people – particularly effeminate men – remains repressive, discriminatory, and violent as a consequence of culture, religion, machismo, and hyper-masculinity (Monterrubio, 2021). It is not surprising that acts of discrimination and violence against gay people during travel take place in the country.

The Survey on Discrimination on the Grounds of Sexual Orientation and Gender Identity, conducted in 2018, based on a sample of 12,331 sexual and gender-diverse people (45.8% gay men) in Mexico, revealed that practically all the people surveyed (96.8%) reported having heard offensive jokes about LGBT people, and

93.3% have witnessed expressions of hatred, physical attacks, and harassment against this population group. It is also reported that 60% of participants felt discriminated against at least once during the 12 months prior to the survey and that one in four people has been unjustifiably denied some right (e.g. education and justice). The survey found that 86.4% of the participants consider that the rights of LGBT people are "little" or "not" respected in Mexico (Conapred, 2019).

Within travel and tourism, several instances of discrimination and violence against people in gay destinations in Mexico can be listed. Cases such as those of two gay men in Los Cabos (Northwest Mexico) who were offended and beaten by two guards of a five star hotel for kissing in the pool in 2005 (Medina, 2005), the recent violent attempt to arrest two Canadian tourists in Tulum (Southeast Mexico) for kissing on the grounds where there were children and families (Varillas, 2021), or the case of a young gay man who was beaten, tortured, burned, and killed when he revealed that he was HIV-positive at a party in the popular international destination of Cancun (Mexican Caribbean) (EFE, 2021) are just illustrations of how homophobia is still present in different destinations within the country.

Methods

The research reported here aims to explore prejudiced attitudes and discrimination acts as experienced by gay men during holidays in Mexico. This study adopted an interpretive social science paradigm. According to Jennings (2001), the interpretive paradigm recognises that there are multiple conceptions and realities of one social phenomenon. Therefore, data need to be collected through an insider's perspective since "[t]hose who have directly experienced the phenomenon under investigation are in the best position to enhance an understanding of its realities and, in critical realist terms, its actualities" (Killion & Fisher, 2018, p. 15). This paradigm was thus considered necessary for understanding how multiple realities and conceptions of prejudiced attitudes and discrimination are subjectively constructed by gay tourists. An interpretive approach was also adopted as it has proved to be fruitful in understanding in-depth the various travel and leisure experiences from the perspective of gay people themselves (Herrera & Scott, 2005; Monterrubio, 2021).

Sexual orientation, particularly one that differs from heterosexuality, is a sensitive topic; as a result, homosexual participants may be more reluctant to participate in research (Hughes, 2000). Previous research has demonstrated that small samples of gay people can be quite productive and effective in meeting exploratory scopes of research (Monterrubio, 2021). Bearing this in mind, ten in-depth interviews with men, self-identified as gay, who had travelled within and/or outside the country were undertaken in Mexico in 2021. Participants were recruited through snowball sampling. This technique is particularly useful when the researcher faces difficulties reaching participants because of the lack of formal or informal network connections (Jennings, 2001). Participants had to be at least 18 years old, self-identify as gay men, and, under their own conceptions and subjectivity, have experienced negative prejudice, discrimination, or violence during travel.

The instrument was an interview guide and included questions to identify the participants' travel patterns (e.g. frequency, destination, and company), conceptions of what a discriminatory act means to them, and how they have experienced prejudice, discrimination, and/or violence during their holidays. Due to the COVID-19 pandemic restrictions, most of the interviews were undertaken via telephone calls or online using Microsoft Teams and Zoom meeting platforms. Two interviews were administered in person at the participants' house and place of work.

All the interviews were audio recorded with participants' consent and later transcribed verbatim for analysis. Each interview was carefully reviewed to identify cases, descriptions, and concrete examples of prejudiced and discriminatory acts. Then such cases were grouped under the specific domains of prejudiced attitudes and discrimination. In order to ensure the participants' anonymity, pseudonyms are used in the following sections.

Findings

Motivations and destination choice

Participants' ages ranged from 23 to 52 years. Eight of them self-identified as gay while two as homosexual. As Hughes (2000) claims, sexual identity is a fluid concept largely defined at a very individual level. Only one of them had any children. All of them reported being unmarried, but seven were in a relationship. While some relationships were recent, others had lasted around 19 years. As seen later, being in a relationship may significantly influence how prejudice and discrimination acts are experienced by gay men. Almost all of the participants held a job in the private sector, and their jobs ranged from general employees to directors. One of them was a student and another worked for the government. With regard to their educational level, two had only a high school diploma, seven held a bachelor's degree, and one had a master's degree.

To contextualise experienced prejudiced attitudes, the interviewees' travel patterns were explored. Most of them take around three holiday trips during the year, although others may travel more often, mainly when both work and leisure purposes intersect. They prefer to travel during summer but also travel during other seasons of the year. Their trips last from three to four days, but some may travel for a whole week. Almost all of them travel for recreational purposes: relaxation, fun, escape from ordinary life or distress, entertainment, physical activity, and culture. This reveals that participants' holiday motivations are diverse.

For most of them, their favourite type of destination is the beach; they claim that the weather and the nightlife are the main pull motivational factors for destination choice. Popular gay destinations in Mexico, such as Cancun, Puerto Vallarta, and Acapulco, were reported among the most frequently visited. According to previous research in the country, such destinations are popular gay destinations not only among Mexican gay men (López et al., 2013) but are also popular among mainstream tourists. However, others also reported visiting places with natural, cultural, and archaeological attributes. For example, Javier, who is 42 years old and travels twice a year, claims, "I like archaeological zones. I like history and to learn how people used to live before". These results suggest that the types of destination among Mexican gay travellers are varied.

The instrument included a question regarding participants' perception as to whether their sexual orientation influences their destination choice and their travel patterns. All but one responded negatively, suggesting that the destinations they choose are not determined by their sexual identity. However, all participants reported going to gay places once at the destination. They said they tend to go to gay or gay-friendly bars, nightclubs, restaurants, and cafés during their holidays. Some of the reasons for visiting gay-friendly places were to experience freedom, socialisation with other gay men, fun, and comfort. Twenty-five-year-old Adrián said, "[a]t gay bars and night clubs, I find people with whom I feel identified because we share the same preferences and likes". Fernando, who travels on average 22 times a year, added, "I go mostly to gay bars and night clubs. They are more comfortable and I feel quite comfortable at those places". David, who is 25 and travels for leisure purposes, clearly states, "I go to those places simply to feel free". This result suggests that while gay men's main push and pull motivations are not strongly influenced by their sexual identity, they tend to search for places in which they can be gay, perhaps more freely, in a comfortable and relaxed environment once at the destination.

Perceived prejudice, discrimination, and violence

Considering that members of the GL community perceive discrimination differently (Ro & Olson, 2020), participants were asked about what they perceive as a discriminatory act in their everyday life. Their perceptions and experiences with regard to discriminatory acts were quite consistent. Some of them would consider it discriminatory, for example, to be denied any type of service, to not be let into an establishment, or to be delivered improper or differentiated service as a result of their sexual orientation. Others, however, associated discrimination directly with violence, both verbal and physical. Acts such as prying eyes, teasing, whispering, disrespecting, being pointed out, insults or even beatings were considered by most to be acts of discrimination that may take place in their ordinary life. Adrián, who says that his experiences with locals and tourists have generally been positive but has suffered acts of verbal violence, described it this way, "[discrimination is] any act of disrespect, physical or verbal aggression. For example, saying some type of words that seek to insult me because of my sexual preference or any physical aggression towards me caused by my sexual preferences".

While many of the participants reported their interactions and experiences with locals and other tourists as satisfactory and positive, they have also been the victims of prejudice during the holidays. Prejudiced acts – including discrimination and both verbal and physical abuse – have been experienced in some way during travel by all of the participants. The manifestations of prejudiced, discriminatory, or violent acts experienced in ordinary environments may be experienced during travel as well. Prejudiced acts were reported mostly as non-physical and these included looks, whispers, and overt insults, and they were experienced mainly when manifestations of affection took place in a public place, especially in the presence of other people. Terms such as *puto, maricón, puñal*, and *amanerado*, which are pejorative slang terms to refer to homosexuals, mainly effeminate homosexual males in Mexico (Domínguez-Ruvalcaba, 2009), are part of the verbal abuse participants have faced during their travel experiences within the country.

When asked if he has been a victim of discrimination or violence during one of his travel experiences, Roberto, a 29-year-old manager, replied:

> Never physically but verbally yes . . . when my partner and I started to travel, we did it by bus. Once the transport staff looked at us strangely, we asked them something and they responded very rudely. I remember that when we wanted to get our baggage at the destination, they said something like "*Putitos, mariconsitos, puñales*, get down your suitcases, I will help you because you are like girls". They used words that humiliate and leave you with a bitter taste during your travel experience.

Similarly, Javier, who is 42 and considers holidays as one of the few opportunities to enjoy, relax, and get rid of stress, reported:

> My partner and I were on a boat on a tour in Bacalar (southeast of Mexico). Then a man began to insult us, he told the service provider that he would not have allowed us to get on. He said that my partner and I were being disrespectful to him and his family. We replied that we were not doing anything wrong and that we also had the right to enjoy the trip. It did not go beyond a verbal attack.

Negative attitudes towards gay tourists may also take the form of physical violence. In such cases, we should note that they mostly come as a result of displays of affection in public, particularly when such acts take place in front of other males and families. They may come from both locals or other tourists. Three participants reported having experienced a physically violent act during at least one of their trips. For example, Tadeo, who is 52, recounted the experience in which he and his partner were holding hands in a bar when four people arrived and began to insult them; it resulted in a fight. According to the participant, the manager of the bar removed the participant and his partner, and those who initially insulted them were allowed to stay at the bar. Sebastián, who often travels with his partner, narrated a similar experience:

> I was on the beach with my partner, we were lying on the sand enjoying the beach and the scenery. Then a couple of foreigners approached, they were

drunk and spoke Spanish. For no reason, they began to insult us, they said "couple of *maricas, amanerados*". We just tried to ignore them, but the guys insisted on insulting us. So, we started to defend ourselves verbally, but they became aggressive. They threw bottles and shoes at us . . . it all ended badly.

Aggressions and discrimination are not exclusive to couples. They are also experienced when being with other gay friends. Braulio, who acknowledges that he sometimes cannot enjoy his travel experiences due to homophobic attitudes, experienced collective discrimination and violence this way:

I was in Acapulco with a couple of friends. We arrived at a very famous bar. At the beginning, the treatment was good, but later three boys began to insult us, to swear. They told us we were *putos*; that we didn't have to be in that place, and that's when a fight started. The security personnel supported us and tried to convince us not to leave, but the discomfort we were experiencing at that time was very great and that is why we ended up withdrawing from the place.

As evidenced earlier, some gay tourists tend to remain passive in terms of their reaction towards discrimination and violence, while others have actively reacted towards people's offences. Some have responded physically towards people's aggressions. This suggests that not all gay tourists are willing to remain silent or subordinated to homophobic acts.

In search of minimising risks, dangers, and possibilities of conflict, gay tourists have developed certain strategies to remain active in the tourism experience. A particular strategy, reported by participants, is disguising their homosexual identity, particularly effeminate and exhibitionist expressions and manifestations of affection with their partners. Braulio, who acknowledged that he cannot fully enjoy his travels due to acts of homophobia, said:

When I travel, I regularly have to hide my sexual orientation to go unnoticed, so that people do not realise that I am gay, to feel good about myself. During my travels, I must take care of myself because of my sexual orientation; in certain places I don't know what kind of people I am going to meet so I can suffer discrimination and insults, and that is not pleasant at all.

Forty-year-old Mariano admitted he has hidden his sexual orientation, not necessarily to avoid discrimination but as a form of respect to families and, in particular, children.

I think that there is discrimination when there is exhibitionism on the part of a person of the gay community. I have seen cases of discrimination, aggression, or things like that when someone is an exhibitionist, but if you behave properly, there is no problem.

Adrián claimed that during his holidays he does not disguise his sexual orientation but recognises that displays of affection towards his partner need to be limited to avoid conflict.

> I do keep respect by not showing much affection with my partner in public spaces. There are families and children and, therefore, it is not necessary to give great demonstrations of love. However, in a gay club this is different. The environment is more active and permissible, and I do not repress my displays of affection there.

Discussion

This study confirms that the motivations of male gay tourists are very similar to those of other forms of tourists (Hattingh, 2021): relaxation, fun, escape, and getting to know other cultures are among the main tourist motivations of the Mexican gay men that participated in this study. These motivations are driving factors that lead to the choice of destinations, in both gay and mainstream tourism. However, the choice of diverse destinations, many of them visited by families and mainstream tourists, places gay tourists in heteronormalised spaces that represent a threat not only for the enjoyment of travelling but also for the construction or reinforcement of their individual and collective gay identity.

In this way, the general idea that tourism is an escape from the restrictions imposed by heteronormativity and an opportunity to express gay identity (Vorobjovas-Pinta, 2018) is not always true. Although there seems to be a growing political and social acceptance of homosexuality, many mainstream tourist spaces – particularly those in which heterosexuality is the norm – are settings where prejudicial attitudes, including manifestations such as discrimination and violence, are part of the experience of gay travellers. Although the participants were not explicitly asked if their experiences of discrimination and violence differed according to the type of space (i.e. gay/non-gay), it seems that prejudice attitudes towards gay tourists are more recurrent in heteronormalised places, that is, in places that are not necessarily popular among gay tourists. In some sociocultural contexts, where homosexuality is still frowned upon and even punishable, heteronormalised tourist spaces can pose significant risks and threats to gay tourists. For some people belonging to sexual and gender diversity, avoiding travel and staying at home means greater security (Monterrubio et al., 2020). As Tadeo mentions, "Here in my town, people see me as normal, but when I go further afield, people call me *puto*. They see me badly".

This study revealed that not all gay men experience discriminatory acts in tourism in the same way. Within gay tourism, there are factors that increase the likelihood of discrimination and violence. This study found that, on the one hand, expressions of affection between gay men in public spaces dominated by heterosexuality increase the risks of being verbally or physically assaulted. These findings then suggest that the benefits of tourism can be achieved mostly by gay men who travel alone or at least who do not show their affection publicly in destinations dominated by heteronormativity. Thus, tourism in mostly heterosexual spaces – which are the vast majority in Mexico and around the world – continues to be only aspirational for many gay men.

Despite the restrictions imposed by heteronormalised tourist spaces, gay men do not always give up tourist trips. Gay travellers are active subjects who react to institutional or social restrictions during their travels. Some of them seek and implement strategies to continue being a part of tourism. Hiding their sexual orientation and avoiding displays of homosexual affection are strategies that allow many gay men to participate in tourism, particularly in destinations where heterosexuality is the norm. This is consistent with Gao's (2021) conclusion that due to social disapproval, some gay men prefer not to travel openly as gay. While this allows them to have access to the benefits of tourism and, above all, reduces the possibilities of discrimination and violence, it must be recognised that it is at the cost of ceasing to be themselves, of denying their identity, and, thereby, of denying their own being. Therefore, the participation of gay men in many destinations is possible as long as it is done as established by heteronormativity.

Conclusion

This research explored prejudice, discrimination, and violent acts as experienced and perceived by gay men during holidays. This was done within a sociocultural context in which homosexuality is still, to some extent, structurally and socially condemned and has been largely excluded from gay tourism studies worldwide.

Based on the empirical evidence obtained, the study concludes that although male gay tourists may visit a wide variety of destinations, their tourist experiences are not free from prejudice and discrimination. Many of the destinations they visit are spaces governed by heteronormativity that require avoiding displays of affection between homosexual couples. Gay or gay-friendly spaces are spaces that, in minimal quantities, offer the option of openly being who they really are. In fact, some gay destinations in Mexico are indeed spaces that do allow gay men to form an identity and experience social inclusion (Bailey, 2021). However, in the larger context of mainstream destinations, gay men's participation in tourism is conditional on not being gay, denying their identity, and therefore denying their existence.

Despite its limitation in terms of the type of sampling adopted, this study contributes to current research by revealing the experiences of gay tourism in non-Western countries (Hattingh, 2021). However, many issues remain unknown. If we consider that certain subgroups tend to be more stigmatised and discriminated against by other members of the gay community (Taywaditep, 2002), the discrimination and violence that gay men experience from other members of the LGBT community during their travels also need to be studied. This will allow us to know how tourism is experienced by the most stigmatised members of group who already discriminated against.

References

Andrade, H., Breda, Z., & Dinis, G. (2021). Is Porto a gay-friendly travel destination? A tourism supply analysis. In O. Vorobjovas-Pinta (Ed.), *Gay tourism. New perspectives* (pp. 185–200). Channel View Publications.

Bailey, E. G. (2021). Is gay tourism more than tourism? A case study of Puerto Vallarta, Mx. *Humanity & Society*. https://doi.org/10.1177/01605976211014013

BBC News. (2019, April 26). *Bolsonaro: Brazil must not become "gay tourism paradise"*. www.bbc.com/news/world-latin-america-48062075, 24/08/21

Beck, E. J., Espinosa, K., Ash, T., Wickham, P., Barrow, C., Massiah, E., Alli, B., & Nunez, C. (2017). Attitudes towards homosexuals in seven Caribbean countries: Implications for an effective HIV response. *AIDS Care*, *29*(12), 1557–1566. https://doi.org/10.1080/09540121.2017.1316355

Chambers, D. (2008). A postcolonial interrogation of attitudes toward homosexuality and gay tourism: The Case of Jamaica. In M. Daye, D. Chambers, & S. Roberts (Eds.), *New perspectives in Caribbean tourism* (pp. 94–114). Routledge.

Clift, S., & Forrest, S. (1999). Gay men and tourism: Destinations and holiday motivations. *Tourism Management*, *20*(5), 615–625. https://doi.org/10.1016/S0261-5177(99)00032-1

CMI. (2019). *24th annual LGBTQ tourism & hospitality survey*. Community Marketing & Insights. Retrieved August 17, 2021, from https://cmi.info/documents/temp/CMI_24th-LGBTQ-Travel-Study-Report2019.pdf

Cohen, T. R., Hall, D. L., & Tuttle, J. (2009). Attitudes toward stereotypical versus counterstereotypical gay men and lesbians. *Journal of Sex Research*, *46*, 1–8. http://dx.doi.org/10.1080/00224490802666233

Conapred. (2019). *Encuesta sobre discriminación por motivos de orientación sexual e identidad de género 2018*. Resumen ejecutivo. Retrieved September 9, 2021, from www.gob.mx/cms/uploads/attachment/file/473668/Resumen_Ejecutivo_ENDOSIG_16-05_2019.pdf

Cox, M. (2002). The long-haul out of the closet: The journey from smalltown to boystown. In S. Clift, M. Luongo, & C. Callister (Eds.), *Gay tourism: Culture, identity and sex* (pp. 151–173). Continuum.

Dahl, S., & Barreto, A. M. (2021). Away from the mainstream: Motivations of travellers seeking alternative forms of LGBT travel. In O. Vorobjovas-Pinta (Ed.), *Gay tourism. New perspectives* (pp. 153–168). Channel View Publications.

Domínguez-Ruvalcaba, H. (2009). From fags to gays. Political adaptations and cultural translations in the Mexican gay liberation movement. In L. Egan & M. K. Long (Eds.), *Mexico reading the United States* (pp. 116–134). Vanderbilt University Press.

EFE. (2021, June 8). *Torturan y asesinan a joven homosexual en Cancún*. El Sol de México.

European Travel Commission. (2018). *Handbook on the lesbian, gay, bisexual, transgender and queer (LGBTQ) travel segment*. European Travel Commission. Retrieved August 17, 2021, from https://etc-corporate.org/uploads/reports/ETC-Handbook-on-LGBTQ-Travel-Segment.pdf

Flores, A. (2014). *National trends in public opinion on LGBT rights in the United States*. The Williams Institute.

Gao, X. (2021). (Re)discovering Chinese lesbian and gay travel. In O. Vorobjovas-Pinta (Ed.), *Gay tourism. New perspectives* (pp. 89–102). Channel View Publications

Hattingh, C. (2021). Understanding African LGBT traveller motivations: A non-Western perspective. In O. Vorobjovas-Pinta (Ed.), *Gay tourism. New perspectives* (pp. 67–88). Channel View Publications.

Hattingh, C., Spencer, J. P., & Venske, E. (2011). Economic impact of special interest tourism on Cape Town: A case study of the 2009 Mother City queer project: Sport and tourism. *African Journal for Physical Health Education, Recreation and Dance*, *17*(3), 380–398. http://dx.doi.org/10.4314/ajpherd.v17i3.71090

Herrera, S. L., & Scott, D. (2005). "We gotta get out of this place!" Leisure travel among gay men living in a small city. *Tourism Review International*, *8*(3), 249–262. https://doi.org/10.3727/154427205774791564

Hogg, M. A., & Vaughan, G. M. (2008). *Social Psychology*. Pearson.

Hughes, H. (1997). Holidays and homosexual identity. *Tourism Management*, *18*(1), 3–7. https://doi.org/10.1016/S0261-5177(96)00093-3

Hughes, H. (2002). Gay men's holiday destination choice: A case of risk and avoidance. *International Journal of Travel Research*, *4*, 299–312. https://doi.org/10.1002/jtr.382

Hughes, H. (2006). *Pink tourism: Holidays of gay men and lesbians*. CABI Publishing.

Hughes, H., Monterrubio, J. C., & Miller, A. (2010). "Gay" tourists and host community attitudes. *International Journal of Tourism Research*, *12*(6), 774–786. https://doi.org/10.1002/jtr.792

Hughes, H. L. (2000). Gay men's holidays. Profit, sex, and identity. *Téoros. Revue de Recherche en Tourisme*, *19*(2), 22–27. https://doi.org/10.7202/1071960ar

Hughes, H. L. (2005). A gay tourism market reality or illusion, benefit or burden? *Journal of Quality Assurance in Hospitality & Tourism*, *5*(2–4), 57–74. https://doi.org/10.1300/J162v05n02_04

Human Rights Watch. (2013). *LGBT rights*. Human Rights Watch. Retrieved August 24, 2021, from www.hrw.org/topic/lgbt-rights

ILGA. (2020). *State-sponsored homophobia 2020: Global legislation overview update*. Retrieved August 24, 2021, from https://ilga.org/downloads/ILGA_World_State_Sponsored_Homophobia_report_global_legislation_overview_update_December_2020.pdf

Jennings, G. (2001). *Tourism research*. Wiley.

Killion, L., & Fisher, R. (2018). Ontology, epistemology: Paradigms and parameters for qualitative approaches to tourism research. In W. Hillman & K. Radel (Eds.), *Qualitative methods in tourism research* (pp. 1–28). Channel View Publications.

Korflür, M., Royo Vela, M., & Ruiz Molina, M. E. (2006). The gay tourism market: A study in Catalonia. *Estudios Turísticos*, *167*, 103–129.

Lawler, S. (2008). *Identity. Sociological perspectives*. Polity Press.

López, J. A. (2017). Los derechos LGBT en México: acción colectiva a nivel subnacional. *European Review of Latin American and Caribbean Studies*, *104*, 69–88. http://doi.org/10.18352/erlacs.10234

López, Á., & Van Broeck, A. M. (2013). *Turismo y sexo en México: cuerpos masculinos en venta y experiencias homoeróticas. Una perspectiva multidisciplinaria*. UNAM.

Markwell, K. (2021). Foreword. In O. Vorobjovas-Pinta (Ed.), *Gay tourism. New perspectives* (pp. xiii–xvi). Channel View Publications.

Marr, R. (2021, July 19). Gay man has jaw "destroyed" with hammer in brutal attack. *MetroWeekly*. Retrieved August 24, 2021, from www.metroweekly.com/2021/07/gay-man-has-jaw-destroyed-with-hammer-in-brutal-attack/

Medina, A. (2005, December 22). Discriminan y golpean a pareja gay en hotel de 5 estrellas en Los Cabos. *La Jornada*. www.jornada.com.mx/2005/12/22/index.php?section=sociedad&article=046n1soc

Monterrubio, C. (2019). Tourism and male homosexual identities: Directions for sociocultural research. *Tourism Review*, *74*(5), 1058–1069. https://doi.org/10.1108/TR-08-2017-0125

Monterrubio, C. (2021). The significance of gay tourism spaces for local gay men: Empirical evidence from Mexico. In O. Vorobjovas-Pinta (Ed.), *Gay tourism. New perspectives* (pp. 34–51). Channel View Publications.

Monterrubio, C., Rodríguez Madera, S. L., & Pérez, J. (2020). Trans women in tourism: Motivations, constraints and experiences. *Journal of Hospitality and Tourism Management*, *43*, 169–178. https://doi.org/10.1016/j.jhtm.2020.04.009

Ong, F., Vorobjovas-Pinta, O., & Lewis, C. (2020). LGBTIQ+identities in tourism and leisure research: A systematic qualitative literature review. *Journal of Sustainable Tourism*, 1–24. https://doi.org/10.1080/09669582.2020.1828430

Poria, Y., & Tailor, A. (2001). "I am not afraid to be gay when I'm on the net": Minimising social risk for lesbian and gay consumers when using the internet. *Journal of Travel and Tourism Marketing*, *11*(2/3), 127–142. https://doi.org/10.1300/J073v11n02_07

Pritchard, A., Morgan, N., & Sedgley, D. (2002). In search of lesbian space? The experience of Manchester's gay village. *Leisure Studies*, *21*(2), 105–123. https://doi.org/10.1080/02614360110121551

Pritchard, A., Morgan, N. J., Sedgley, D., Khan, E., & Jenkins, A. (2000). Sexuality and holiday choices: Conversations with gay and lesbian tourists. *Leisure studies*, *19*(4), 267–282. https://doi.org/10.1080/02614360050118832

Ram, Y., Kama, A., Mizrachi, I., & Hall, C. M. (2019). The benefits of an LGBT-inclusive tourist destination. *Journal of Destination Marketing & Management*, *14*, 100374. https://doi.org/10.1016/j.jdmm.2019.100374

Ro, H., & Olson, E. (2020). Gay and lesbian customers' perceived discrimination and identity management. *International Journal of Hospitality Management*, *84*. https://doi.org/10.1016/j.ijhm.2019.102319

Rosenbaum, M. S., Ramirez, G. C., & Kim, K. (2020). From overt to covert: Exploring discrimination against homosexual consumers in retail stores. *Journal of Retailing and Consumer Services*, *59*, 102426. https://doi.org/10.1016/j.jretconser.2020.102

Secretaría de Turismo. (2018). *Turismo LGBT*. Retrieved August 24, 2021, from www.sectur.gob.mx/gobmx/wp-content/uploads/2018/05/TURISMO-LGBT.pdf

Spartacus. (2021). *Gay guide Mexico*. https://spartacus.gayguide.travel/goingout/north america/mexico

Taywaditep, K. J. (2002). Marginalization among the marginalized. *Journal of Homosexuality*, *42*(1), 1–28. https://doi.org/10.1300/j082v42n01_01

United Nations World Tourism Organization. (2017). *Second global report on LGBT tourism*. World Tourism Organization. Retrieved August 18, 2021, from www.hospitalitynet.org/file/152008162.pdf

United Nations World Tourism Organization. (2021). *International tourism highlights, 2020 edition*. https://doi.org/10.18111/9789284422456

Van Laer, K., & Janssens, M. (2011). Ethnic minority professionals' experiences with subtle discrimination in the workplace. *Human Relations*, *64*(9), 1203–1227. https://doi.org/10.1177/0018726711409263

Varillas, A. (2021, February 25). Policías de Tulum detienen a pareja gay por besarse en la playa. *El Universal*. www.eluniversal.com.mx/estados/policias-de-tulum-detienen-pareja-gay-por-besarse-en-la-playa

Vorobjovas-Pinta, O. (2018). Gay neo-tribes: Exploration of travel behaviour and space. *Annals of Tourism Research*, *72*, 1–10. https://doi.org/10.1016/j.annals.2018.05.008

Vorobjovas-Pinta, O. (Ed.). (2021). *Gay tourism. New perspectives*. Channel View Publications.

Waitt, G., & Markwell, K. (2006). *Gay tourism: Culture and context*. Routledge.

Wilson, A. (2019, June 6). LGBT tour operator faces death threats over Ethiopian trip. *The Guardian*. www.theguardian.com/travel/2019/jun/06/lgbt-tour-operator-faces-death-threats-over-ethiopia-trip

10 Doing gender well and differently

The case of women managers in tourism

Inês Carvalho and Carlos Costa

Introduction

Management, hierarchies, divisions of labour, and sexuality are usually gendered within organisations (Hearn, 2000), in that the "advantage and disadvantage, and control, action and emotion, meaning and identity are patterned through, and in terms of, a distinction between male and female, masculine and feminine" (Acker, 1990, p. 146). Organisations are not only gendered, but they reinforce gender differences, gender power relations, and the male-dominated gender order. Organisations are places where male power is produced and reproduced (Collinson & Hearn, 2005; Hearn & Collinson, 2006), and hierarchies in organisations are an expression of traditional gender power relations (Acker, 1988). Organisational processes influence how workers perceive themselves as gendered and have an impact on gender relations at many levels, as well as images and beliefs about men and women, masculine and feminine in society. For example, women do not correspond to the notion of the "ideal" unencumbered worker who has no imperatives outside the organisation (Acker, 2012).

Although women make up the majority of the tourism workforce worldwide, they tend to be concentrated at the bottom, while men are disproportionately represented in upper-level echelons (Carvalho et al., 2014). In tourism, a sharp horizontal and vertical segregation is underpinned by strong sociocultural barriers and traditional gender roles (Cave & Kilic, 2010). This inequality can still be observed despite the increase in women's participation in tourism higher education (Costa et al., 2012). In this context, it is relevant to study gender power relations in tourism management.

"Leadership" and "management" are not gender-neutral concepts but rather models that reflect the "male norm". Masculine images and values are so deeply embedded in managerial discourse and organisational practices that they often appear to be "normal" or even official ways of doing business in organisations (Collinson & Hearn, 1994; Hearn, 2010). This poses obstacles to women managers, who must struggle to be regarded as legitimate leaders. In fact, women who want to be perceived as credible leaders may face conflicting expectations concerning their gender role and their managerial role.

DOI: 10.4324/9781003255413-12

Mavin and Grandy's (2012) conceptualisation of doing gender "well" and "differently" is proposed as a useful tool to understand such contradictions of gender role expectations. For women, doing gender well means conforming to the expected (feminine) behaviour for their sexed bodies socially perceived as female, while doing gender differently corresponds to contradicting such gender role expectations, for example, in management styles. While men can act in congruence with their sex category, women have to find a balance between doing gender well and differently in order to be perceived as effective leaders. In other words, they must simultaneously meet gender role expectations (e.g. motherly and nurturing) and masculine constructions of leadership (e.g. risk-taking and ambitious) (Mavin & Grandy, 2012).

This study seeks to answer the following main question: "How do women managers in the tourism sector do or re-do gender in the different contexts of their lives?" The purpose of this study is to analyse how female top-level managers do, undo, or re-do gender and to what extent they are unsettling the gender binary in different contexts of their lives. The specific objectives include the following:

- Analysing the consequences of doing gender well and differently, specifically challenging or confirming both constructions of management and expectations of gender roles; and
- Analysing to what extent these women are opening up new possibilities for understanding and doing gender.

In-depth semi-structured interviews were carried out with 24 female senior managers in Portuguese hotels and travel businesses. Instead of focusing on similarities and differences between women and men as leaders, this study uses gender as an analytical category to understand the ambivalent, fluid, and contradictory nature of doing gender for women managers (Mavin & Grandy, 2012). It focuses on interviewees' multiple ways of "doing gender" and gendered constructions of management and leadership. Mavin and Grandy's (2012) conceptualisation of "doing gender well" and "doing gender differently" is used in order to understand how women confirm and/or challenge gender role expectations, as well as gendered constructions of management.

Literature review

Sex, gender, and the gender order

While "gender" is a term still in the making and its definitions are often contested, it has been mostly used to establish a distinction with the term "sex"'. In general terms, "sex" concerns the biological differences between men and women (e.g. genitalia or chromosomal typing) and involves the categorisation of people as either male or female based on biological criteria (Mavin & Grandy, 2012; Oakley, 1972). "Gender" refers to the sociocultural constructions of these biological differences, such as the different social roles that are attributed to women and men (i.e. "feminine" versus "masculine") (Oakley, 1972).

The concept of gender highlights that many of the differences between men and women are not strictly natural or biological but are also influenced by social, historical, and political processes (Hearn et al., 2012). Gender can change at different periods in history, since it depends on culture, ethnicity, religion, education, class, as well as on the geographic, economic, and political environment (Organisation for Economic Co-operation and Development, 1999). The importance of regarding gender as socially constructed is that femininity and masculinity are not seen as either absolute or true (Wahl, 2001). Hence, gender is not a consequence of our "essential" sexual nature. It is not a variable, a set of traits, a "natural" property, or a possession of individuals but rather a product of "social doings" (West & Zimmerman, 1987, p. 129), constructed and accomplished in everyday interactions with others.

Gender also signifies relationships of power (Scott, 1986). In doing gender, men do dominance while women do deference (Goffman, 1967, as cited in West & Zimmerman, 1987). Men are positioned as the norm (Alvesson & Billing, 1997) while women are conceived as the "Other" (Butler, 2004). This serves to maintain a hierarchical structure between the sexes (Patterson et al., 2012b). Connell (1987) uses the phrase "gender order" to refer to "a historically constructed pattern of power relations between women and men and definitions of femininity and masculinity" in society as a whole (pp. 98–99). The gender order is not immanent in biology, but it is rather a historical response to human reproduction (Connell, 1987). Although gender differences are constructed, they are used to reinforce the idea of "essential" differences between women and men. This legitimates hierarchical arrangements and "naturalises" the gender order. The gender stratification system is bolstered and perpetuated by its apparent legitimacy (Chafetz, 1988). Organisations also have a gender order that reflects the power balance between men and women. This gender order is related to the gender order of society and cannot be separated from it because both reproduce each other (Wahl & Holgersson, 2003).

Doing gender well and differently

For West and Zimmerman (1987), doing gender is unavoidable. Doing gender consists in managing what is perceived to be expressions of feminine and masculine "natures": it is "the activity of managing situated conduct in light of normative conceptions of attitudes and activities appropriate for one's sex category" (West & Zimmerman, 1987, p. 127). Doing gender can be understood as conforming to gender role expectations of appropriate behaviour for one's perceived sex category, reflecting the sexual division of labour and the gender hierarchy of society. The outcome of "doing gender" is seen either as gender-appropriate or as gender-inappropriate, as individuals fail or succeed in meeting gendered societal expectations. While Butler (2004) claims that gender can, and should, be undone, several authors contend that this belief is over-optimistic and simplistic (Mavin &

Grandy, 2011; West & Zimmerman, 2009). Rather than undone, gender should be *redone* or *done differently* (Mavin & Grandy, 2012; West & Zimmerman, 2009).

Mavin and Grandy (2011, 2012) propose a conceptualisation of doing gender "well" and "differently" to better understand such contradictions in gender role expectations. Doing gender "well" can be described as:

> For a woman to do gender well or appropriately, as evaluated against and accountable to her sex category, she performs expected feminine behaviour through a body that is socially perceived to be female. For a man, to do gender well or appropriately, as evaluated against and accountable to his sex category, he performs expected masculine behaviour, through a body that is socially perceived to be male. In that way, there is congruence and balance between the perceived sex category and gender behaviour, and femininity (or masculinity) is validated.
>
> (Mavin & Grandy, 2011, pp. 3–4)

Hence, doing gender well means conforming to expected (masculine or feminine) behaviours for one's own sexed body (socially perceived as male or female), while doing gender differently corresponds to contradicting such gender role expectations. While individuals can do gender differently and unsettle gender binaries by enacting masculinity or femininity, respectively, they remain constrained and restricted by gender binaries (Mavin & Grandy, 2012). The understanding of doing gender well and differently cannot be separated from sex category, since it is according to the external mark of sex that someone is perceived as doing gender, either well or differently (Mavin & Grandy, 2011, 2012). Hence, the body cannot be ignored in the constructions of gender, because it is an integral part of doing gender. West and Zimmerman's (1987) conceptualisation of gender was revolutionary because it reframed gender as a variable and dynamic process and no longer as a fixed status (Jeanes et al., 2011).

Women managers "doing gender" well and differently

Although leadership is usually defined from a gender-blind or gender-neutral perspective (as if gender was irrelevant for its definition), nowadays several scholars agree that the typical notion of leadership has been constructed as masculine and mirrors the male norm (Due Billing & Alvesson, 2000; Patterson et al., 2012b; Wahl, 1998). Management and leadership positions are masculinised by being constructed around male norms in such a way that it becomes hard to separate between leadership and men (Eagly & Carli, 2008; Mavin et al., 2014).

This way, "masculinity and men are permitted the luxury of invisibility" (Patterson et al., 2012a, p. 402), while women and all that is non-masculine become visible as the "Other" (Butler, 2004; Patterson et al., 2012a). Therefore, women might be regarded as illegitimate or less credible leaders (Patterson et al., 2012b). While male managers are more likely to describe their own management style as "being themselves" (Wahl, 2010), women have to make more effort to do gender differently in order to be recognised or taken seriously. They need to "build" confidence and reputation, instead of being assumed as being confident and reputable, since confidence and reputation are masculine traits (Patterson et al., 2012b). While women's gender identity does not reinforce their power within the organisation, male leadership and male gender identity confirm and boost each other (Wahl, 1998). However, the same behaviours that are perceived as positive when demonstrated by male leaders (e.g. assertiveness and ambition) may be perceived as negative when demonstrated by a woman in the same position (Mavin, 2009), because they contrast with stereotypical understandings of women and "create incongruity with their socially perceived female body" (Patterson et al., 2012a, p. 398).

While women in service-based work and female-typed jobs (e.g. tourism jobs) are regarded as good workers when they do gender well – by showing friendliness, politeness, and dressing in a feminine way – women leaders need to find the right balance of doing gender well and differently in order to be perceived as effective leaders, due to the incongruency between gender and management roles (Mavin & Grandy, 2012). Wahl (1998) noted that women perceive a conflict between being feminine and being business-like. While women who aspire to become managers are criticised for their lack of authority, women managers are criticised for being too masculine. In both cases, the result is that women are regarded as less suitable for management work (Wahl, 1998, 2001). Hence, in order to be perceived as credible leaders, women may need to balance feminine and masculine expressions in their clothing, language, and behaviour (Wahl, 1998).

Mavin and Grandy's (2011, 2012) conceptualisation of doing gender "well" and "differently" is a useful tool to understand such contradictions in management and gender role expectations. While male leaders can act in congruence with their gender category, women who want to be perceived as effective leaders need to find the right balance between doing gender well and differently. They simultaneously need to meet gender role expectations (e.g. motherly and nurturing) and masculine constructions of leadership (e.g. risk-taking, ambitious (Mavin & Grandy, 2012).

By analysing how gender is done well and differently, it is possible to understand senior women's experiences and how their simultaneous enactments of masculinities and femininities can disrupt the gender order and unsettle gender binaries over time (Mavin & Grandy, 2012). This framework may unveil some hidden aspects of gender and highlight how the gender binary contributes to maintaining existing practices and values. This understanding of gender recognises individual agency to accept or reject gender social role expectations while acknowledging that women remain constrained by the gender binary (Mavin & Grandy, 2012; Patterson et al., 2012b).

Despite criticism on the concept of gender (Hearn et al., 2012), it is useful as an analytic category for theorising the positions and relationships between men and women in society. The idea that gender is not a result of our "essential" nature but rather a social construction is central to the present study. Gender, here, is understood as a dynamic process, which is manifested in daily interactions, discourse, laws, and institutional practices. Socially constructed gender differences "naturalise" the gender order. The belief underlying this investigation is that although the purpose of "undoing gender" seems overly optimistic, it may be possible to unsettle gender binaries and challenge the gender order, over time. Capturing how gender is done well and differently also allows for the recognition of the ambivalent, fluid, and contradictory nature of doing gender and offers new possibilities for the gender binary to be disrupted (Mavin & Grandy, 2011, 2012).

Methodology

The data presented here reflect the results of the qualitative part of a broader mixed-methods study. The main research aim of that study was to examine how women reach top-level management positions in tourism and how they are affected by multiple gendered contexts in their lives. In this study, we included both women climbing the corporate ladder in large businesses and women in leading positions in small- and medium-sized enterprises.

Semi-structured in-depth interviews were carried out with 24 top-level female managers in hotels, travel agencies, and tour operators in Portugal (Table 10.1). These women provided details about their experiences with gender issues

Table 10.1 Research participants.

Interviewee (Fictitious Names)	Status in Employment	Sector	Children
Ana	Employee	Hotel	Yes
Andreia	Employer	Hotel	Yes
Beatriz	Employee	Travel business	Yes
Cláudia	Employer	Hotel	No, but would like
Cristina	Employer	Travel business	No
Diana	Employer	Hotel	Yes
Dulce	Employer	Travel business	Yes
Francisca	Employee	Hotel	Yes
Graça	Employee	Hotel	No
Helena	Employee	Hotel	Yes
Laura	Employer	Travel business	Yes
Luísa	Employee	Hotel	No
Margarida	Employee	Hotel	No, but would like
Maria	Employer	Travel business	Yes
Matilde	Employee	Travel business	Yes
Natália	Employer	Travel business	No
Paula	Employer	Travel business	Yes
Raquel	Employee	Hotel	Yes (pregnant)
Rita	Employee	Travel business	Yes
Sara	Employer	Hotel	Yes
Sofia	Employer	Travel business	Yes
Sónia	Employee	Hotel	Yes
Tânia	Employer	Travel business	Yes
Teresa	Employee (also employer)	Hotel	None

throughout their careers. They were selected on the basis of stratified purposeful sampling combined with snowball sampling. Hence, the sample reflected the distribution of women managers across several categories of business dimensions. Interviews were carried out face-to-face, by phone, or Skype. The sampling method used sets limits on the generalisation of the results to a broader population.

Thematic analysis was combined with elements of narrative analysis in order to capture the fluidity of individual experiences. While thematic analysis searches for themes across the whole dataset, narrative analysis searches for themes within each individual interview. Following each woman's individual life story could jeopardise women's anonymity. However, a sense of continuity across individuals is not retained (Braun & Clarke, 2006), and consistencies and contradictions in women's discourses could not be fully grasped with thematic analysis alone. Therefore, some elements of narrative analysis were introduced to capture the fluidity of individual experiences. NVivo was used to organise the themes for subsequent analysis. For ethical reasons, the identity of the interviewees was masked during the transcription stage, and they were attributed fictitious names, which are used in the present article.

In this investigation, validity is understood as the result of the reflexivity of the researcher and the dialogical intersubjectivity through communicative validation, with both other researchers and the research participants (Kvale & Brinkmann, 2009). Our view is that the understanding of a phenomenon is always partial and that there is no single truth (Lincoln et al., 2011). Participants' accounts were taken as evidence of the meanings experienced by them. In order to increase the reliability of the study, some research participants were interviewed twice while others were sent follow-up questions by e-mail to better clarify their experiences.

Findings

"Doing gender" and "doing management" well and differently

Doing gender differently may challenge traditional gender stereotypes and essentialist notions of women as inferior and hence contribute to disturbing the current gender order. Throughout the interviews, research participants revealed that they were aware of the stereotypical expectations of women as less competent, less confident, or weaker. Maria believed that opportunities are not the same since "a man arrives and rules"[1] and is assumed as competent from the beginning. Several participants shared this belief that women need to be very capable in order to be accepted, recognised, and regarded as equals. Therefore, they consider that women have to work harder, make more effort, show competence and availability, or be better than men in order to be as visible, credible, and as recognised as them. Only then can they reach the same position and earn the same respect and recognition:

> I think that the only way of a woman asserting herself, feeling less discriminated against, and more approved of, is to be successful and commit herself

to work, but this requires redoubled efforts, because . . . she'll always have that burden of . . . "she's a woman and may get pregnant".

(Cláudia)

Sara adds, "I have the feeling that sometimes it looks like we have to work more to prove we are as competent or more competent". Hence, women need to distance themselves from feminine stereotypes, such as weakness and lack of ability and confidence, to be perceived as effective and highly professional leaders.

Some women have managed to challenge the gender hierarchy by being determined and asserting their position in the organisation, by refusing to do minor tasks, or by not being afraid of being outspoken among men. Matilde acknowledges, "You need to work your way up, you need to elbow your way to the top". Hence, these women "do gender differently" by resorting to certain masculine behaviours, such as being more assertive, particularly at the beginning of their careers. Rita explains,

> When we really want to change something, we have to fight for it, we have to assert ourselves, and we have to present arguments that we're an added value for the company, or that they can really bet on us, that we can give as much as, or more than, a man.

However, doing gender differently is not always intentional. It may be a by-product of responding to heavy work requirements or trying to approximate oneself to the notion of the unencumbered "ideal" worker (Acker, 2012), who is constantly available to meet work demands. By effectively responding to these work requirements and expectations, they end up "doing gender differently", as expressed by Ana: "I love working here, my second home is [the hotel]. I spend more time here than at home. My home is to sleep and not much more, and to play a bit with my daughter. So, I feel fine here".

Doing gender differently may also be a result of women embracing adventures and risky challenges in their careers, thus unintentionally dismantling traditional gender role expectations. Some of these women consider it important to take risks, be adventurous, and accept challenges, not only for career advancement but also to maintain passion and avoid monotony. For example, some women make career decisions that decrease their earnings, because they were motivated by the challenge. This notion breaks with gender stereotype, in the sense that women are not just professionals, careerwise, they are also in it for the adventure.

In this way, by doing gender differently, either intentionally or unintentionally, women reject some of the traditional gender role expectations that hamper their external image as professional individuals.

> Women in management positions are still regarded in a less positive way, we need to assert ourselves to overcome that . . . I think it's a lot about having the required availability. But from the moment you show up, you have that

availability, and that you're willing to win and advance, that issue is overcome, and you're regarded as equal (Graça).

Maria adds,

> Only when they saw that I worked hard and seriously would they respect me ...... The oldest [men] ... still have that taboo and prejudice ... "is she competent?". Some never said this to me clearly, but almost indirectly ... "You, young lady, should be at home enjoying your son", like, go to the kitchen, pots and pans, and stuff. Many wouldn't do this openly anymore, but in an unconscious way we feel this, I felt this. ... Now I feel that I'm very respected, very acknowledged for my career, for my skills ... but it was hard to get here.

Doing gender differently challenges essentialist notions of men and women and disrupts stereotypes of women as inferior, unavailable, or more family-oriented. Therefore, it contributes to unsettling the gender binary.

However, doing gender differently does not defy traditional ways of doing management. In fact, the idea that women need to do gender differently to be perceived as efficient managers may, in some cases, reinforce the association between masculinity and management. Maria's case illustrates this:

> When you start having a lot of these meetings [with only or almost only men], it's good that you can talk with confidence about politics, or mobile phones, or light alloy wheels, mostly football results, otherwise you won't open your mouth during the first half-hour. And when you're in a position of strategic negotiation, this leaves you, from the beginning, in a weak bargaining position and weakens you during the negotiation. ... So, I had to learn ... I don't know anything about football, but I do check the results before these meetings. ... It's enough, I don't need to go much deeper than this.

The more entrenched the male culture is in their organisations, the more women feel that, in order to be recognised, they have to do gender differently by trying to speak "men's language" or by being more assertive and imposing themselves. Maria continues, "You have to be sure of yourself, and as a woman, either you get there and say 'I know what I'm doing here, I know more than you, even if you bend over backwards, you're not going to make it', otherwise, forget about it".

The interviewees' accounts suggest that women adopting typical masculine behaviours are more common in male-dominated organisations. In organisations where women are better represented at the top and where masculine values are less pervasive, women seem to have more room to defy the traditional ways of doing management and to do management differently by doing gender well (e.g. by using a "different" language, not allowing for sexist jokes, favouring the attainment of goals over presenteeism, or understanding employees' work-life balance needs). Francisca explains,

> I confess that in the team I work for and report to, all female directors in this department are also mothers, and perhaps for that reason they understand why you sometimes have to leave at seven sharp or half past six, or why you have to take your kid to the doctor, and therefore I don't feel any discrimination for having a baby.

Maria was critical of the way leadership is done and advocated that less emphasis should be put on availability and that "feminine traits" should be more valued. "Men think that those positions should be filled by someone with immense availability . . . and they underestimate our skills, our intuition, our sixth sense, our diplomacy". Hence, this is a claim for doing leadership differently. Having the freedom to "do gender well" challenges gendered and masculinised constructions of leadership. However, if organisations expect women to display certain feminine traits, this may lead to the reinforcement of gender stereotypes and constrain the possibilities of what women should be like as managers (e.g. "motherly" or "emotional labourers") (Due Billing & Alvesson, 2000). Women's management opportunities should not be constrained by expectations that they act specifically "as women".

Female entrepreneurs seemed to have more freedom to combine multiple ways of doing gender, as observed in Mavin and Grandy (2012) and Patterson et al. (2012a). Entrepreneurship may grant women more autonomy in the way they intertwine masculine and feminine behaviour. Being an entrepreneur allowed Diana to do management differently by doing gender well (e.g. by being feminine, kind, and nice). In fact, most women detached themselves from the stereotypical "unfeminine", "unemotional", and "workaholic" businesswoman.

The women entrepreneurs interviewed experienced greater fluidity between doing gender well and differently. For example, some entrepreneurs stated that their organisations had a "family-like" atmosphere where they could bring their children to work, and, thus, make the boundaries between the public and private spheres more fluid. Moreover, some of the interviewees who were entrepreneurs did not enjoy a period of maternal leave at home but kept involved in their businesses while nursing their children, since they found it hard to delegate their responsibilities. This confirms the idea that in women entrepreneurial-led organisations, there is greater acceptance of multiple ways of doing gender and greater opportunities for women to do gender well and differently, as also observed by Mavin and Grandy (2012) and Patterson et al. (2012a).

For most research participants, clothing is important in order to look, simultaneously, professional and feminine but not the "wrong kind of feminine", and in part to control sexual advances from men in work-related contexts Maria says

> I have to be very careful . . . because if I show a bit more cleavage or something more provoking in some situations, like tougher negotiations, it's complicated. Because he won't be listening to what I'm telling him, it gives rise to other types of conversation, you see. . . . you have to cut out all these distractions because you need to be fully focused.

Hence, female managers balance feminine and masculine expressions in their behaviour in order to be regarded as effective and credible leaders, as also observed by Patterson et al. (2012a) and Wahl (1998).

Doing gender "well" and "differently" at the intersection of work and family

It is also important to investigate the conceptualisation of "doing gender well" and "doing gender differently" at the intersection of women's family and work spheres. Most women regarded themselves as both leaders and mothers, thus challenging the idea that management is incompatible with motherhood and opening up opportunities for doing gender well and differently.

The fact that most participants wanted to "have it all" (i.e. a family and a career) shows how women combined doing gender well (by raising a family) with doing gender differently (by investing in their careers). This may contribute to slowly dismantling the notion of the "ideal worker" as someone who is unencumbered by family responsibilities and totally available for organisational commitments (Acker, 2012). However, although doing gender differently is a way to highlight women's professionalism, it may lead to feelings of guilt when women's professional and caregiving roles clash. Rita explains,

> I can tell you about one that affected me a lot, . . . when I became a mum . . . I was already in operations management at the time, and I had to split my maternity leave into two parts. I had to do the high season, and I had to leave my little daughter, only two months old, and stop breast-feeding.

Beatriz adds, "I had to fight a lot . . . I didn't dedicate myself [to my children] the way I should have".

Spousal support is also a factor in a woman's ability to do gender differently. A minority of women have husbands or partners that not only understand their wives' career demands but also support them and share responsibilities at home, which is crucial to enabling their careers. In these "companionate marriages" (Hearn et al., 2008), both partners did gender differently and challenged the gendered norm. In a few cases, gender roles were somewhat reversed at home, with husbands or partners being less career-oriented or having greater work flexibility than the women interviewed. Ana clarifies, "My child was very sick but I've never missed a day of work. . . . My husband can miss work while I can't, especially if we're talking about summer, I can't".

Concerning the participants whose husbands did not share tasks equally at home, the most frequent response to the unequal division of tasks was resignation.

> We [women] always do most [of the housework], there's no way . . . we are going to be labelled as cleaners for the rest of our lives. It's never going to be the man . . . but I don't have any hard feelings
>
> (Laura).

Six participants were divorced, some of them due to their husband's lack of acceptance of their careers. As Beatriz explains, "My husband started not to accept that I spent so many hours working. So, that was a moment of disharmony that ended in divorce".

Discussion and conclusion

The conceptualisation of doing gender as doing gender "well" and "differently" proposed by Mavin and Grandy (2011) is an adequate tool for a better understanding of the paradoxes inherent in women's ways of "doing gender" and "doing management". This conceptualisation is useful to understand how research participants confirm and/or contradict gendered constructions of management and gender role expectations in the different contexts of their lives. It also allows for the recognition of the fluid and paradoxical nature of doing gender.

Doing gender differently is a way for women exercising their agency, either intentionally or unintentionally. One can think of agency as the possibilities for resistance, subversion, and remodelling of gender identities in emancipatory ways (McNay, 2000). By doing gender differently, women disturb the gender binary and traditional gender stereotypes, thus challenging essentialist notions of women as inferior, unadventurous, unavailable, or more family-oriented. This is in line with previous studies (e.g. Liu et al., 2020). Doing gender differently may be particularly important at the beginning of their careers, until women prove their competence, as also observed by Patterson et al. (2012b). However, doing gender differently may reinforce the association of management with masculinity and leave the "male norm" unquestioned. In fact, women in organisations with a more entrenched male culture are more likely to feel that they have to be strict or authoritarian in order to be acknowledged. In contrast, in companies with a weaker male culture, women have more room to defy the traditional ways of doing management and do management differently by doing gender well.

Women entrepreneurs also seem to have greater autonomy to do gender well and differently, which corroborates previous literature (Mavin & Grandy, 2012; Patterson et al., 2012a). Patterson et al. (2012a) observed that descriptions of entrepreneurial leadership begin to establish a bridge between descriptions of masculinity and femininity. In contrast, masculine hegemony has permeated literature of its founding disciplines, that is, entrepreneurship and leadership. Although masculinities are still preponderant, the recognition of the need of intertwining masculinities and femininities is a sign of progress, from a gender perspective (Patterson et al., 2012a).

Whereas having the freedom to do gender well may challenge gendered and masculinised constructions of leadership, the expectation that women managers behave like women may constrain their possibilities as managers and construe them as "motherly" or "emotional labourers" (Due Billing & Alvesson, 2000, p. 155). The construction of an alternative feminine notion of leadership essentialises gender as biologically determined, reinforces gender stereotypes, limits women to behave specifically as women, and does not challenge the male norm or the gender social order.

Doing gender well and differently in the family context (i.e. raising a family while simultaneously investing in one's career) may contribute to unsettling the notion of the "ideal worker" (Acker, 2012) as someone with no family responsibilities. However, this does not erase the fundamental incompatibility between both roles, since doing gender differently for the sake of professionalism may, in some circumstances, leave women feeling guilty for having prioritised their work over their family responsibilities, even when they are in "companionate" partnerships and marriages.

According to Bosak and Sczesny (2011), people's beliefs about the erosion of perceived incongruity between women and leaders may undermine gender roles in the future. Combining multiple ways of doing gender may not only reinforce but also disturb both gender and management-leadership stereotypes. The findings of this study suggest that women have some sort of individual agency to accept or reject gender social role expectations (Patterson et al., 2012b). Although women remain constrained by the gender binary (Mavin & Grandy, 2012) and cannot truly "undo" gender, they can still unsettle gender stereotypes, which may, over time, challenge the gender order. Capturing how gender is done well and differently allows for the recognition of the fluid and paradoxical nature of doing gender. Instead of becoming entangled in the paradox, it is important to highlight the bringing together of individual agency with social structures to allow for a constant reflection on ambiguity and contradictions. This might be helpful to disturb the hierarchical nature of the gender binary, as argued by Brink and Stobbe (2009).

Over time, it is essential that mentality and cultural changes take place. This can be achieved not only through awareness-raising practices but also by setting an example. Women's balanced representation in political and decision-making bodies is crucial to achieve change and undo gender prejudice and gender stereotypes. Education can also be an important tool to impart such values to citizens from a young age. Other measures could be creating mentorship programmes for women tourism professionals, giving more visibility to successful women to speak at tourism events and ensuring that women are well-represented on public-private tourism councils, committees, and advisory boards (United Nations World Tourism Organization, 2011). Esping-Andersen (2005) contends that if men had a more "female" life cycle by also having interruptions in their careers, employers' gender-asymmetric expectations would be neutralised, and gender-specific discrimination in the labour market would be weakened. Hence, policy measures such as shared parental leave could approximate men and women's pattern of career breaks and ways of "doing gender".

Although the tourism industry in Portugal is feminised (Carvalho et al., 2014) and, to a certain extent, may "open doors" for women, it is still far from being a truly "women-friendly" industry. It is important to raise gender awareness of the stakeholders in this field so that it is possible to see through the apparent gender neutrality of the sector and gradually attain structural and cultural changes in organisations and improvements in terms of gender equality. Making subtle processes visible may have an impact on the daily workings of organisations, as observed by Kantola (2008). In fact, high visibility and low legitimacy of inequalities may enhance the possibilities for change while social movements may contribute to both high visibility and low legitimacy (Acker, 2006). Stainback et al. (2010) argue that changes towards equality are more likely to be linked to pressures on organisational fields than to direct pressures on specific workplaces. There is evidence of "mimetic isomorphism" across industries, which, through inertia, leads to the institutionalisation of gender and other social inequalities. Hence, it is important to act, not only at the level of individual workplaces but also at the industry level (Stainback et al., 2010, p. 240).

It is also crucial to monitor the evolution of women's representation in leadership positions in the tourism sector, as well as their distribution across all hierarchical levels. Wider sectorial organisations, such as the United Nations World Tourism Organization or the World Travel and Tourism Council, could also be involved in such actions. In addition, it is important to approach power structures and engage in a "quantitative" discourse about the percentage of women on boards or collect data as a goal in itself (Lombardo & Meier, 2007). Therefore, it is important to include gender experts and civil society actors in the change process.

Finally, although gendered prejudice spans across organisational borders and cannot be easily pinpointed in society and within the interdependencies with other organisations, organisations are a crucial place where gender power relations are enacted and gendered images are produced and reproduced. Hence, tourism organisations can either be places where inequalities are reproduced, or "microcircles" of resistance where gendered identities become more fluid, gendered power is more equally redistributed, and gendering processes are challenged. For example, it is possible to confront the way work is being done. Practices, such as scheduling meetings outside normal working hours or carrying out important negotiations outside the workplace during the weekend or at night, should be discouraged since they disproportionately affect workers with family responsibilities. Such practices perpetuate traditional gender roles and are exclusionary towards women. Besides, business trips should be scheduled whenever possible with considerable antecedence so that workers can make the necessary arrangements in their private lives to accommodate work requirements. While some types of flexibility benefit the employer more than the employee (Costa et al., 2017), some sort of flexibility is part of a supportive work environment and is important for work-family balance. Another aspect is that work-life balance policies should not only target professionals or managers but all workers, so as not to further increase the burden of low-wage mothers. Organisations should also encourage networking activities that are inclusive of women and minorities, and discourage male-only social events (Williams et al., 2012).

Note

1 Adapted from the Portuguese idiomatic expression: "O homem chegou e reinou", meaning that someone stepped straight to a position of power or status immediately, "upon arrival", without having to prove themselves.

References

Acker, J. (1988). Class, gender and the relations of distribution. *Signs*, *13*(473–497).
Acker, J. (1990). Hierarchies, jobs, bodies: A theory of gendered organizations. *Gender & Society*, *4*(2), 139–158.
Acker, J. (2006). Inequality regimes: Gender, class, and race in organizations. *Gender & Society*, *20*(4), 441–464.
Acker, J. (2012). Gendered organizations and intersectionality: Problems and possibilities. *Equality, Diversity and Inclusion: An International Journal*, *31*(3), 214–224.
Alvesson, M., & Billing, Y. D. (1997). *Understanding gender and organisations*. SAGE Publications.
Bosak, J., & Sczesny, S. (2011). Exploring the dynamics of incongruent beliefs about women and leaders. *British Journal of Management*, *22*(2), 254–269.
Braun, V., & Clarke, V. (2006). Using thematic analysis in psychology. *Qualitative Research in Psychology*, *3*(2), 77–101. https://doi.org/10.1191/1478088706qp063oa
Brink, M., & Stobbe, L. (2009). Doing gender in academic education: The paradox of visibility. *Gender, Work and Organization*, *16*(4), 451–470.
Butler, J. (2004). *Undoing gender*. Routledge.
Carvalho, I., Costa, C., Lykke, N., & Torres, A. (2014). An analysis of gendered employment in the Portuguese tourism sector. *Journal of Human Resources in Hospitality & Tourism*, *13*(4), 405–429.
Cave, P., & Kilic, S. (2010). The role of women in tourism employment with special reference to Antalya, Turkey. *Journal of Hospitality Marketing and Management*, *19*(3), 280–292.
Chafetz, J. S. (1988). The gender division of labor and the reproduction of female disadvantage: Toward an integrated theory. *Journal of Family Issues*, *9*(1), 108–131.
Collinson, D. L., & Hearn, J. (1994). Naming men as men: Implications for work, organizations and management *Gender, Work and Organization*, *1*(1), 2–22.
Collinson, D. L., & Hearn, J. (2005). Men and masculinities in work, organizations, and management. In M. Kimmel, J. Hearn, & R. W. Connell (Eds.), *Handbook of studies on men & masculinities* (pp. 289–310). Sage.
Connell, R. W. (1987). *Gender and power: Society, the person and sexual politics*. Polity Press.
Costa, C., Bakas, F. E., Breda, Z., Durão, M., Carvalho, I., & Caçador, S. (2017). Gender, flexibility and the "ideal tourism worker". *Annals of Tourism Research*, *64*, 64–75.
Costa, C., Carvalho, I., Caçador, S., & Breda, Z. (2012). Future higher education in tourism studies and the labor market: Gender perspectives on expectations and experiences. *Journal of Teaching in Travel & Tourism*, *12*(1), 70–90.
Due Billing, Y., & Alvesson, M. (2000). Questioning the notion of feminine leadership: A critical perspective on the gender labelling of leadership. *Gender, Work & Organization*, *7*(3), 144–157.
Eagly, A. H., & Carli, L. L. (2008). *Through the labyrinth*. Harvard Business School.
Esping-Andersen, G. (2005). Final remarks: A jobless and childless Europe? In T. Boeri, D. D. Boca & C. Pissarides (Eds.), *Women at work – An economic perspective* (pp. 268–274). Oxford University Press.
Hearn, J. (2000). On the complexity of feminist intervention in organizations. *Organization*, *7*(4), 609–624.
Hearn, J. (2010). *Equality, growth, sustainability: Adding some more missing ingredients to the mixture*. Paper presented at the Equality, Growth and Sustainability – Do they mix?
Hearn, J., & Collinson, D. (2006). Men, masculinities and workplace diversity/diversion. In A. M. Konrad, P. Prasad, & J. K. Pringle (Eds.), *Handbook of workplace diversity* (pp. 299–322). Sage.

Hearn, J., Jyrkinen, M., Piekkari, R., & Oinonen, E. (2008). "Women home and away": Transnational managerial work and gender relations. *The Journal of Business Ethics*, *83*(1), 41–54.
Hearn, J., Metcalfe, B. D., & Piekkari, R. (2012). Gender, intersectionality and international human resource management In G. Ståhl, I. Björkman, & S. Morris (Eds.), *Handbook of research on international human resource management* (pp. 509–531). Edward Elgar.
Jeanes, E. L., Knights, D., & Martin, P. Y. (Eds.). (2011). *Handbook of gender, work & organization*. Wiley.
Kantola, J. (2008). 'Why do all the women disappear?' Gendering processes in a political science department. *Gender, Work and Organization*, *15*(2), 202–225.
Kvale, S., & Brinkmann, S. (2009). *InterViews: Learning the craft of qualitative research interviewing* (2nd ed.). SAGE.
Lincoln, Y. S., Lynham, S. A., & Guba, E. G. (2011). Paradigmatic controversies, contradictions, and emerging confluencies, revisited. In N. K. Denzin & Y. S. Lincoln (Eds.), *The SAGE handbook of qualitative research* (pp. 97–128). Sage.
Liu, T., Li, M., & Wu, M. (2020). Performing femininity: Women at the top (doing and undoing gender). *Tourism Management*, *80*, 104130. https://doi.org/10.1016/j.tourman.2020.104130
Lombardo, E., & Meier, P. (2007). European union gender policy since Beijing: Shifting concepts and agendas. In M. Verloo (Ed.), *Multiple meanings of gender equality: A critical frame analysis of gender policies in Europe* (pp. 51–75). Central European University Press.
Mavin, S. (2009). Navigating the labyrinth: Senior women managing emotion. *International Journal of Work Organisation and Emotion*, *3*(1), 81–83.
Mavin, S., & Grandy, G. (2011). Doing gender well and differently in dirty work: The case of exotic dancing. *Gender, Work & Organization*, *20*(3), 232–251.
Mavin, S., & Grandy, G. (2012). Doing gender well and differently in management. *Gender in Management*, *27*(4), 218–231.
Mavin, S., Grandy, G., & Williams, J. (2014). Experiences of women elite leaders doing gender: Intra-gender micro-violence between women. *British Journal of Management*, *25*(3), 439–455.
McNay, L. (2000). *Gender and agency: Reconfiguring the subject in feminist and social theory*. Polity.
Oakley, A. (1972). *Sex, gender and society*. Temple Smith.
Organisation for Economic Co-operation and Development. (1999). *DAC guidelines for gender equality and women's empowerment in development co-operation*. OECD.
Patterson, N., Mavin, S., & Turner, J. (2012a). Envisioning female entrepreneur: Leaders anew from a gender perspective. *Gender in Management: An International Journal*, *27*(9), 395–416.
Patterson, N., Mavin, S., & Turner, J. (2012b). Unsettling the gender binary: Experiences of gender in entrepreneurial leadership and implications for HRD. *European Journal of Training and Development*, *36*(7), 687–711.
Scott, J. (1986). Gender: A useful category of historical analysis. *American Historical Review*, *91*, 1053–1075.
Stainback, K., Tomaskovic-Devey, D., & Skaggs, S. (2010). Organizational approaches to inequality: Inertia, relative power, and environments. *Annual Review of Sociology*, *36*, 225–247.
United Nations World Tourism Organization. (2011). *Global report on women in tourism 2010*. UNWTO.
Wahl, A. (1998). Deconstructing women and leadership. *International Review of Women and Leadership*, *4*(2), 46–60.

Wahl, A. (2001). From lack to surplus. In S. E. Sjöstrand, J. Sandberg, & M. Tyrstrup (Eds.), *Invisible management. The social construction of leadership* (pp. 126–148). Thomson.
Wahl, A. (2010). The impact of gender equality on management and leadership: Reflections on change and resistance. In L. Husu, J. Hearn, A. M. Lämsä, & S. Vanhala (Eds.), *Leadership through the gender lens* (pp. 1–20). Hanken Research Reports.
Wahl, A., & Holgersson, C. (2003). Male managers' reactions to gender diversity activities in organizations. In M. Davidson & S. Fielden (Eds.), *Individual diversity and psychology in organizations* (pp. 313–329). Wiley.
West, C., & Zimmerman, D. H. (1987). Doing gender. *Gender and Society*, *1*(2), 125–151.
West, C., & Zimmerman, D. H. (2009). Accounting for doing gender. *Gender & Society*, *23*(1), 112–122.
Williams, C. L., Muller, C., & Kilanski, K. (2012). Gendered organizations in the new economy. *Gender & Society*, *26*(4), 549–573.

11 Exploring obese people's tourist experiences

A search for an accessible, bias-free experience

Yaniv Poria, Arie Reichel, and Jeremy Beal

Introduction

At the backdrop of the series of studies reported here is the growing size of the obese people (herein OP) travel segment and the attempts to improve their visitor experience and consequently, their quality of life. From 2011 to 2014, OP made up 36.5% of the adult population in the United States, and current trends indicate that this rate is on the rise (Ogden & Clementi, 2010). According to the most recent Behavioral Risk Factor Surveillance System data, adult obesity rates in the United States now exceed 35% in 9 states, 30% in 31 states, and 25% in 48 states (State of Childhood Obesity, 2019). If the proportion of obese visitors to tourist attractions matches that of the general population, then one third of all visitors are obese. To date, surprisingly, both industry and academia have paid relatively little attention to this rapidly growing travel segment.

There seems to be a lack of understanding of the nature of the tourist experience of people whose body might be a barrier to full enjoyment and participation. The research project presented here is inspired by studies highlighting the role of the body in tourism and hospitality (Crouch, 2000; Harris & Small, 2013; Pons, 2003; Pritchard & Morgan, 2011; Veijola & Jokinen, 1994), as well as the call to include ethical and justice theories in tourism research (Jamal, 2019). Specifically, this chapter relies on studies indicating that people's appearance could serve as a trigger for inducing seclusion from the tourism and travel experience (Poria, 2006; Poria & Taylor, 2001). In particular, we rely on the social model of disability that concerns the inclusion of all members of society in participation in tourism, including people with disabilities (McCabe, 2019).

Obesity is yet to be thoroughly investigated by tourism scholars (Lewis & Van Puymbroeck, 2008) despite previous studies clearly demonstrating that people's tourist experience is affected by their physical appearance (Berdychevsky, Gibson, et al., 2013; Berdychevsky, Poria, et al., 2013; Small, 2007). Moreover, the inclusion tenet is congruent with legislation, driving the industry to be attuned to disenfranchised segments of the population (Poria et al., 2010). In addition, the growing competition in tourism markets pushes toward exploring new, unserved target niche audiences. This is surprising given the high visibility of obesity and the considerable media coverage it has received since 2008 (Lewis & Van

Puymbroeck, 2008). One example of this media attention is the wide coverage of airlines' discriminatory policies and actions toward OP (e.g. Stephenson et al., 2018). Hence, theoretical, ethical, social, and business-marketing rationales render research about the travel and tourist experience of OP. The tenet underlying this study is that all members of society have the right to participate in tourism (McCabe, 2019) and that it is a management responsibility to actively prevent their exclusion.

Literature review

Obesity as a disability

It should be noted that OP are often considered people with disabilities given the multiple physical challenges they confront (Chang et al., 2017; Kim, 2019). This is consistent with the United Nations Convention on the Rights of Persons with Disabilities, which recognises their rights in many areas, among them involvement in leisure activities (Pagán, 2012). With regard to participation in cultural life, recreation, leisure, and sport, Article 30 identifies the right of persons with disabilities to enjoy access to places for cultural performances or services, such as theatres, museums, cinemas, libraries, and tourism services (Darcy & Dickson, 2009). Article 30 was interpreted in various ways by numerous nations, leading to diverse legislations systems (see, e.g. Americans with Disability Act, 1990; The Law of People's Republic of China on the Protection of Disabled Persons, 1990).

Two models of disability are commonly adopted in tourism studies: the medical/individual model and the social model (Darcy & Buhalis, 2011). The underlying assumption for the medical/individual model is that the disabled person is a "subject" who can be treated by knowledgeable professionals who espouse "the dichotomy of normal/abnormal" (Darcy & Buhalis, 2011, p. 25). In contrast, underlying the social model is the assumption that disability is the outcome of a socially constructed environment. The social model, as applied in the current research project, views disability as part of human diversity. In some cases, the social model expands into the concept of diversity emanating from notions such as intersectionality and decolonial thinking (Desbiolles, 2020). This implies that OP, as well as other well-accepted "disabilities", are part of human diversity. The social model is in line with the principles underlying social tourism (McCabe, 2019) and universal design, both of which aim to prevent people's exclusion (Preiser & Ostroff, 2001). Clearly, adopting the social model approach would contribute to the understanding of the OP's body impact, travel experience, and quality of life (Sirgy, 2010; Uysal et al., 2013). Accordingly, OP tourists' self-reports of their perceptions, feelings, and emotions play a major role in this study.

The body in travel and tourism

The role of the body has been recognised as important for the conceptualisation of the tourism experience (Berdychevsky et al., 2015; Veijola & Jokinen, 1994).

People's body or their perception of their body has an impact on the time frame before a visit, as well as during a visit. For instance, people with mobility disabilities or blind tourists (Poria et al., 2010) may not be able to enter certain tourist attractions due to accessibility issues. Moreover, tourists' own perception of their body and their physical appearance have an impact on their travel patterns. Poria (2008) found that women who are not satisfied with their body appearance are less likely to consume massage services during their vacation. Indeed, the importance assigned to tourists' subjective perception of their body highlights the rationale for adopting a research approach that takes into account participants' feelings and emotions. Specifically, this study relies on Pritchard and Morgan's (2011) argument that the body should not be conceptualised as "a simple material reality, but as a complexly constructed set of social discourses" (p. 154).

Studies in environmental psychology and human geography reveal that public space is not open to all "bodies" (Poria & Oppewal, 2005). In accordance, Veijola and Jokinen (1994) argue that tourism is not open to all visitors. However, there are few empirical studies that relate OP's body impacts on the tourist experience. This is surprising, as this segment of the population is increasing, and OP can be easily identified – they cannot hide their obesity.

Perceptions of obesity

Aside from its numerous physical health risks, obesity, and OP's body image are linked to psycho-social issues (Blodorn et al., 2016). Historically, a person's large body was a means to signify capital and social echelon (Bourdieu, 1984). However, due to changes in modern Western capitalistic societies, there seems to be a trend to associate OP with limited social capital and negative images. OP, in many circumstances, have become pariahs. Prejudice against them can be compared to symbolic racism, based on the common notion that OP do not follow traditional values of hard work, authority, and self-discipline. Moreover, they do not follow puritan work ethics. In addition, the belief that "people get what they deserve" leads to a multitude of negative attitudes (Crandall, 1994, p. 884).

Furthermore, recent research indicates that OP body signifies discrimination, prejudice, stigmatisation, and seclusion. Accordingly, OP are viewed as stupid, unhealthy, academically unsuccessful, socially inept, unhygienic, lazy, lacking in self-control, and morally lax (De Brún et al., 2014; Hebl et al., 2009; Lewis et al., 1997). The stigma attached to OP has also been known to result in bullying and discrimination in areas such as education, health care, and employment (De Brún et al., 2014). It should be noted that the stigmas are also prevalent among OP, a sentiment akin to "self-hate". For example, according to Ogden and Clementi (2010), many OP experience their weight in profoundly negative ways. This is attributed to living in a society that stigmatises their condition in terms such as "freak", "hate", "blob", and "disgust", which reflect the pervasively negative impact on their physical appearance.

In the series of studies reported in this chapter, the emphasis is on hearing the authentic voice of OP. This perspective is congruent with the growing interest in the concept of the body in tourism and hospitality studies and with critical research approaches (Crouch, 2000; Crouch & Desforges, 2003; Harris & Small, 2013; Pons, 2003; Pritchard & Morgan, 2011; Veijola & Jokinen, 1994). The body is viewed as a sociocultural entity inscribed with meaning, and thus, the tourist experience moves beyond being a cognitive experience to being a corporeal and emotional one. Consequently, the body is a powerful issue in OP's tourist experience, one that cannot be underestimated or absent from the OP tourism depiction and analysis. This is especially significant given the role of "beautiful people" who are visible and viable in most travel advertisements, leading viewers to believe that it is only those who look fit that deserve to have access to a tourist's paradise (Pritchard & Morgan, 2011).

In spite of the growing attention to secluded segments of tourism, there is a dearth of empirical attempts to study the nature of OP's tourist experiences. Comparing OP experiences in various servicecapes and tourism environments will further shed light on the nature of their travel experience and the challenges they face, hence enriching the current body of tourism knowledge. Moreover, it is expected that findings might be beneficial to travel and tourism organisations in their attempt to serve OP.

OP's study supposition

The main research supposition is centred around body size, specifically, that OP physical appearance will impact their travel and tourism experience, especially in regard to their interaction with the physical environment. It was assumed, however, that the social stigma attached to OP would not play a major role, because tourism environments are supposedly attributed to anonymity, hence allowing people to look or behave differently (Poria & Taylor, 2001; Uriely & Belhassen, 2006). This presumably reduces the effect of every day's social stigmas and norms on OP during the tourist experience (Berdychevsky et al., 2015). These assumptions are also supported by studies indicating that tourism provides a shelter from today's social norms and social stigmas (Berdychevsky et al., 2013).

The chapter is an attempt to integrate a set of previous studies to gain insight into various elements of the travel and tourism experience of OP. Specifically, accumulated reported experiences of OP in flights (Poria & Beal, 2017), hotels (Poria et al., 2021), restaurants (Poria, Shani, & Beal, 2019), theme parks (Poria et al., 2020), and museums (Poria et al., 2019), will be analysed in an attempt to form a coherent depiction of what it means to be an OP involved in travel and tourism experiences. In line with the social model of disability (Swain et al., 1997), solutions for creating an enabling environment are explored.

Methodology

Due to the exploratory nature of the research questions and the attempt to provide participants with the opportunity to authentically reflect on their own experience, a qualitative methodology was applied. This approach followed studies by Berdychevsky et al. (2013) and Poria (2006), who deemed it especially suitable when addressing personal and sensitive issues (Small & Darcy, 2011).

Most of the 36 participants in the study came from Virginia, USA, where this study was conducted. Potential participants were contacted through Craigslist, which seems to be the most suitable website due to its popularity. The ad offered OP $20 for their participation; all those who responded ended up participating. It was mentioned explicitly in the ad that only people whose body mass index (herein BMI) was higher than 35 should respond. For ethical reasons, participants were not asked about their weight (all participants were aware of their BMI). During the interviews, almost all participants revealed their weight and BMI. The participants (20 men and 16 women) ranged in age from 22 to 46; 22 of them self-reported a BMI of 30–35 (moderately obese) and 14 had a BMI of 35 or higher (obese or morbidly obese).

The in-depth semi-structured interviews were conducted by two of the authors. It was the decision of the interviewer whether to add additional questions based on the interview flow. The interview was grounded on studies elucidating the significant role of remembering noteworthy parts of past vacations, including unpleasant emotional experiences (Fuchs et al., 2015; Torres et al., 2017), as well as studies highlighting the importance of memorable moments on the perception of the tourist experience (Poria et al., 2007). The interviews were all recorded with the participants' permission. To raise the level of cooperation and rapport, the interviewer explained that the study was designed to provide insights that would be disseminated as widely as possible with the aim of improving OP travel and tourist experiences. It was specifically mentioned that the aim of the researchers is to enrich hotel and tourism literature, as well as to provide meaningful information for practitioners to ensure better quality service to OP, allowing them full participation in the tourism experience. Participants were offered the opportunity to conduct the interview in a location where they would feel comfortable, either at home or in a public place. In most cases, participants preferred to conduct the interviews in restaurants or coffee shops close to their home.

Topics in the interview included participants' travel and visitation patterns, experiences related to their body size, difficulties and obstacles imposed by their body size, and ways they were able to overcome these challenges. During the interviews, which lasted an average of 80 minutes, participants were asked to recall negative and positive experiences associated with their obesity. Additionally, they were asked to offer solutions that might improve OP travel/tourist experiences. Participants were then asked to refer to the experiences of other OP they knew and to answer "what-if" questions (e.g. "What would you do to improve OP restaurants/museums experiences if you were a restaurant/museum manager?"). In addition, they were asked, if possible, to compare their tourist experiences before and after they had become obese. Participants often referred to their leisure experiences within their local community.

As noted earlier, the interviewees were asked about experiences that are crucial to the tourist experience: flights, hotels, restaurants, theme parks, and museums.

They referred also to issues such as travel to/from the destination, the hotel stays, and components of the visit (restaurants, theme parks, and museums). Capturing and integrating these five experiences will provide a holistic view on OP travel experiences. Flights and hotel experiences were the easiest to retrieve and report, and indeed, most of the interviews centred on these issues. Participants referred to their experience in Virginia, as well as other destinations in the United States (e.g. Florida, West Virginia, Washington, DC, New York, and Las Vegas). To protect participants' anonymity, names have been removed, and only when gender and body size (obese/morbidly obese) were relevant to a particular finding was this information added.

Data analysis was conducted simultaneously with the process of data collection, subjecting the notes and transcripts to thematic content analysis (Braun & Clarke, 2006). During data analysis, the researchers achieved a high level of agreement in the categorisation process. The analysis was done according to the tourism settings (i.e. museum, flight) and the difficulties/barriers (i.e. social and physical) the participants confronted. Malam (2004) argued that the researchers' personal characteristics impact their studies. Accordingly, it should be noted that the researchers are non-obese, white males, while two of the three are non-American.

Main findings

The study presents four themes that run through the data. These include OP interaction with the physical environment, the presence of other tourists, the difference between the various tourist experiences, and handling the tourist experience.

OP interaction with the physical environment

The findings indicate that in many tourists' settings, the physical environment does not fit the participants' bodies. OP referred to various elements of the travel and tourism servicecape that negatively impact their experiences, elements that people of average size would probably not even have noticed, for example, the chair size in restaurants and bars ("Obese people just can't sit on a bar chair. We need two"), or the aisle on a plane ("Sorry, the aisle is too narrow for me"); the size of the hotel bathroom; the size of the toilets on the plane ("you can't imagine how difficult it is for obese people to use the plane's toilets"); the hotel bed size and height; and the distance between the chair and the table in the hotel room. This incompatibility between OP body size and the physical environment has a clear negative impact on the tourist experience. Yet, such challenges to inclusion were often received by OP with a sense of understanding, and at times even with a touch of humour. Apparently, participants did not have expectations that the environment would fully suit their body size, as in one comment about the chair in a restaurant: ". . . unfortunately, the chairs in the restaurant [are] aimed at people with one ass only. I have two asses. I can't sit in [a] one-ass chair". The incongruity between the body size and the physical servicecape was most evident in in-flight experiences. OP felt a considerable sense of inconvenience due to their inevitable physical contacts with fellow passengers ("I am so big that I inevitably touch those sitting next to me").

Participants also referred to their weight as a major challenge, suggesting that it prevents them from being able to walk long distances or walk quickly. While perhaps not evident to the common visitor to museums, OP reported walking to distant bathrooms as an exhausting experience. The same frustration was expressed in airports in terms of the need to reach the gates of connecting flights ("It's very difficult for obese people to walk long distances in a very short time. As far as walking, we are like old people"). In this context, participants apparently felt that their physical difficulties were associated with profuse sweating that caused them considerable shame and inconvenience, as well as being wet and malodorous ("We [OP] sweat more than thin people. You can't imagine how embarrassing it is to sweat so much while you are sitting next to someone else"). This, in turn, caused them to shun the physical proximity and company of other people.

The presence of other tourists

The presence of other tourists was revealed to be the main factor affecting OP tourist experiences, often resulting in self-afflicted seclusion. Apparently, the study's main supposition that tourist anonymity is a shield against discrimination or a feeling of exclusion has to be rejected. Specifically, other visitors' gaze or staring were found to be crucial in understanding both OP travel and local leisure experiences. The staring of the "others" was interpreted by the participants as an accusation for choosing to be obese, becoming people with disabilities who enjoy government disability support and "take other people's money". Almost all participants reported they felt that others looked down at them, as if they were people who chose to be obese ("People think that we choose to be obese. That we are unemployed. That we are lazy. That we are bad parents").

The epitome of embarrassment came at attractions where, as some OP were waiting in line with their children, they were pulled out of the line by members of the staff. The reason being body size limits. In reminiscing such distraught scenes, participants interpreted the look of others as if they were happy for their blight and rejection. One participant said: "when I left the line [in the theme park], as I could not enter the cabin in the mountain train, I saw that others were looking at me enjoying this show". Indeed, the gaze of other tourists caused the participants, in certain cases, to seclude themselves from certain components of the tourist experience and avoid participation.

Such gazes are likely to form a major barrier for a fully satisfying tourism experience. For example, to escape the gaze of other tourists, participants avoided going to hotel gyms, swimming pools, or beaches ("There is no chance that I'll go the hotel swimming pool if there is someone around; 'I'll never go the hotel gym. It's so embarrassing. Just imagine how people will stare at me. The fat woman who is trying to lose weight"). This gaze was also a factor that prevented OP from joining guided tours in museums ("I don't want to be the one that everyone waits for. Looking at him. Blaming him for being late"), and influenced OP to drive instead of flying ("If it's a short flight, I'd rather take my car and avoid the airport, the security check and the flight. It's a hassle for someone like me").

Difference between the various tourist experiences

Apparently, there are noticeable differences between the various servicecapes experiences. Participants reported considerable differences between museums, on the one hand, and all other tourist experiences. The museum experience was unique in the sense that it provided a servicecape where obesity does not seem to play a dominant negative role ("Museums are like paradise for obese people"). Despite close physical proximity while waiting in lines and around exhibits and given the long walks along museums corridors, participants suggested that their obesity barely affected their museum experience. Interviewees reported feeling protected from others' gaze, because the clientele are well educated ("Those going to museums know that not all obese are lazy and unemployed"). Moreover, OP felt there was an implicit "educated, erudite on-site code of behaviour". Specifically, interviewees noted that visitors were interested in the exhibits and that staring at other visitors is against the museum's social code of behaviour.

In contrast, OP maintained that in other tourist servicecapes (e.g. airplanes, hotels, restaurants, and theme parks) it was socially acceptable to stare at each other, consequently forming a sense of seclusion. Interviewees reported that the most unpleasant, noticeable, and accusing stares took place in restaurants. On such occasions, participants felt they were blamed for enjoying their food when they should be limiting their caloric intake or being involved in healthier, calorie-burning activities. Some suggested that they felt that others expected them not to eat in a restaurant, as if such dining were a "crime" ("At restaurants I feel that people scold me for enjoying eating").

Although not a subject originally intended to be included in the research project, some participants referred to the race issue, viewing it as a significant factor affecting the tourist experience. Specifically, some interviewees indicated a clear preference for leisure environments with African American clientele or service providers ("If I have any problem during the check-in process, I'll look for obese black women. They are much nicer. They won't look at me as if I am disgusting"). Participants argued that the presence of African Americans made them feel more at ease, relaxed, and welcome, as they seemed not to show judgement, prejudice, or hostility towards OP. For example, one participant (a morbidly obese woman) referred to the line before boarding the plane:

> If they want me to board the plane with the group of people with disabilities, they should approach me in private and ask me to do so. The best will be if an Afro-American woman does it. They [African Americans] do not think that obese people are ugly or disgusting.

Another participant adds: "Black men like big women. They hate skinny women. Only white men like them".

The presence of the participants' close friends was also an important factor for understanding their tourist experience. When they were with people who knew them well, they felt less subjected to the stigma attached to OP ("My friends know me. They know who I am"). In these cases, they felt less restricted and limited. For example, in local restaurants and in the company of familiar people, they did not order "healthy foods", which they described as a compromise that is not tasty. Also, they felt more comfortable going to the beach or a local/community swimming pool in their home environment along with people who knew them and, they felt, who shielded them from stares.

Differences were found between male and female participants. When relating to the hotel experience, almost all female participants revealed that they were ashamed to show their body, even in their private room. Some insisted on turning off the lights or going to bed before their partner ("You may not believe, but my husband never saw me naked"). Contrary, a few women revealed that in public spaces (e.g. hotel swimming pools) they were proud of their body and felt attractive. This pattern was not found among the male participants.

Handling the tourist experience

Participants have adopted several modes of behaviour to overcome the difficulties they face when travelling. To avoid the disturbing and accusing staring of others, OP attempt to blend into the environment ("I try to hide myself from others") by sitting far from the centre or avoiding crowds. For example, in airplanes, they prefer to board first and sit in the first/last rows, where presumably less passengers can stare at them. In other locations, the OP's tactic is to leave quietly to ensure minimal exposure to others ("I am the last one to leave the plane").

Generally speaking, although OP would appreciate special help, only a few participants stated that they would ask for minor preferential treatment to improve the quality of their tourist experience, such as asking for a chair that would fit their size. They rationalised their behaviour by suggesting that they felt embarrassed to identify themselves to the service providers, who might perceive them as people with disabilities. Asking for help from the crew may cause other passengers to stare at them. It should be noted, however, that several participants referred to themselves as "people with disabilities", claiming that obesity should be classified as a disability. Accordingly, they came forward and asked in advance for special arrangements to assist them during their visit. For example, they reserved wheelchairs or golf carts (in airports) or accessible hotel rooms. These participants argued that, in tourism settings, OP should be approached and treated by the site's management as people with disabilities.

Discussion

In the variety of servicecapes explored, it became obvious that OP felt a strong sense of social exclusion. While Small and Harris (2012) argued that tourism is a right for "all the world's inhabitants" (p. 686), not all people have access to this right (Small et al., 2008), and this is specifically true for OP. Furthermore, Small and Harris (2012) claimed that tourism settings seem to attract "beautiful people" and that those who do not fit this image are not "welcome in paradise" (p. 687). The current study's findings indicate that tourism is not fully open for OP and that the gatekeepers are the other guests who ostracise OP by their gaze. Clearly, McCabe's (2019) question "tourism for all?" (p. 61) resonates in these findings. Only museums serve as havens for OP, specifically as the prevailing norm is contrary to staring at other people.

In their tourist pursuits, OP confront numerous challenges arising from their body size. These challenges can be divided into two: an incongruity between the individual body dimensions and the physical environment and others' gaze as an accusation of being obese (Lin & Fu, 2020). It is argued that the tourist experience, which often provides leisure time accorded by being anonymous, is less applicable to OP. The stigmas attached to one's physical appearance are obvious and explicit.

The findings add to the literature on stigmas towards OP. It was found here that OP believe that they are stigmatised as individuals who make a conscious, deliberate decision to be disabled, and do not make the effort to lose weight in order to be healthy and productive members of society. The combination of the stigmas for which OP feel internally, coupled with scrutinised gazes, is a major source of reservation, contempt, and prejudice. Apparently, OP feel that others believe they are not supposed to have the requisite purchasing power for a vacation.

Though participants emphasised the difficulties arising from social pressures emanating from the presence of others, the impact of the physical environment should not be overlooked. It was found that often the physical environment did not fit OP body size (e.g. size of an airplane seat, hotel towels, and restaurant tables). The difficulties faced by OP in dealing with the physical environment seem to be comparable to studies on tourists with disabilities (Poria et al., 2010). Both groups cannot stand for a long time or walk long distances in order to gain the full experience of the site. In both cases, the tourists confront reduced mobility affecting the tourist experience.

The literature on the tourist experience often emphasises the function of anonymity. The foreign location is often viewed as a "liminal environment" (Uriely & Belhassen, 2005, 2006), hence enabling activities that would be unacceptable in a home environment. The desire and, indeed, the wish for anonymity were found in studies focusing on the motives for tourism (Berdychevsky et al., 2013; Uriely & Belhassen, 2005, 2006). The findings described here clearly contradict the literature analysing the anonymity elements in relation to OP.

The findings also indicate that obese women feel more at ease interacting with African American service providers and, in a leisure environment, with African American men. This corresponds with studies that suggest that obese African Americans are less concerned about their weight and have a higher level of satisfaction with their body (Kumanyika et al., 1993) and that issues of race and gender should be considered when studying the social realms of obesity (Paeratakul et al., 2002)

The study also supports the adoption of the social model of disability in the analysis of obese tourist experience (Darcy & Buhalis, 2011; Desbiolles, 2020;

McCabe, 2019). It is the individual's perception of the socially constructed environment that affects OP's travel experiences. It is rare that tourism literature emphasises tourist-to-tourist interaction as a barrier to tourist experience (Darcy & Buhalis, 2011). As noted in this particular study, other tourists are indeed a considerable barrier to a full, positive experience (Eichhorn & Buhalis, 2011).

It is argued that, in the context of tourism, obesity could be conceptualised as a social disability. Following Maddox and Leiderman (1969) and Goering (2015), OP tourists shun other tourists out of a desire to hide from scrutiny, criticism, and stigmas. Clearly, social disability plays a crucial role that affects OP's ability to be involved in tourism and, consequently, their quality of life (Palmeira et al., 2016). In sum, the studies' findings highlight another form of disability – social disability resulting from the stigmas attached to one's looks.

Following Ford and Eiser's (1995, p. 323) description of "situational disinhibition" as the feeling of being a different person on holiday, it was found that OP are devoid of such an experience, as they are subject to others' gaze. Moreover, it is argued that OP do not regard tourism as permissive and playful (Turner, 1982). Hence, obesity could be conceptualised as a form of discrimination, preventing people from participating in tourism. We should recognise that tourism spaces are not only gendered and sexualised (Jordan & Aitchison, 2008) but also affected by body size. This study indicates that people's body is a central facet of the social realm, which should be highlighted when conceptualising the tourist experience. Apparently, OP are not thin enough to pass through the tourism gate.

Managerial implications

Our studies reveal that the tourism industry is not yet attuned to the OP experience. It seems that major stakeholders in the tourism industry have not yet fully comprehended their responsibility in providing an equality of offerings to all tourists (Darcy et al., 2020). As far as the experiences investigated here, as well as in previous studies on barriers to accessing tourism (Eichhorn & Buhalis, 2011), it is suggested that tourism and travel organisations should provide OP with information about accessibility. For example, theme parks should inform their obese visitors about attractions that are accessible in terms of body dimensions. Restaurants should inform their guests about the size of chairs and whether chairs and tables are fixed to the floor. An adaptation should also be made for OP. For example, hotels should provide OP with bigger bathrobes and towels that will facilitate a gratifying hospitality experience. Other suggestions include opportunities to board airplanes before other passengers and be offered cart service at airports, seat-belt extensions, and various sitting options in restaurants for those who prefer a more secluded section. The findings indicate that such specialty services should be provided as discreetly as possible, without raising the attention of other visitors. It is possible for organisations to consider adopting a strategy of co-creation (Rachão et al., 2020) by involving OP in the planning and designing of tourism and travel offerings. As noted earlier, often minor changes can solve or minimise the incompatibility between the obese patron and the environment.

Current technological improvements allow tourism organisations to provide their customers with the option to identify themselves as obese in advance (e.g. when making online hotel reservations). This information could assist management in providing obese customers with a better tourist experience and, hopefully, spare them embarrassment. Moreover, service providers should recognise that OP are mobility challenged and may need special accommodations

It is suggested here that although this study focused on OP, the implications may be relevant for other segments of the population which attempt to hide themselves from others, as well as those who have mobility difficulties. The implementations should be conducted in a sensitive and responsible way relying on the ideas of universal design to promote inclusive participation in tourism (Preiser & Ostroff, 2001).

Limitations and future research

Due to the research approach adopted, no indication of this study's statistical representativeness can be made. Most of the participants live in Virginia, a state marked by high rates of obesity (Byrnes, 2021). Moreover, the findings are based on participants who chose to reveal their own experience. Following the development of the body of knowledge on OP tourism, future studies should adopt a quantitative research approach, examining, for example, non-OP's attitudes toward obese tourists. Further research could focus on OP's tourist experience in other countries and cultures where attitudes toward body image differ in comparison to the Western world (Thomas & Thomas, 2002; Zhang et al., 2018). Additional studies could investigate other types and forms of OP tourism (e.g. business travel) and obese children and adolescents tourism experience (Lewis & Van Puymbroeck, 2008). Finally, future studies may examine whether the study's findings are relevant for the conceptualisation of tourist experiences for other groups whose appearance may make them targets of stigmatisation, leading to a sense of seclusion (Eichhorn et al., 2008). Such studies will enrich our understanding of the role of the non-standard body in the tourist experience and provide a more holistic view on OP tourist experiences.

References

American with Disability Act. (1990). *An overview of the Americans with Disabilities Act.* https://adata.org/factsheet/ADA-overview

Berdychevsky, L., Gibson, H., & Poria, Y. (2015). Inversions of sexual roles in women's tourist experiences: Mind, body, and language in sexual behaviour. *Leisure Studies, 34*(5), 513–528.

Berdychevsky, L., Poria, Y., & Uriely, U. (2013). Hospitality accommodations and women's consensual sex. *International Journal of Hospitality Management, 34,* 169–171.

Blodorn, A., Major, B., Hunger, J., & Miller, C. (2016). Unpacking the psychological weight of weight stigma: A rejection-expectation pathway. *Journal of Experimental Social Psychology, 63,* 69–76.

Bourdieu, P. (1984). *Distinction: A social critique of the judgement of taste.* Harvard University Press.

Braun, V., & Clarke, V. (2006). Using thematic analysis in psychology. *Journal of Qualitative Research in Psychology, 13*(2), 77–101.

Byrnes, H. (2021). This is where Virginia childhood obesity ranks in the US. *Northern Virginia's Leading News Source*. Retrieved June 18, 2021, from www.insidenova.com/news/state/this-is-where-virginia-childhood-obesity-ranks-in-the-us/article_62827637-97a3-540f-858f-75128ea889a2.html

Chang, V. W., Alley, D. E., & Dowd, J. D. (2017). Trends in the relationship between obesity and disability, 1988–2012. *American Journal of Epidemiology, 186*(6), 688–695.

Crandall, C. S. (1994). Prejudice against fat people: Ideology and self-interest. *Journal of Personality and Social Psychology, 66*(5), 882–894.

Crouch, D. (2000). Places around us: Embodied lay geographies in leisure and tourism. *Leisure Studies, 19*(2), 63–76.

Crouch, D., & Desforges, L. (2003). The sensuous in the tourist encounter: Introduction: The power of the body. *Tourist Studies, 3*(1), 5–22.

Darcy, S., & Buhalis, D. (2011). Conceptulising disability. In D. Buhalis & S. Dracy (Eds.), *Accessible tourism: Concepts and issues* (pp. 21–45). Channel View Publications.

Darcy, S., & Dickson, T. (2009). A Whole-of-Life approach to tourism: The case for accessible tourism experiences. *Journal of Hospitality and Tourism Management, 16*(1), 32–44.

Darcy, S., McKercher, B., & Schweinsberg, S. (2020). From tourism and disability to accessible tourism: A perspective article. *Tourism Review, 75*(1), 140–144.

De Brún, A., McCarthy, M., McKenzie, K., & McGloin, A. (2014). Weight stigma and narrative resistance evident in online discussions of obesity. *Appetite, 72*, 73–81.

Desbiolles, F. H. (2020). Diversity in tourism: A perspective article. *Tourism Review, 75*(1), 29–32.

Eichhorn, A., & Buhalis, D. (2011). Accessibility: A key objective for the tourism industry. In D. Buhalis & S. Darcy (Eds.), *Accessible tourism: Concepts and issues* (pp. 46–61). Channel View Publications.

Eichhorn, V., Miller, G., Michopoulou, E., & Buhalis, D. (2008). Enabling disabled tourists? Accessibility tourism information schemes. *Annals of Tourism Research, 35*(1), 189–210.

Ford, N., & Eiser, R. (1995). Sexual relationships on holiday: A case of situational disinhibition? *Journal of Social and Personal Relationships, 12*, 323–339.

Fuchs, G., Chen, P. J., & Pizam, A. (2015). Are travel purchases more satisfactory than nontravel experiential purchases and material purchases? An exploratory study. *Tourism Analysis, 20*(5), 487–497.

Goering, S. (2015). Rethinking disability: The social model of disability and chronic disease. *Current Review of Musculoskeletal Medicine, 8*(2), 134–138.

Harris, C., & Small, J. (2013). Obesity and hotel staffing: Are hotels guilty of "lookism"? *Hospitality & Society, 3*(2), 111–127.

Hebl, M. R., King, E. B., & Perkins, A. (2009). Ethnic differences in the stigma of obesity: Identification and engagement with a thin ideal. *Journal of Experimental Social Psychology, 45*(6), 1165–1172.

Jamal, T. (2019). Tourism ethics: A perspective article. *Tourism Review, 75*(1), 221–224.

Jordan, F., & Aitchison, C. (2008). Tourism and the sexualisation of the gaze: Solo female tourists' experiences of gendered power, surveillance and embodiment. *Leisure Studies, 27*(3), 329–349.

Kim, S. (2019). Washington State Supreme Court rules that obesity is a disability. *Forbes*. Retrieved July 18, 2019, from www.forbes.com/sites/sarahkim/2019/07/18/washington-state-supreme-courts-obesity-disability/?sh=589863f4d274

Kumanyika, S., Wilson, J. F., & Guilford-Davenport, M. (1993). Weight related attitudes and behaviors of black women. *Journal of American Diet Association, 93*, 416–422.

Law of the People's Republic of China on the protection of disabled persons. (1990). Order of the President no. 36 promulgated as of May 15, 1991. http://en.hbjz.net/view/534.html

Lewis, R. J., Cash, T. F., Jacobi, L., & Bubb-Lewis, C. (1997). Prejudice toward fat people: The development and validation of the Antifat Attitudes Test. *Obesity Research*, *5*(4), 297–305.

Lewis, S. T., & Van Puymbroeck, M. (2008). Obesity-stigma as a multifaceted constraint to leisure. *Journal of Leisure Research*, *40*(4), 574–588.

Lin, B., & Fu, X. (2020). Gaze and tourist-host relationship – state of the art. *Tourism Review*, *76*(1), 138–149. https://doi.org/10.1108/TR-11-2019-0459

Maddox, G. L., & Leiderman, V. (1969). Overweight as a social disability with medical implications. *Journal of Medical Education*, *44*, 214–220.

Malam, L. (2004). Embodiment and sexuality in cross-cultural research. *Australian Geographer*, *35*(2), 177–183.

McCabe, S. (2019). "Tourism for all?" Considering social tourism: A perspective paper. *Tourism Review*, *75*(2), 61–64.

Ogden, J., & Clementi, C. (2010). The experience of being obese and the many consequences of stigma. *Journal of Obesity*, 1–9, 429098. http://dx.doi.org/10.1155/2010/429098

Oppewal, H., & Poria, Y. (2005). A new medium for data collection: online news discussions. *International Journal of Contemporary Hospitality Management*, *15*(4), 232–236.

Paeratakul, S., White, M. A., Williamson, D. A., Ryan, D. H., & Bray, G. A. (2002). Sex, race/ethnicity, socioeconomic status, and BMI in relation to self-perception of overweight. *Obesity Research*, *10*(5), 345–350.

Pagán, R. (2012). Time allocation in tourism for people with disabilities. *Annals of Tourism Research*, *39*(3), 1514–1537.

Palmeira, L., Pinto-Gouveia, C., & Cunha, M. (2016). The role of weight self-stigma on the quality of life of women with overweight and obesity: A multi-group comparison between binge eaters and non-binge eaters. *Appetite*, *105*, 782–789.

Pons, P. O. (2003). Being-on-holiday: Tourist dwelling, bodies and place. *Tourist Studies*, *3*(1), 47–66.

Poria, Y. (2006). Tourism and spaces of anonymity: An Israeli lesbian woman's travel experience. *Tourism*, *54*(1), 33–43.

Poria, Y. (2008). Gender – A crucial neglected element in the service encounter: An exploratory study of the choice of hotel masseur or masseuse. *Journal of Hospitality & Tourism Research*, *32*(2), 151–168.

Poria, Y., & Beal, J. (2017). An exploratory study about obese people's flight experience. *Journal of Travel Research*, *56*(3), 1–11.

Poria, Y., Beal, J., & Reichel, A. (2019). The only place where people don't judge other people's body: Obese people's museum experience. *Tourism Management Perspectives*, *31*, 159–164.

Poria, Y., Beal, J., & Reichel, A. (2020). The joy of riding or walk of shame? The themepark experience of obese people. *European Journal of Tourism Research*, *24*, 2412–1417.

Poria, Y., Beal, J., & Shani, A. (2021). "I am so ashamed of my body": Obese guests' experiences in hotels. *International Journal of Hospitality Management*, *92*, 102728.

Poria, Y., Butler, R., & Airey, D. (2007). Understanding tourism – Memorable moments in a complex timeframe. *Asian Journal of Tourism and Hospitality Research*, *1*(1), 25–38.

Poria, Y., Reichel, A., & Brandt, Y. (2010). The flight experiences of people with disabilities: An exploratory study. *Journal of Travel Research*, *49*(2), 216–227.

Poria, Y., Shani, A., & Beal, J. (2019). Size doesn't matter? An exploratory study of the public dining experience of obese people. *Journal of Hospitality and Tourism Management*, *39*, 49–56.

Poria, Y., & Taylor, A. S. (2001). "I'm not afraid to be gay when I am on the net": Minimising social risk for lesbian and gay consumers searching for hotel related information. *Journal of Travel and Tourism Marketing*, *11*(2/3), 127–142.
Preiser, W. F. E., & Ostroff, E. (2001). *Universal design handbook*. McGraw-Hill.
Pritchard, A., & Morgan, N. (2011). Tourist bodies, transformation and sensuality. In P. Bramham & S. Wagg (Eds.), *The new politics of leisure and pleasure* (pp. 153–168). Palgrave Macmillan. https://doi.org/10.1057/9780230299979_10
Rachão, S. A. S., Breda, Z., Fernandes, C., & Joukes, V. (2020). Food-and-wine experiences towards co-creation in tourism. *Tourism Review*. https://doi.org/10.1108/TR-01-2019-0026
Sirgy, M. J. (2010). Toward a quality-of-life theory of leisure travel satisfaction. *Journal of Travel Research*, *49*, 482–495.
Small, J. (2007). The emergence of the body in the holiday accounts of women and girls. In A. Pritchard, M. Ateljevic, & I. Harris (Eds.), *Tourism and gender: Embodiment, sensuality and experience* (pp. 73–91). CABI.
Small, J., & Darcy, S. (2011). Understanding tourist experience through embodiment: The contribution of critical tourism and disability studies. In D. Buhalis & S. Darcy (Eds.), *Accessible tourism: Concepts and issues* (pp. 73–97). Channel View Publications.
Small, J., Harris, C., & McIntosh, A. (2008, February 11–14). "Whose body is welcome in paradise?", CAUTHE 2008 Conference: Where the bloody hell are we? *Surfers Paradise*. Retrieved September 29, 2021, from www.academia.edu/24656572/Whose_Body_Is_Welcome_in_Paradise?auto=citations&from=cover_page
Small, J., & Harris, G. (2012). Obesity and tourism: Rights and responsibilities. *Annals of Tourism Research*, *39*(2), 686–707.
State of Childhood Obesity. (2019). *Obesity rates: Adults*. Retrieved February 2020 from https://stateofchildhoodobesity.org/adult-obesity/
Stephenson, C., Lohmann, G., & Spasojevic, B. (2018). Stakeholder engagement in the development of international air services: A case study on Adelaide Airport. *Journal of Air Transport Management*, *71*, 45–54.
Swain, J., Finkelstain, V., French, S., & Oliver, M. (1997). *Disabling barriers – Enabling environments*. Sage.
Thomas, F. C., & Thomas, P. (2002). *Body image: A handbook of theory, research, and clinical practice*. Guilford Press.
Torres, E. N., Wei, W., & Hua, N. (2017). Towards understanding the effects of time and emotions on the vacation experience. *Tourism Review*, *72*(4), 357–374.
Turner, V. (1982). *From ritual to theatre: The human seriousness of play*. PAJ Publications.
Uriely, N., & Belhassen, Y. (2005). Drugs and tourist's experiences. *Journal of Travel Research*, *43*(3), 238–246.
Uriely, N., & Belhassen, Y. (2006). Drugs and risk taking in tourism. *Annals of Tourism Research*, *33*(2), 339–359.
Uysal, M., Perdue, R. R., & Sirgy, J. M. (2013). *Handbook of tourism and quality-of-life research*. Springer Business Science.
Veijola, S., & Jokinen, E. (1994). The body in tourism. *Theory, Culture & Society*, *11*, 125–151.
Zhang, L., Qian, H., & Fu, H. (2018). To be thin but not healthy – The body-image dilemma may affect health among female university students in China. *PLOS ONE*, *13*(10), e0205282. https://doi.org/10.1371/journal.pone.0205282

12   50 Shades of discrimination

Commercial kink in hospitality and tourism

Craig Webster

Introduction

In Western countries, there have been substantial changes in attitudes towards sex, sexuality, and gender roles. The first step in the shift in attitudes was instigated by the biological revolution of effective oral contraceptives in the 1960s when the Food and Drug Administration, in the United States, approved oral contraception for public use (Christin-Maitre, 2013). The result was that vaginal intercourse was effectively separated from the high risk of reproduction (Bullough & Bonnie, 1990). This led to a rethinking of the relationships between the sexes and instigated the sexual revolution, leading to a different outlook on sex and the role of sexuality in society. Eventually, some changes trickled down to non-heterosexuals, leading to greater legal recognition of same-sex marriages, now accepted in approximately 30 countries and territories in the world (Pew, 2019a). The legal acceptance of same-sex marriages also seems to have been met with social acceptance in most advanced economies. The shift has been quick, as in 2004 only about 31% of the US public accepted same-sex marriage (Pew, 2019b), while 2021 data show that this figure was 70% (McCarthy, 2021). The figures illustrating the acceptance by Canadians are similar (CROP, 2017). These social and political shifts regarding acceptance of same-sex marriage would suggest a wider acceptance or tolerance of non-mainstream heterosexual practices in the developed world.

Despite such a substantial change in attitudes towards same-sex relations and marriage, there is another sexual minority that has not been embraced and accepted by the public of developed countries as widely. Here, I will look upon "kinksters", including bondage, discipline, dominance, and submission (BDSM) practitioners, groups that generally do not have a receptive general public that will accept their sexual lifestyles/practices and thus have to remain "in the closet" when practising their lifestyles. While the success of E. L. James' (2012) *Fifty Shades of Grey* and subsequent franchising of books and films would suggest that kink has gone mainstream, there is ample evidence that kink is still a risky endeavour and that kinksters run the risk of suffering negatively from discrimination. In this chapter, I will discuss these sexual minorities, look into the ways in which they largely practise their lifestyle undercover, and address the ramifications, since they would otherwise face substantial discrimination when practising their lifestyles openly.

What are kink and BDSM and how many are into it?

The history of sex and sex practices will illustrate that many participants seem out of the ordinary or odd to many (see, e.g. Peakman, 2016). However, what is ordinary and excepted may change fairly drastically from one society to another, as well as over time, such as the general acceptance of same-sex relations in most developed countries. However, change does not happen overnight nor is it accepted globally by all societies. It should be noted that same-sex marriage seems to be legally sanctioned by the most developed countries in the world (Human Rights Campaign, 2021), meaning that for most countries that are not in Europe and North America (and also much of Latin America), such marriages are not officially recognised, and presumably, the societies are not supportive of such marriages/sexual relations. This fact illustrates what is fairly obvious, that what is accepted and mainstream in terms of sexual practices and relations in one place in the world may not be acceptable or mainstream in another.

The language used to explain those sexual practices that are outside of the host society's view of what is normal or acceptable has been explained elsewhere (Webster, 2020), but what is noteworthy is the vagueness of the language used to define the behaviours that constitute kink. "Kink" seems to be the umbrella term that refers to practices that are considered odd or quirky and are related to sexuality. Indeed, Nichols (2006) simplified the definitional intricates of dealing with the multitude of sexual behaviours that are considered apart from mainstream practices as "BDSM (bondage and discipline, dominance and submission, sadism and masochism) and fetishism, all of which fall under what has been termed kink" (p. 282). A similar loose and vague notion is echoed by Rehor (2015), who defined the umbrella term "kink" as

> unconventional sensual, erotic, and sexual behaviour including BDSM-related behaviours (physical and psychological stimuli including bondage, discipline, dominance, submission, sadism, and masochism), exhibitionistic behaviours (arousal by being observed by others), voyeuristic behaviours (arousal by observing others), fetishistic behaviours (arousal by objects), and others.
>
> (p. 826)

The lack of a central authority to define what the terms "kink" and "fetish" mean for those who study such expressions of sexuality creates a situation in which the component language should be investigated in terms of what these words mean in English. The word "kink" itself is defined by one leading dictionary as "a mental or physical peculiarity" or "unconventional sexual taste or behaviour" (Merriam-Webster, 2019b, n.p.), among other definitions. The term itself suggests the peculiar or unconventional in reference to sexuality. Literature seems to support the use of the word "kink" as referring to those things that are not accepted by the dominant culture as being mainstream (Miller, 2021; Shahbaz & Chirinos, 2016).

Another concept associated with "kink" is "fetish". One definition from a major dictionary for a "fetish" is "an object or bodily part whose real or fantasised presence is psychologically necessary for sexual gratification, and that is an object of fixation to the extent that it may interfere with complete sexual expression" (Merriam-Webster, 2019a, n.p.). While the mainstream view on sexuality may view the human foot in a non-sexual way, some fetishists place a great amount of value on the foot and see it in a very sexual way. There are many other fetishes that could be included, such as an attraction to stockings, urophilia (attraction to urine), or gerontophilia (attraction to older persons). Those who find an object or fixation that seems peculiar but that plays a large role in their sexuality would be included, probably, in the definition of a kink.

Another related, but separate, concept is that of BDSM, which is another general term that includes activities and components that include a set of power relationships in terms of the practice of sexuality (Hébert & Weaver, 2014, p. 49). For example, the person who is being tied up in a bondage scenario would probably be considered to be in a submissive position relative to the person who applies the bondage. A person being flogged in a discipline situation would be someone who would be considered to have greater power, and thus the right to inflict flogging as a punishment. In general, BDSM relations seem to suggest differences in power and authority between those practising various scenarios. But these practices may be non-sexual, as there are people who identify as "asexual" but are also BDSM practitioners (Sloan, 2015).

These terms make a great deal of sense, but when put into practice can become less than precise. The issue lies with regard to that which is sensory and that which is sexual or linked with sexuality. For example, there is a practice in which a person may enjoy being used as a piece of furniture or ashtray (usually ashes are discarded into a person's mouth) by another person. As such, a person may find some satisfaction in terms of being treated as a furniture/ashtray. While this does not seem to be overtly sexual, it does seem to be odd or something particularly outside the mainstream. However, there is likely some aspect of kink or BDSM at play in such a scenario, as the person who plays the role of the furniture/ashtray would likely do this as a submissive act to someone who uses them and feels some sexual attraction to them. So, while being used as furniture/ashtray may not be overtly sexual, there is an element of BDSM present, assuming there is a dominant or submissive role for those engaging in the behaviour. There are some other sensory elements at play, such as those who enjoy the feeling of balloons on their skin and prefer to be touched/tickled by balloons if the person doing the tickling were attractive to the person being tickled.

While the terms "kink", "fetish", and "BDSM" are not synonyms, they are related and are often used interchangeably since they are all concepts linked with sexuality and sexual practices that are beyond the pale of what polite society accepts as normal. There is no real definitive authority that defines and guides the use of language, making it essentially imprecise in terms of referring to these practices. However, it is important to understand that the language used to define the groups, and these larger communities that identify as being part of "kink" or "BDSM", is important if only to understand that their significant common identifying factor is that they are identified by practices that are not mainstream and that if not directly sexual, are linked with sexuality and the expression of sexuality.

Kink/BDSM can be an occasional sexual practice, a sexual identity, or even a lifestyle (Kolmes et al., 2006). There will be many who have quirky attractions and practices that may not recognise that this makes them part of a group, or may develop tastes that are more mainstream over time, leaving quirky practices behind them in a historical sense. So, in terms of estimating how many people are kinky, fetishists, or practitioners of BDSM, the changes in social perceptions of what is not mainstream, the changes in a person's practices and predilections over time, and the self-awareness of what they like in their personal lives play a confounding role on the estimation of the population's size.

There have been attempts to estimate the size of the population that is "kinky". In terms of simply trying to estimate those that have kinky thoughts, research indicates that there is substantial evidence that there is a sizable percentage of the population (Joyal et al., 2015; Joyal & Carpentier, 2017). Joyal and Carpentier (2017) surveyed over 1,000 Quebec respondents and found evidence that about a third of the respondents indicated that they had done various activities that would normally be considered kinky, and about one-half had fantasies that would be considered kinky. In a large survey by Durex (2005), the condom company, surveys were administered in 41 countries and found that about 5% of the respondents admitted taking part in sadomasochism in their sex lives. In addition, about 20% admitted to having experiences in their sex lives that included the use of masks, bondage, or blindfolds. Moreover, Richters et al. (2008) estimate that about 2% of their Australian sample has some experience in BDSM practices, and Holvoet et al. (2017) (from a Belgian sample) derived figures that suggest about 10% of the population could be considered kinksters. Herbenick et al. (2017), in a study of the US population, estimate that 20–30% of the population has engaged in kinky practices in their sex lives, including spanking or bondage.

How many people in a population may be considered to be kinky or have a predilection to be a BDSM practitioner seems to hover somewhere between 2% of the population to about a third of the population, if this includes those who have taken part in kinky/BDSM practices. However, if kinky thoughts/fantasies are considered, about half of the population has kinky tendencies, assuming the Quebec findings can be applied to other developed societies. These data are very imprecise and hard to operationalise but suggest that many people have quirks in their private/sexual lives that is considered outside of what is socially acceptable.

The study of kink and its application in leisure studies

Psychologists seem to be those in academic circles most interested in studying kink/BDSM, and the literature on the topic has developed a great deal in recent years (see, e.g. Ardill & O'Sullivan, 2005; Bauer, 2014; Baumeister, 1997; Chaline, 2010; Connolly, 2006; Cross & Matheson, 2006; Dunkley & Brotto, 2018; Dymock, 2012; Hébert & Weaver, 2014; Holt, 2016; Moser, 1988; Moser & Levitt, 1987; Nichols, 2006; Pitagora, 2017, Richters et al., 2008; Sandnabba et al., 1999; Weinberg et al., 1984; Yost & Hunter, 2012). Much of the literature deals with the ways that people enter into kink practices, how they learn about kink practices, and how relationships function when such practices are generally frowned upon.

For example, Moser and Levitt (1987) found that over a quarter of the kinksters surveyed "came out" even before their first experiences with kink, and that about a quarter of their sample had experienced sadomasochism by the age of 16. In addition, the research shows that over 9% of sadomasochists surveyed identified as such by the time they were ten years old (Sandnabba et al., 1999). The research suggests that many kink practitioners have a long-standing predisposition towards kink, so it is likely an innate predilection instead of a choice. Moreover, the general findings of these studies illustrate that the practitioners of kink/BDSM appear to be well-adjusted, in terms of their mental health (Lindemann, 2011; Richters et al., 2008; Wismeijer & van Assen, 2013).

Other researchers are more interested in the subculture/community of those who are practitioners and the resulting distinct subculture (see, e.g. Bezreh et al., 2012; Meeker, 2013; Weinberg, 2006; Weinberg & Falk, 1980). Findings indicate that for many of the practitioners, kink/BDSM is just another pastime and simply considered a leisure activity in which they take part (Newmahr, 2010; Williams & Prior, 2015; Williams et al., 2016). Baumeister (1997) and Cross and Matheson (2006) find that this leisure pursuit is just another way to escape the stresses of life, as would be the case for many other pastimes.

There is some indication that many who are kinksters do not always feel free to express their association with the practices or lifestyle in an open way. Wright (2006) illustrates that there is good reason to not be open about association with kink, since her research documents a number of cases in which people suffer from harassment, violence, and discrimination, largely because kink practices seem to resemble violence or abusive behaviour to many in society. The fear of discrimination and violence are likely reasons that about 70% of practitioners are at least partially closeted (Wright, 2006). Kolmes et al. (2006) found that even disclosing an interest in kink to therapists can be problematic, since many therapists would confuse kink practices with abusive relationships and indications of prior experiences of abuse. Since there are costs to disclosing participation in kink, the decision of being open about having kink-related interests is often complex (Bezreh et al., 2012). Indeed, the fear of discrimination among kink practitioners seems to be an understandable consideration, as such most tend to keep their interests private.

There is a small and growing literature that looks into the pursuits of kinksters/BDSM practitioners linked with hospitality and tourism. Graham et al. (2016) and Weiss (2006) have made mention of the social outings of kinksters, illustrating the social function of their events. There is also very specialised literature that looks into the munch, a social event particular to the kink/BDSM community. In this literature, the motivations and methods of those who organise the events (Webster, 2018; Webster & Ivanov, 2019) and those who attend the social events of the community (Webster & Ivanov, 2019; Webster & Klaserner, 2019) are assessed. There is a great deal of speculation about the commercialisation of munch events (see, e.g. Webster & Ivanov, 2019), but there is also speculation that providing BDSM practitioners with the products and services that they want within a commercial market has not been fully exploited (see, e.g. Tomazos et al., 2017; Webster, 2020).

The study of kink/BDSM, from different perspectives, seems to indicate several things. First, there is the indication that kink/BDSM practitioners tend to be well-adjusted people who use kink/BDSM as a leisure practice to blow off steam, as one would any leisure practice. Second, there is some indication that there are already substantial social and other events/activities associated with the subculture/community and that these events/activities have the potential for commercial exploitation.

In the closet and discrimination

The stigma of being associated with kink is very real (De Neef et al., 2019). As such, there is a tendency for members of the community to remain in the closet (Hoff & Sprott, 2009; Shahbaz & Chirinos, 2016). The fear of "coming out" and being open about kink is not necessarily exaggerated. For example, in 2014, the Canadian Broadcasting Corporation dismissed a well-known radio host, Jian Ghomeshi, because it came to light that the host was known to be involved in BDSM (Keenan, 2014). In the United Kingdom, a woman alleged in court that she was dismissed from her job as a midwife for wearing jewellery around her neck that included a BDSM symbol (Fae, 2011). In New Jersey, Kristen Hyman, a police officer, was dismissed after videos came to light in which she had illustrated her skills as a dominatrix in films, years before becoming an officer. She claimed that she simply considered the role as an acting job (Inside Edition, 2018). In a high-profile case, a United Nations weapons inspector, Jack McGeorge, was pressured to resign when it was made known that he was a BDSM practitioner (Noah, 2002). While a great deal of this seems to be anecdotal, it does appear that the stigma of being associated with kink/BDSM may have severe repercussions for many, and there are instances in which association with kink/BDSM has hurt people professionally and, likely, personally.

The law, as well, is not necessarily helpful, as "morality clauses" in employment contracts are usually vaguely worded and can be understood to include association with kink/BDSM as grounds for dismissal from a job (Keenan, 2014). US legislation does not protect people who are associated with kink practices or lifestyle, so such dismissals may be legal (Keenan, 2014). Indeed, many of the practices of BDSM may not be protected by some interpretations of the US Constitution (Volokh, 2016). Additionally, there is some indication that association with kink can be an issue in civil court in the case of child custody proceedings (Klein & Moser, 2006). There are many other instances in which kinksters may also face discrimination by the law (Ridinger, 2006).

There are some widely known practices in the kink community that are designed to protect the identity of those who attend kinkster events. For example, Webster (2018) illustrates that the organisers of munches consider the choice of venues, suggest the use of street clothes to allow for conversations among attendees with little reason to believe that others would overhear suggestive discussions, and shun overt uses of kink symbols and clothing at such events held in public. There is also an indication that even at kink events, such as munches, only about 65% of participants use their real names consistently (Webster & Klaserner, 2019) and may sometimes wear masks to shield their identity. This suggests that even within a supportive environment of like-minded participants, many at such events still do not feel confident and safe enough to identify themselves. There may be a functional reason for a person not using her/his real name at an event, such as using a pseudonym to create an identity that may be more interesting/exotic/sexy to others, but it also serves a very practical use, making it harder to connect people to a social group in which there may be real negative repercussions for having such an association. In short, kinksters are a sexual minority with individuals who have good reason to hide their predilections in many developed countries, and this stands in contrast to gays/lesbians who are generally met with indifference or at least a lack of open hostility to their sexual practices.

Hospitality/leisure and kink

There has been very little research that has laid out how kinksters socialise and how businesses can cater to their needs. The most recent, and most thorough, is Webster (2020) who investigated the various institutions of kink to illustrate that the kink/BDSM subculture has a number of different types of events. Table 12.1 summarises the very real differences between play and non-play events, since they require radically different environments in which to operate. It can be seen that the non-play events require very little capital but run the risk of taking place where the identities of people attending can be made public. The methods used in such cases are assisted by the choice of venue and the enforcement of rules that are used to ensure that no undue attention is brought to those in attendance with overt use of BDSM symbols or flamboyant attire. However, in the more private venue of a dungeon, such rules are not needed.

Table 12.1 Kink events types and characteristics.

Event Type	Likely Venue	Dress Code	Participation	Likely Activities
Non-Play Events: munch, slosh, kinky drinkies, liquid munch	Restaurant/bar/pub/online (since 2020)	Street dress	Open to public	Food, drink, general socialising
Play Events: generic play parties, theme-specific play parties, workshops, conferences, training events, competition	Public dungeon, private home, private club, swinger club	Street dress, costume theme, anything goes up to full nudity	Open or by invitation, depending on event and venue	General socialising, general kink play, non-sexual kink, play according to theme, anything imaginable

Source: Modified from Webster (2020).

The dungeon is "a room or space designated specifically for BDSM play or BDSM scenes" (Kinkly, 2021, n.p.); however, there are private and public dungeon spaces. Particular kinksters may have dungeons in their home, typically in basements, while "public dungeons can be found in fetish studios, sex workspaces, sex clubs, warehouses, and nightclubs (sometimes during specific fetish parties and themed nights) and are usually open to the public" (Kinkly, 2021, n.p.). Dungeons will often include various forms of furniture that are used for different needs of kink/BDSM practitioners, such as a St. Andrew's cross (a large cross to which people are often tethered) and other furniture for bondage and flogging, meaning that dungeons and their substantial furniture are not necessarily mobile. The dungeon is a social space, but because of the public's attitudes towards kinksters, dungeons generally attempt to remain as inconspicuous as possible. However, there are some exceptions, such as London's Torture Garden, an establishment that has been in existence for decades and is well-known to kinksters.

There are a substantial number of businesses that cater to the tourism, leisure, and hospitality needs of kinksters. For example, La Domaine Esemar is a facility in rural New York State that has been in existence since the 1990s. It offers "bed and dungeon" visits, catering to a distinct type of tourist/leisure traveller. A visitor may pay for the services of a dominant or a submissive as well as the expected food and lodging, offering visitors an immersive kink experience with others in a rural setting. A similar, but much larger, facility is in the Czech Republic, the Other World Kingdom (2019), which is a facility dedicated to female domination in a 16th-century chateau on a 3-hectare (7.4 acre) estate and has been in operation since the 1990s.

Apart from these two notable facilities, other commercial enterprises create opportunities for travel and leisure activities for kinksters. A notable one is Kink-BNB, which is an analogy to AirBNB but designed with the kinkster in mind, allowing kinksters to identify kink-friendly facilities for travellers and, typically, identifying homes for rent with dungeons in them. Dark Odyssey offers events in kink at various venues around the United States. Typically, their events take over a hotel venue and offer speakers and training on kink-related topics. Domme Trips, run by female dominants, offers annual events in the Caribbean in which a person can pay to attend either as a dominatrix or a submissive for the stay. Camp Crucible offers an annual camping event in which kinksters camp together and have various kink-friendly activities.

The travel, tourism, and hospitality services offered to the modern kinkster, by necessity, remains largely underground or at least not very visible to the non-kinkster. The businesses here are just some examples of what is currently available. While some larger enterprises are offering kinkster travel and leisure services, it is likely the smaller scale commercial dungeons that are supplying much of the need of the kinkster subculture.

Commercial opportunities and discrimination

Kinksters are, and will likely continue to be, discriminated against for the foreseeable future, and this will play a role in shaping the tourism-related products that they demand from the market. For kinksters, there are issues that are almost insurmountable. First, they live in societies in which they are a clear minority, since one of the basic elements of defining a kinkster is based upon the quirkiness of the practices and desires of the individual. Second, many of the practices of kink may not be particularly legal. For example, while tickling a person with a balloon may not be illegal in many places, restraining people with handcuffs or flogging a person may not be legal. Indeed, even when some practices may be consensual and legal (e.g. a person manipulating another person's breathing or flogging a person), an outsider viewing the behaviour could identify the practice as dangerous, suggestive of an abusive relationship, or simply find the practice too shocking to permit in a civilised society. Therefore, many practices of kink will emote a visceral reaction, and this will prevent large-scale commercialisation of kink products in the open.

Fortunately for those involved in kink, the practitioners can blend into the general population very well and are not particularly easy to identify. Thus, in the age of the internet, the community of kinksters can function as never before. Yet, it seems that kinksters will never really be fully included in the mainstream of polite society and will always be at risk of suffering from discrimination.

Tourism, as an industry, can cater to some of the needs of kinksters but will require some knowledge and flexibility to supply kink practitioners with the products and services that they need. First, tourism services have to recognise the possible cost of being identified as a member of this community, as their reputation may be on the line when serving as a venue for kinksters and the careers of many kink practitioners can be jeopardised. Second, tourism services have to understand and recognise that many practices of kink/BDSM may be shocking, in a questionable grey area with regard to legality, or hold risks that may be greater than they are willing to accept. Thus, tourism services have to understand the risks, not only with the revelation of the identities of participants but the types of risks and liabilities that may occur when serving as a venue for kink. As such, training and a recognition of best practices to ensure safety would create a sense of safety for participants and venues.

Kinksters are unlikely to fight discrimination, as they are a diffuse and hard to define minority in any society. At any rate, fighting discrimination is unlikely to be very fruitful when they, by definition, are individuals with sexual tastes outside the mainstream. When faced with discrimination, they are likely to continue to remain undercover in their societies, use subtle symbols to identify each other in public, attend events that are only known to other kinksters, and keep many of their sexual predilections hidden from the non-kinky world in which they inhabit. However, there are many commercial opportunities to meet the demand for kinky services in hospitality and tourism (Tomazos et al., 2017; Webster, 2020).

References

Ardill, S., & O'Sullivan, S. (2005). Upsetting an applecart: Difference, desire and lesbian sadomasochism. *Feminist Review*, *80*(1), 98–126.

Bauer, R. (2014). *Queer BDSM intimacies: Critical consent and pushing boundaries*. Palgrave MacMillan.

Baumeister, R. F. (1997). The enigmatic appeal of sexual masochism: Why people desire pain, bondage, and humiliation in sex. *Journal of Social and Clinical Psychology, 16*(2), 133–150.

Bezreh, T., Weinberg, T. S., & Edgar, T. (2012). BDSM disclosure and stigma management: Identifying opportunities for sex education. *American Journal of Sexuality Education, 7*(1), 37–61.

Bullough, V. L., & Bonnie, B. (1990). *Contraception: A guide to birth control methods*. Prometheus Books.

Chaline, E. R. (2010). The construction, maintenance, and evolution of gay SM sexualities and sexual identities: A preliminary description of gay SM sexual identity practices. *Sexualities, 13*(3), 338–356.

Christin-Maitre, S. (2013). History of oral contraceptive drugs and their use worldwide. *Best Practice & Research Clinical Endocrinology & Metabolism, 27*(1), 3–12.

Connolly, P. H. (2006). Psychological functioning of bondage/domination/sado-masochism (BDSM) practitioners. *Journal of Psychology and Human Sexuality, 18*(1), 79–120.

CROP. (2017). *Are you in favour of same-sex marriage? 74% of Canadians and 80% of Quebecers support it*. Retrieved September 26, 2021, from www.crop.ca/en/blog/2017/207/

Cross, P. A., & Matheson, K. (2006). Understanding sadomasochism: An empirical examination of four perspectives. *Journal of Homosexuality, 50*(2–3), 133–166.

De Neef, N., Coppens, V., Huys, W., & Morrens, M. (2019). Bondage-discipline, Dominance-submission and sadomasochism (BDSM) from an integrative biopsychosocial perspective: A systematic review. *Sexual Medicine, 7*(2), 129–144. https://doi.org/10.1016/j.esxm.2019.02.002

Dunkley, C. R., & Brotto, L. A. (2018). Clinical considerations in treating BDSM practitioners: A review. *Journal of Sex & Marital Therapy, 44*(7), 701–712.

Durex. (2005). *2005 global survey results*. Retrieved September 26, 2021, from www.data360.org/pdf/20070416064139.Global%20Sex%20Survey.pdf

Dymock, A. (2012). But femsub is broken too! On the normalisation of BDSM and the problem of pleasure. *Psychology and Sexuality, 3*(1), 54–68.

Fae, J. (2011, August 16). Believing in bondage. *The Guardian*. www.theguardian.com/commentisfree/2011/aug/16/bondage-bdsm-consensual-slavery

Graham, B. C., Butler, S. E., McGraw, R., Cannes, S. M., & Smith, J. (2016). Member perspectives on the role of BDSM communities. *Journal of Sex Research, 53*(8), 895–909.

Hébert, A., & Weaver, A. (2014). An examination of personality characteristics associated with BDSM orientations. *Canadian Journal of Human Sexuality, 23*(2), 106–115.

Herbenick, D., Bowling, J., Fu, T.-C., Dodge, B., Guerra-Reyes, L., & Sanders, S. (2017). Sexual diversity in the United States: Results from a nationally representative probability sample of adult women and men. *PLOS ONE, 12*(7), e0181198. https://doi.org/10.1371/journal.pone.0181198

Hoff, G., & Sprott, R. A. (2009). Therapy experiences of clients with BDSM sexualities: Listening to a stigmatized sexuality. *Electronic Journal of Human Sexuality, 12*(9), 30–54.

Holt, K. (2016). Blacklisted: Boundaries, violations, and retaliatory behavior in the BDSM community. *Deviant Behavior, 37*(8), 917–930.

Holvoet, L., Huys, W., Coppens, V., Seeuws, J., Goethals, K., & Morrens, M. (2017). Fifty shades of Belgian gray: The prevalence of BDSM-related fantasies and activities in the general population. *Journal of Sexual Medicine, 14*(9), 1152–1159. https://doi.org/10.1016/j.sxm.2017.07.003

Human Rights Campaign. (2021). *Marriage equality around the world*. Retrieved September 26, 2021, from www.hrc.org/resources/marriage-equality-around-the-world

Inside Edition. (2018, February 13). Kristen Hyman, the cop fired over role as dominatrix in video, determined to get back on the force. *Inside Edition*. www.insideedition.com/kristen-hyman-cop-fired-over-role-dominatrix-video-determined-get-back-force-40694

James, E. L. (2012). *Fifty shades of Grey*. Vintage Books.

Joyal, C. C., & Carpentier, J. (2017). The prevalence of paraphilic interests and behaviors in the general population: A provincial survey. *The Journal of Sex Research, 54*(2), 161–171.

Joyal, C. C., Cossette, A., & Lapierre, V. (2015). What exactly is an unusual sexual fantasy? *Journal of Sexual Medicine, 12*(2), 328–340.

Keenan, J. (2014). Can you really be fired for being kinky? Absolutely. *Slate*. https://slate.com/human-interest/2014/10/the-jian-ghomeshi-case-echoes-many-kinksters-worst-fears-being-outed-and-fired.html

Kinkly. (2021). *Dungeon*. Retrieved September 23, 2021, from www.kinkly.com/definition/653/bdsm-dungeon

Klein, M., & Moser, C. (2006). S/M (sadomasochistic) interests as an issue in a child custody proceeding. *Journal of Homosexuality, 50*(2–3), 233–242. https://doi.org/10.1300/J082v50n02_11

Kolmes, K., Stock, W., & Moser, C. (2006). Investigating bias in psychotherapy with BDSM clients. *Journal of Homosexuality, 50*(2–3), 301–324. https://doi.org/10.1300/J082v50n02_15

Lindemann, D. (2011). BDSM as therapy? *Sexualities, 14*(2), 151–172.

McCarthy, J. (2021, June 8). Record-high 70% in U.S. support same-sex marriage. *Gallup*. Retrieved September 26, 2021, from https://news.gallup.com/poll/350486/record-high-support-same-sex-marriage.aspx

Meeker, C. (2013). Learning the ropes: An exploration of BDSM stigma, identity disclosure, and workplace socialization. In M. S. Plakhotnik & S. M. Nielsen (Eds.), *Proceedings of the 12th annual South Florida education research conference* (pp. 134–141). Florida International University. Retrieved September 26, 2021, from http://education.fiu.edu/research_conference/

Merriam-Webster. (2019a). *Fetish*. Retrieved September 26, 2021, from www.merriam-webster.com/dictionary/

Merriam-Webster. (2019b). *Kink*. Retrieved September 26, 2021, from www.merriam-webster.com/dictionary/

Miller, K. (2021). *Kink vs. Fetish: What's the difference? Here's what experts say*. Retrieved September 20, 2021, from www.health.com/sex/kink-vs-fetish-whats-the-difference

Moser, C. (1988). Sadomasochism. *Journal of Social Work and Human Sexuality, 7*(1), 43–56.

Moser, C., & Levitt, E. E. (1987). An exploratory-descriptive study of a sadomasochistically oriented sample. *Journal of Sex Research, 23*(3), 322–337.

Newmahr, S. (2010). Rethinking kink: Sadomasochism as serious leisure. *Qualitative Sociology, 33*(3), 313–331.

Nichols, M. (2006). Psychotherapeutic issues with kinky clients: Clinical problems, yours and theirs. *Journal of Homosexuality, 50*(2–3), 281–300.

Noah, T. (2002, December 3). Pleasure, pain, and Saddam Hussein: A meditation on recreational violence. *Slate*. https://slate.com/human-interest/2014/10/the-jian-ghomeshi-case-echoes-many-kinksters-worst-fears-being-outed-and-fired.html

Other World Kingdom. (2019). Retrieved September 26, 2021, from www.owk.cz/who.php

Peakman, J. (2016). *The pleasure's all mine: A history of perverse sex*. Reaktion Books.

Pew Research Center. (2019a). *Gay marriage around the world*. Retrieved September 26, 2021, www.pewforum.org/2017/08/08/gay-marriage-around-the-world-2013/

Pew Research Center. (2019b). *Changing attitudes on gay marriage*. Retrieved September 26, 2021, from www.pewforum.org/fact-sheet/changing-attitudes-on-gay-marriage/

Pitagora, D. (2017). No pain, no gain? Therapeutic and relational benefits of subspace in BDSM contexts. *Journal of Positive Sexuality*, *3*, 44–54.

Rehor, J. E. (2015). Sensual, erotic, and sexual behaviors of women from the "kink" community. *Archives of Sexual Behavior*, *44*(4), 825–836. https://doi.org/10.1007/s10508-015-0524-2

Richters, J., de Visser, R. O., Rissel, C. E., Grulich, A. E., & Smith, A. M. (2008). Demographic and psychosocial features of participants in bondage and discipline, "sadomasochism" or dominance and submission (BDSM): Data from a national survey. *The Journal of Sexual Medicine*, *5*(7), 1660–1668.

Ridinger, R. B. (2006). Negotiating limits: The legal status of S/M in the United States. *Journal of Homosexuality*, *50*(2–3), 189–216. https://doi.org/10.1300/J082v50n02_09

Sandnabba, N. K., Santtila, P., & Nordling, N. (1999). Sexual behavior and social adaptation among sadomasochistically oriented males. *The Journal of Sex Research*, *36*(3), 273–282.

Shahbaz, C., & Chirinos, P. (2016). *Becoming a kink aware therapist*. Routledge.

Sloan, L. J. (2015). Ace of (BDSM) clubs: Building asexual relationships through BDSM practice. *Sexualities*, *18*(5–6), 548–563. https://doi.org/10.1177/1363460714550907.

Tomazos, K., O'Gorman, K. D., & MacLaren, A. C. (2017). From leisure to tourism: How BDSM demonstrates the transition of deviant pursuits to mainstream products. *Tourism Management*, *60*, 30–41.

Volokh, E. (2016, March 4). No constitutional right to engage in consensual BDSM sex. *Washington Post*. www.washingtonpost.com/news/volokh-conspiracy/wp/2016/03/04/no-constitutional-right-to-engage-in-consensual-bdsm-sex/

Webster, C. (2018). Fifty shades of organizing kinkster events: Munch events in the BDSM community. *International Journal of Hospitality and Event Management*, *2*(1), 19–37.

Webster, C. (2020). Kinky people need kinky events: Kinkster events and kink/BDSM products in hospitality and tourism. In D. C. Parry & C. W. Johnson (Eds.), *Sex and leisure: Promiscuous perspectives* (pp. 127–143). Routledge.

Webster, C., & Ivanov, S. (2019). Events are bound to happen: Spank you very much. *Event Management*, *23*(4–5), 669–684.

Webster, C., & Klaserner, M. (2019). Fifty shades of socializing: Slosh and munch events in the BDSM Community. *Event Management*, *23*(1), 135–147.

Weinberg, M. S., Williams, C. J., & Moser, C. (1984). The social constituents of sadomasochism. *Social Problems*, *31*(4), 379–389.

Weinberg, T. (2006). Sadomasochism and the social sciences: A review of the sociological and social psychological literature. *Journal of Homosexuality*, *50*(2), 17–40.

Weinberg, T., & Falk, G. (1980). The social organization of sadism and masochism. *Deviant Behavior*, *1*(3–4), 379–393.

Weiss, M. D. (2006). Working at play: BDSM sexuality in the San Francisco Bay area. *Anthropologica*, *48*(2), 229–245.

Williams, D. J., & Prior, E. E. (2015). Wait, go back, I might miss something important! Applying Leisure 101 to simplify and complicate BDSM. *Journal of Positive Sexuality*, *1*, 63–69.

Williams, D. J., Prior, E. E., Alvarado, T., Thomas, J. N., & Christensen, M. C. (2016). Is bondage and discipline, dominance and submission, and sadomasochism (BDSM) recreational leisure? A descriptive exploratory investigation. *Journal of Sexual Medicine*, *13*(7), 1091–1094. https://doi.org/10.1016/j.jsxm.2016.05.001

Wismeijer, A. A. J., & van Assen, M. A. L. M. (2013). Psychological characteristics of BDSM practitioners. *The Journal of Sexual Medicine*, *10*(8), 1943–1952.

Wright, S. (2006). Discrimination of SM-identified individuals. *Journal of Homosexuality*, *50*(2–3), 217–231. https://doi.org/10.1300/J082v50n02_10

Yost, M. R., & Hunter, L. E. (2012). BDSM practitioners' understandings of their initial attraction to BDSM sexuality: Essentialist and constructionist narratives. *Psychology and Sexuality*, *3*(3), 244–259.

13 But where is your wife? Reflections of a gay tourist in a heteronormative environment

Amit Kama

A matronly lady, who runs a bed & breakfast (B&B) in Ireland, welcomed me to her home. Situated in the wonderful countryside of evergreen vistas, it was exactly what I needed and something to which I looked forward. Even the obstinate rain was blessed in the eyes of someone who lives in the Middle East where rain is quite uncommon. I made the reservation for a room in her home some weeks earlier indicating that we were a couple. When my husband of 23 years came out of the rented car she cried out: "But where is your wife?". She then led us to a twin-room instead of the double-room I initially thought I was booking. I certainly do not wish to accuse the proprietor of blatant homophobia but to convey how a trip to a rural location can be overshadowed by a single utterance. This taken-for-granted assumption that all guests are (or should be) heterosexual is shared by most non-LGBT (lesbian, gay, bisexual, transgender) persons. This assumption is grounded in the heteronormative ideology that accrues various benefits (material as well as symbolic) to heterosexuals while donning various sanctions to anyone who is not. These sanctions vary from homophobic violence to legal discrimination, from discomfort at the company of LGBT to being "blind" to their existence. The Irish B&B owner, following this heteronormative perception, could not realise or anticipate that a booking couple is not necessarily non-same-gender. We simply caught her off-guard. This vignette demonstrates ubiquitous questions that my husband and I, like countless other same-gender couples, grapple with: do we really need to come out? When? At the time of booking a room or upon checking-in? Will we be unwelcome or frowned upon? In this chapter, I will strive to show how being a gay tourist has implications on many levels, from the decision of travelling to the choice of a proper venue.

Introduction

I am writing now with great caution and apprehension. Indeed, I feel as if I am entering a veritable minefield. Metaphorical as well, as real mines are everywhere: from the starting point of writing about gay men as if they were one monolithic group, through the obvious neglect of other groups that are nowadays routinely (and even mindlessly) assembled under the LGBT acronym, to issues of theoretical and empirical soundness and reliability that may accrue from this personal narrative. I wish to stress from the beginning that I am fully aware of these pitfalls, yet I hope and believe that my readers will be, at least, able to get a glimpse into the universe of experiences that a gay man encounters and lives through during the process of becoming and being a tourist in a foreign land. I am employing here two verbs – to become and to be – that may seem a bit unconventional in this context. It is my strong belief that tourism is a liminal stage: in between and in betwixt quotidian routines. One must not only prepare and plan for the overseas visit, but one also needs to construct a sort of identity while being a tourist, which is not necessarily the same in everyday life. In other words, one must invest various sources (particularly financial and time) in the planning of the trip and then adopt an identity for it. The identity is one of a foreigner, limited in language proficiency, and outside the norm of daily practices (e.g. work and family). The entire process, naturally, begins with the basic questions: should I travel? Where to? In the following pages, I wish to address these issues in the context of gay men.

Why only gay men? I have been politically active in Israeli LGBT struggles for equality and social change since the early 1980s. In the subsequent decades, Israel has made tremendous strides (that are beyond the scope of this chapter) in the legal, political, social, and cultural arenas concerning the LGBT community (see, e.g. Gross, 2015; Harel, 2000; Hartal, 2020; Kama, 2011). As one of the leaders of this change, I have been closely involved with myriad of gay men. After some 20 years in the forefront, I decided to turn to academia and research the group in which I felt deeply entrenched and embedded while surely being careful not to trespass the invisible line of going too "native" (Lewin & Leap, 1996). Since 2000, I have been extensively studying various aspects of gay men: sports, leisure, politics, media consumption, and so on. This chapter is focused on only gay men, not just because they constitute the group I am most familiar with but mainly because other groups of the LGBT acronym face different challenges and undergo different experiences (e.g. Poria, 2006).

Here, a serious caveat is in strict order. Studying, researching, and writing about a social group, especially one that has been socio-historically constructed as an ultimate "Other" (more about this soon), may erroneously reflect its conceptualisation as homogenous or monolithic. Most positivistic researchers envelop whole groups under strict titles that diminish and annihilate individuality and heterogeneity. Qualitative researchers and phenomenologists may also err in assuming their subjects' similarities are stronger than their idiosyncrasies. It is certainly unavoidable to write about a group rather than about individuals, and in the subsequent pages I will also write as if "gay men" is an actual umbrella term that assumes they are all the same. Moreover, I am going to employ my own personal autobiographical vignettes to make some general comments. And, yet, it should be remembered that gay men do not constitute a homogeneous social group. Writing about them as if they were one seamless collection may be rightly construed as simplification, generalisation, and stereotypisation. Their only common denominators are their gender and sexual orientation. I would also add that the main and fundamental characteristic that distinguishes gay from non-gay men is the ever-present issue of identity management and its corollary, namely, the question of coming out.

Coming out is not only a crucial element of being gay, but it also has ramifications in the act of playing the tourist role (about which I will elaborate later). Countless scholarly papers and books (e.g. Dank, 1979; Sedgwick, 1990; Troiden, 1993) have been looking into the mechanism by which a gay person (in this case, lesbians and bisexual men and women undergo identical processes (Morris, 2008)) discloses his sexual orientation to others. This is a life-long practice because in every encounter and communication with another person, the gay individual asks himself: does s/he have to know about me? Should I come out to her/him? And, of course, there are calculations of symbolic and material gains versus sanctions and losses: will I be physically or emotionally harmed or abused? Will our relationship be enhanced and more intimate? And the like. The conceptualisation of the intensity of the role and vitality of coming out is rooted in the late 1960s American gay and lesbian liberation organisations. Many other cultures have embraced the idea that coming out is psychologically healthy and politically meaningful (Kama, 2000). However, in recent years, younger generations tend to integrate their sexual orientation within their identity in a way that does not necessitate coming out or diminishes the need to do so (Gray, 2009; Seidman et al., 1999). They tend to be more open and comfortable about their sexuality. They expect the same from travel providers, to the extent that it should not even be an issue. Perhaps, we are now entering a post-sexual-identity politics where one's sexual orientation and gender identity do not comprise a basic element of the self to be continuously grappled with. Perhaps younger generations will not have to deal with the questions this chapter poses. At any event, I am writing this chapter from the perspective of a very much alive and kicking sexual identity politics.

For me, as an elderly gay man, being gay is paramount among the various components of my identity. My perceptions of self and the surrounding social world emanate from a strong sense of otherness and from a long history of encountering homophobia – that is, a set of cognitive and affective attitudes and behaviours exhibited by individuals or social groups against LGBT (Sears, 1997) – at home, in school, in academia, and in many other instances where being gay constitutes an obstacle. I grew up in a world where homosexuality was a moral sin, a psychological aberration, and a crime. Until I was 28, the law in Israel condemned homosexuality with up to ten years of imprisonment. For me, coming out is always in the threshold of my consciousness, and contemplating it is forever part and parcel of my relations with others. Furthermore, in my mind, there is always an altercation with the slogan "Why do you need to flaunt your homosexuality?"

Another element that characterises gay men of my generation is the need, very similar to other minority group members, to seek others like me in every social situation. Growing up in a small town in the desert in the 1960s–1970s meant that the feelings of isolation were acute: are there any other boys who are like me? Additionally, since no LGBT were present in the public sphere and media representations were null, there were no role models to whom I could aspire. A desolate, lonely, and futile life was the only option for me. When I gradually got involved in a gay and lesbian organisation and met others like me, I realised that my gloomy expectations could turn into a hopeful future. This was a revelation that actually changed my life course. However, the early background was so profoundly ingrained in my psyche and that my sexual orientation became salient to this day. I forever look around me to see that I am not alone, that there are other men who feel like me. I assume that many LGBT people of my generation seek the company of other LGBT people in order to alleviate the overwhelming sense of otherness so entrenched in their selves. I will elaborate on how this aspect is relevant to tourism later on.

LGBT tourism studies

Recent decades have witnessed a burgeoning academic interest in LGBT individuals and communities. Vast empirical and theoretical literature has inundated various disciplines that delve into a large array of aspects pertaining to their identity, social relations, politics, representations, and so on. The emerging academic interest in LGBT tourism is quite new in this rich field, though in fact it mostly focuses on gay men (Vorobjovas-Pinta & Hardy, 2016), and my present contribution obviously only adds to this bias. LGBT tourism is considered to be a significant market segment, accounting for US$165 billion globally[1] (Gay European Tourism Association, n.d.). Given this number, it is no wonder the subject has caught the attention of both researchers and business firms.

The study of LGBT tourism can be traced to the publication of the first academic article (Holcomb & Luongo, 1996) and the first book on this subject matter (Clift et al., 2002). Since these pioneering scholars have paved the way for studying the nexus between tourism and LGBT identities, needs, and practices, innumerable publications covered a vast array of aspects: from its economics and material revenues to critique of the commercialisation of Pride parades; from sex tourism to gentrification of erstwhile "gay ghettos"; from the myth of the "gay dollar" to homophobic tropical destinations. In other words, quite a few scholars from around the globe and various disciplines have lately been conducting analyses that are meant to understand and apprise the motivations, destination selection, actual experiences of LGBT tourists, and the new markets that are aimed at this so-called "lucrative" niche. Due to brevity constraints, I can neither enumerate nor summarise this field here (see, e.g. Clift & Forrest, 1999; Guaracino & Salvato, 2017; Hartal, 2019; Holcomb & Luongo, 1996; Howe, 2001; Hughes, 2004; Kama & Ram, 2020; Pritchard et al., 2000; Puar, 2002; Waitt & Markwell, 2006; Waitt et al., 2008; Weeden et al., 2016).

The academic and business interests in LGBT tourism simultaneously address two aspects: on the one hand, attention is given to the special needs of LGBT travellers, especially concerning their need for inclusion and feelings of safety (to be discussed later). On the other hand, they accentuate the widely held notion that gay men constitute a lucrative market since they are believed to be a high-income group who leads a leisure-oriented lifestyle and, thus, spend more money as tourists. Consequently, they are a prime target for the tourism industry. Gay men are frequently considered a wealthy segment (Guaracino, 2007; Peters, 2011) since, like other males, they enjoy a higher income than females, are mostly single, and can accumulate and allocate higher financial resources for leisure activities and conspicuous consumption. According to these prevalent opinions, gay couples also benefit from being DINK (dual income, no kids) households. In other words, single gay men, whatever their job or income, can potentially allocate a bigger share of their earnings for leisure activities. They do not have obligations to invest funds for the rearing and future of offspring, and they are at liberty to spend their money for their own enjoyment and gratification in the present. The same applies to DINK couples who are a highly coveted consumer sector in the tourism industry.

Tourism studies, by and large, take these positions for granted and assume that what Waitt et al. (2008, p. 781) call the "pink travel economy" is indeed more profitable. Despite these widely held beliefs, several studies have found them to be nothing but a myth (Badgett, 2003; Vorobjovas-Pinta & Hardy, 2016). Reviewing the literature shows that much of the research has focused on White, wealthy, urban, middle-class, gay men without children, and therefore, it is biased in the economic context.

While drawing on LGBT as a distinct target population may be seen as a breakthrough in the otherwise dominant heteronormativity of tourism studies (Waitt et al., 2008), it may run the danger of narrowing the discussion into an exclusive niche of a "gay ghetto" (Guaracino & Salvato, 2017). Despite the fact that the LGBT group is heterogenic comprising of various sub-groups, ethnic and other minorities, it seems that most of the studies address, primarily, only a distinct subgroup, namely, White, educated, and affluent gay men. In other words, in spite of the umbrella term commonly used, lesbians, bisexuals, and transgender people are less studied (Ginder & Byun, 2015). Vorobjovas-Pinta and Hardy (2016) argue that current knowledge of LGBT tourism overlooks societal transformations and legal developments that have affected the very circumstances of LGBT tourism. It may seem that in the third decade of the 21st century, conditions and circumstances in this context are rapidly improving, and LGBT tourism is entering a new, brave phase. However, in the present chapter, I wish to shed light on some aspects of being a gay tourist from my own personal experiences.

Motivations for overseas travel

LGBT tourism is, *inter alia*, the result of lifelong experiences of LGBT people being disenfranchised, discriminated against, and the target of heterosexist practices (the wide-ranging array of formal, legal, and governmental practices that discriminate against and exclude LGBT) and homophobia (cognitive and affective attitudes, and behaviours exhibited by individuals or social groups against LGBT (Sears, 1997)). LGBT tourism is distinguished from non-LGBT tourism because it constitutes an outlet to relieve and alleviate minority stress, which evolves from prejudice, rejection, hiding one's sexual orientation, and discrimination that create a hostile and stressful environment (Meyer, 2003) that many LGBT individuals suffer on a daily basis. It is meant to present an opportunity to escape into LGBT-friendly circumstances where LGBT are welcomed and homophobic hostilities or threats are minimised, and to enjoy the ability to behave freely and independently of oppressive societal sanctions felt at home. LGBT holidays can also mean a way to construct and validate individual and collective identities (Hughes, 2002). Indeed, "gay travel motivations usually arise from the opportunity to feel free and a possibility to articulate 'gayness' in a non-judgmental space . . . and a sense of belonging to a particular community" (Vorobjovas-Pinta & Hardy, 2016, p. 412).

In sum, gay tourists prefer destinations celebrated as friendly – that is, spatial concentrations of venues, accommodations, and events that cater to gay people, where socialising with predominantly or exclusively other gay men is easy and safe and where the host culture, city, and/or state are not threatening (Guaracino & Salvato, 2017; Hughes & Deutsch, 2010; Vorobjovas-Pinta & Hardy, 2016) – thus becoming famous sites whose reputation is consolidated via personal communication (i.e. friends who have been there and recommend them) and the tourism industry itself (especially through travel guides [to be discussed later]).

I probably personify the ultimate White, affluent, bourgeois gay stereotype discussed earlier. My daily life is not strife with problems, but for many years I have been enjoying planning trips overseas and travelling. I dare even say that, beyond the fun, I NEED to go abroad three to four times a year. The past year and a half of COVID-19 restrictions proved to me how desperately I miss my trips. They are almost bare necessities. Tel Aviv, where I live, despite being a gay-friendly city (Ram et al., 2019) feels suffocating. Israel and Tel Aviv are relatively small in size and population. Moreover, Israeli society is very close-knit and many individuals are in overlapping role relationships, for instance, when my student's mother was in my high school class or when my colleague was my commander in my military service. Wherever one goes, they are bound to meet someone who knows them or has an indirect connection with someone else they know. Coming out in these circumstances usually means that the information about being LGBT – which is supposed to be discreet or a secret meant solely for the other party – can easily be passed on to others. The act of disclosure may, and does, start a chain of gossip. For example, I was 23 and, with a vigorously pounding heart, visited (for the first time) a clandestine gay bar in Tel Aviv, where I moved after too many years in a small desert town. When I visited my parents some weeks later, my father told me that their neighbour heard from her brother-in-law that he saw me entering a shady bar: "What does this mean? Are you homosexual"? he asked in disbelief. Consequently, I need to be in places where I can walk the streets holding my husband's hand and where we can go to gay venues and feel more at ease. Where a kiss between two men is not frowned upon. Where I can be anonymous and not worry about the diffusion of information about me.

My proclivity is not unique. Some years ago, I (Kama, 2014) wrote that one of the most distinctive aspects of the leisure patterns of Israeli gay men, of all walks of life and segments, is relatively frequent and short visits abroad, particularly to big cities and/or "gay Meccas" (Jeffrey et al., 2017; Waitt & Markwell, 2006), such as Berlin, Mykonos, Amsterdam, New York, or Barcelona. In these unique sites, public displays of affection, as a prime example, are not chastised or frowned upon. This phenomenon has historical roots when Israel offered few leisure opportunities for gay men. But even today, there are only a very few gay establishments, where gay men can feel at ease in a public space. European and American big cities offer many attractions for every taste and appetite. Such Western urban centres provide gay tourists with a sense of emancipation. They are havens where one can feel free, liberated, and, not less importantly, enjoy anonymity and play various roles (e.g. sexual practices, such as S&M or special subcultures such as the Leather scene) far away from prying, albeit friendly, eyes. Anonymity abroad is vital for Israeli gay men of two kinds: those who are still "closeted" and wish to keep their homosexuality covert and those whose practices and tastes (sexual and otherwise) are meant to be discreet.

But, at the same time, the very attractiveness of the "gay meccas" also means that gay tourists may limit their visits to only metropolitan centres at the price of eschewing rural places. For instance, I frequently try to combine a visit to a big city with travelling in the countryside. As an inquisitive anthropologist, I always look out for other gay men. While there are plentiful gay men in the city, their number dwindles dramatically in rural areas. In other words, I believe that the clear benefits and attractiveness associated with the city, versus homophobia associated with rural areas, dramatically affect gay tourists' itineraries and, ultimately, may limit their willingness and capacity to explore uncharted territories.

Homophobia

Homosexual men have been pariahs since time immemorial. Their identity has been tainted and stigmatised. Their existence, emotions, and sexual practices have been persecuted by religious churches, legal and state authorities, and the scientific establishment. They have been put to death by stoning or hanging. They have been jailed. They have been subjected to various psychological methods to cure them. Forever on the fringes of "normal", "healthy", and "respectful" society, homosexuals were fundamentally outcasts. They have been both concretely and symbolically annihilated. Two ground-breaking developments occurred in the second half of the 20th century: namely, depathologisation and decriminalisation of homosexuality (Garnets & Kimmel, 1993). Consequently, momentous changes have been evolving in the past 60 years that have resulted in the relative inclusion of gay men into mainstream society. Mainstream society is now more inclined to embrace gay men and accept their individual, as well as collective identities. Social, cultural, legal, and judicial institutions – from the court to the media, from the family to the workplace – have lately integrated them into their midst. However, anti-gay sentiments, attitudes, and practices – labelled homophobia – are not over yet.

Cairo, the Egyptian capital city, is, in principle, next door to me but actually light years away. Some years ago, I wanted to attend a major conference held in Cairo. But for a long time, I had been reading about police raids on gay venues and violent attacks and arrests of gay men (Outright Action International, 2001). It was with an understandable trepidation that I decided to go. After decades of being totally out of the closet at home, I now had to camouflage two fundamental elements of my identity: being gay and Israeli. I first had to hide any external "gay characteristics", that is, to leave at home my pink t-shirts and rainbow stickers. Although I was interested in meeting local gay men, I feared to do it. I was back in the suffocating closet. Secondly, Egyptians just love to ask tourists: "Where are you from?" Israel was most probably not a good answer, I thought. Canada seemed like a practicable solution. "Canada number one!", everyone joyfully exclaimed. In short, to avoid homophobia and anti-Israel sentiments I was, for a week, a Canadian heterosexual man.

Moscow was on the top of my travelling list for a long while. In 2013, Russian President Vladimir Putin signed a new federal law prohibiting propaganda of non-traditional sexual relationships. The anti-propaganda law not only is interfering with the right to freedom of speech and assembly but also instils second-class citizenship in the Russian LGBT community (De Kerf, 2017). The ramifications of this law, as well as information about rampant anti-gay violence, were clear to me as a tourist: stay put in the closet! Like my visit to Cairo, my two visits to this wonderful city were shrouded with unease and anxiety. In order to fulfil my dream, I had to conceal my true identity: despite being a rather well-known gay activist in Israel, the visits to these cities obliged me to instantly hide back in the closet. These trips were like a time capsule for me; I had to return to the 1980s when being openly gay meant being susceptible to penalties.

I certainly have the option not to visit clearly homophobic sites. For example, research conducted in 2016 shows how sexuality has a major influence on British LGBT tourists, with one in three LGBT travellers feeling they are treated differently due to their sexuality when on holiday and two-thirds refusing to visit somewhere with an unwelcoming attitude towards the LGBT community (Kutschera, 2018). But then, a big chunk of the globe – the vast majority of African, Central American, Middle Eastern, and several Asian countries that exhibit homophobia and/or hold official anti-LGBT laws or policies[2] – will be out of bounds for me. In other words, travelling to avowedly homophobic sites seems not to be a smart move, or, at the very least, it imposes strictures on my identity.

These two vignettes, albeit very striking, are not the norm when travelling to and in liberal countries. Homophobia is not an inevitably blatant or palpable violent or aggressive reaction to LGBT individuals and their lives. It can masquerade itself in nuanced and subtle manners. The aforementioned Irish lady serves as a paradigmatic example. I know that many check-in clerks were somewhat surprised to see that my partner is a man and, yes, we did book a double bed. The same story repeats itself every single time my partner and I go through airport security and passport control: "Are you travelling together? What is the relationship between you two?" The irony of this tale is that homophobic reactions are dwarfed by racism. My partner is quite dark-skinned, and he is usually taken aside for further (oral and body) investigations.

I guess my readers can empathise with the feeling of unease upon such (even fleetingly) frowning. It also means that wherever and whenever I travel and check in, I involuntarily need to come out, to repeatedly wear my homosexuality on my sleeve. Not that I mind very much that the person behind the reception counter, the cleaning maid, or the border officer realise I am gay, but it does mean that my sexual identity is always present, even when it does not have to be.

Again and again, people, even close non-homophobic friends, ask me: "Why is being gay relevant at all when you travel?" In principle, it is not and perhaps should not be. But, within the context of an overall climate of explicit unease, or, at the very least, of subtle eyebrow-raising gestures, as I demonstrated earlier, being gay is not quite "transparent" in the sense that one's being gay needs to be negotiated. I wish to reiterate: homophobia exists every time a gay tourist is compelled to come out to complete strangers who need to either embarrassedly or nonchalantly manage and cope with this new (unexpected) information. In other words, while coming out is fundamentally a voluntary act initiated by an individual's perception that disclosure of his sexuality is needed or called for (e.g. to enhance and bolster a relationship), the aforementioned instances are imposed on him. This enforced disclosure may trigger reactions from the service personnel who may not be sensitive or welcoming, not to say prejudiced or intolerant. To sum up, scholars (e.g. Ginder & Byun, 2015; Want, 2002) have already noted that discrimination and prejudices against the LGBT community are still rampant in many places around the world; a fact that problematises the very basis of LGBT tourism.

Gay-friendly venues and guidebooks

When my husband and I visited Montreal, we checked in at a gay hotel. The reception clerk promptly informed us that it was a men's only establishment. We smiled since this was exactly what we were looking for. I then climbed the stairs, while my partner was slow with his heavy suitcase. When he finally entered the room, there was another guy there behind me (whom I unknowingly believed to be my partner), who cried out: "But I was here first!". "No, sir, I've been with him for many years . . .". This funny incident exemplifies the atmosphere of camaraderie and solidarity typical of gay establishments. It is here where a gay traveller can instantly feel at home away from home. There is no need to negotiate his identity or be on the lookout for unpleasant reactions.

In light of the above discussions, most LGBT tourists prefer destinations celebrated as LGBT friendly, where they can, and do, feel safe from harassment, be it street violence or anti-LGBT policies. Indeed, perceptions of safety comprise key factors in the decision-making process for LGBT tourists (Pritchard et al., 2000; Ram et al., 2019). Gay-friendly spaces are havens providing a sense of safety and thus are preferable destinations for LGBT tourists (Weeden et al., 2016). In short, the existence of these spaces is inextricably linked to virtue of their relatively counterhegemonic norms and relative safety. Non-LGBT tourists can, and do, enjoy their vacations regardless of their sexual orientation. Being the hegemonic majority, they face no sanctions for being heterosexuals.

For me, these issues are also of immense importance: will my holiday be marred by insecurity or isolation? Will I feel like Dafydd, "the only gay in the village"? Visiting a "gay Mecca" promises not only a sense of inclusion but also a means to make new friends with whom there is always a common ground to establish a relationship. These relationships can be a brief sexual adventure, they can last for the duration of the trip, and/or become stable, long-term friendships. For example, I met my Danish friend while having breakfast in a gay hotel in Madrid. Breakfasts in a hotel or B&B can be a genuine litmus test: the hustle and bustle of a mass of aloof and unapproachable heterosexuals versus more intimate camaraderie of gay individuals and couples. A fundamental common denominator among them can cultivate and nurture a sense of strong togetherness.

One of the means for establishing, consolidating, and publicising LGBT-friendly places is guidebooks. For many years, these were printed as hefty books but are now available only online (Luongo, 2002). Two of the most famous guides are the American *Damron* (https://damron.com/) published since 1964 and the German *Spartacus International Gay Guide* (https://spartacus.gayguide.travel/) published since 1970. These guides provide detailed information on a city/country, in the context of LGBT rights, and then LGBT-owned catalogues and LGBT-friendly venues, such as accommodations, saunas, dancing clubs, cafes, restaurants, sex clubs, and cruising areas. In other words, they offer survival strategies for LGBT tourists. Knopp and Brown (2021) claim that cities are the guides' building blocks, and thus, these guidebooks are mainly urban in nature. They communicate particular notions of what LGBT space is and function as way-finding tools to help readers navigate.

Pride parades

Pride parades have been established as a cornerstone of LGBT communities around the globe. They are modelled after the transformative parade of 1969 in New York, celebrating LGBT achievements and pride and calling for equality under the law and for social and self-acceptance. The Parades seek to create a solid community and honour the history of the LGBT rights movement. They have recently been utilised by various cities to attract LGBT tourists for two main objectives. First, for LGBT individual participation to "provide opportunities . . . to reaffirm his particular sexual identity, his membership in an imagined community, and to actively contribute to the production of a cultural form" (Waitt & Markwell, 2006, pp. 217–218). These carnivalesque rites of passage, despite being "magnets for commercialisation" (Kates & Belk, 2001, p. 392), "result in social legitimisation of gay and lesbian community" (Ibid., p. 415). Second, for the organising authority (mostly, a city hall), such events constitute a source of hefty income and are considered to be economically lucrative. Official sponsorship and endorsement of Pride events result from the acknowledgement that these events not only attract large numbers of tourists who spend money during their visit, but they can also lead to further visits. It is, thus, not surprising to learn that in 2016–2017, the world federation of Pride organisers, InterPride (n.d.), identified over 900 Pride parades worldwide.

While Pride parades attract vast numbers of LGBT and non-LGBT supporters from home and abroad (Kama & Ram, 2020), they also generate negative responses among LGBT groups, particularly from queer critics. Chasin (2001) laments the "selling out" of the LGBT movement for equality and civil rights and the rise of a consumeristic culture that infuses this community. She notes that the political concept of Pride has been commodified and turned into a consumeristic apparatus. Duggan (2002) calls this rather new phenomenon "homonormativity", which is a politics that challenges neither heteronormative assumptions nor neoliberal capitalism. Homonormative LGBT pursue and aspire for assimilation within the social and political order without challenging the status quo. In the same vein, Johnston (2005) voices a blatant critique of the commodification and commercialisation aspects of the parades alongside her uneasiness with the homonormalisation and policing of the queer community. Pride parades symbolise two opposite discourses: on the one hand, they express an inclusive political and social agenda, and on the other hand, they represent a neo-liberal consumption phenomenon and a practice of commercialisation. Therefore, LGBT participation in these events provides not only opportunities to identify with their community but also a source of income for the organising authority (Waitt & Markwell, 2006).

I have never been interested in travelling abroad to take part in a Pride parade. Solidarity with my peers in another country is politically vital, but personally unappealing and, thus, does not constitute a motivation for travelling. I agree with the aforementioned critics that these events have become a sheer manifestation of capitalist logic and serve neo-liberal forces that have very little to do with LGBT political battles. What I find particularly intriguing (and surely disturbing) is that Pride events have become a sort of an empty symbol. Heteronormative hegemony, and its establishments, have domesticated a political opposition and succeeded in taming LGBT individuals and communities into docile consumers who enjoy one day of carnivalesque exhibition of naked bodies.

Final notes

The world today is unfathomably different from the one I inhabited when I began travelling abroad. When the *Spartacus* guide listed sites as AYOR (at your own risk), gay men, like me, had to carefully manoeuvre their steps to avoid potential violence or police raids: when even the photocopy of this guide was risky (e.g. when flying to China in 1991, I was told that I better destroy these copies before landing!); when small hotel owners claimed they were full when they realised who we were; and when booking flights and hotel rooms was done only by my travel agent. And yet, I never stopped looking for other travellers with whom I have an instant bond, with whom I don't need to explain anything. I do still feel that I am being (even innocuously) Othered and stigmatised.

Homophobia and heterosexism – like other forms of prejudice and discrimination – cannot end instantaneously. The world today is surely more tolerant and accepting of LGBT people than 20 years ago, but remnants of anti-gay sentiments are still prevalent. I assume that many tourism personnel still take for granted that their guests are universally heterosexual and may be at a loss with LGBT clients. Diversity and sensitivity training programmes for all tourism industry employees can bolster their awareness of their attitudes and behaviour while giving them practical ideas on how to accommodate and accept LGBT without letting them feel Othered. Such training can teach employees how to overcome stereotypes and unconscious biases and how to be respectful and sensitive. Tourism scholars have been, lately, alert to similar issues (e.g. Hurst et al., 2020; Vikena et al., 2021), but it seems they mostly contribute to the conceptualisation of cultural sensitivity in the contexts of ethnicity or nationality. These should be "translated" into the domain of sexuality to offer a better understanding of LGBT travellers' needs and sensitivities.

Notes

1 The figure was released in 2013. No updated information could be found.
2 At least 69 countries have national laws criminalising same-sex relations between consenting adults. See map: http://internap.hrw.org/features/features/lgbt_laws/

References

Badgett, M. L. (2003). *Money, myths, and change: The economic lives of lesbians and gay men*. University of Chicago Press.

Chasin, A. (2001). *Selling out: The gay and lesbian movement goes to market*. Palgrave Macmillan.

Clift, S., & Forrest, S. (1999). Gay men and tourism: Destinations and holiday motivations. *Tourism Management, 20*(5), 615–625. https://doi.org/10.1016/S0261-5177(99)00032-1

Clift, S., Luongo, M., & Callister, C. (2002). Introduction. In S. Clift, M. Luongo, & C. Callister (Eds.), *Gay tourism: Culture, identity and sex* (pp. 1–14). Cengage Learning.

Dank, B. M. (1979). Coming out in the gay world. In M. P. Levine (Ed.), *Gay men: The sociology of male homosexuality* (pp. 103–133). Harper & Row.

De Kerf, J. (2017). Anti-gay propaganda laws: Time for the European Court of Human Rights to overcome her fear of commitment. *Journal of Diversity and Gender Studies, 4*(1), 35–48. www.jstor.com/stable/10.11116/digest.4.1.2

Duggan, L. (2002). The new homonormativity: The sexual politics of Neoliberalism. In R. Castronovo & D. D. Nelson (Eds.), *Materializing democracy: Toward a revitalized cultural politics* (pp. 194–175). Duke University Press.

Garnets, L. D., & Kimmel, D. C. (1993). Introduction: Lesbian and gay male dimensions in the psychological study of human diversity. In L. D. Garnets & D. C. Kimmel (Eds.), *Psychological perspectives on lesbian and gay male experiences* (pp. 1–51). Columbia University Press.

Gay European Tourism Association. (n.d.). *The importance of the LGBT travel market*. Retrieved June 20, 2021, from www.geta-europe.org/guru1-LGBT-market.php

Ginder, W., & Byun, S. E. (2015). Past, present, and future of gay and lesbian consumer research: Critical review of the quest for the queer dollar. *Psychology & Marketing, 32*(8), 821–841. https://doi.org/10.1002/mar.20821

Gray, M. L. (2009). *Out in the country: Youth, media, and queer visibility in rural America*. New York University Press.

Gross, A. (2015). The politics of LGBT rights in Israel and beyond: Nationality, normativity and queer politics. *Columbia Human Rights Law Review, 46*(2), 81–152. https://ssrn.com/abstract=3065040

Guaracino, J. (2007). *Gay and lesbian tourism: The essential guide for marketing*. Elsevier.

Guaracino, J., & Salvato, E. (2017). *Handbook of LGBT tourism and hospitality: A guide for business practice*. Harrington Park Press.

Harel, A. (2000). The rise and fall of the Israeli Gay Legal Revolution. *Columbia Human Rights Law Review, 31*(2), 443–471.

Hartal, G. (2019). Gay tourism to Tel-Aviv: Producing urban value. *Urban Studies, 56*(6), 1148–1164. https://doi.org/10.1177/0042098018755068

Hartal, G. (2020). Israel's LGBT movement and interest groups. *Oxford Research Encyclopedia of Politics*. https://doi.org/10.1093/acrefore/9780190228637.013.1295

Holcomb, B., & Luongo, M. (1996). Gay tourism in the United States. *Annals of Tourism Research, 23*(2), 711–713. https://doi.org/10.1016/0160-7383(95)00090-9

Howe, C. (2001). Queer pilgrimage: The San Francisco homeland and identity tourism. *Cultural Anthropology, 16*, 35–61. https://doi.org/10.14506/

Hughes, H. L. (2002). Gay men's holiday destination choice: A case of risk and avoidance. *International Journal of Tourism Research, 4*(4), 299–312. https://doi.org/10.1002/jtr.382

Hughes, H. L. (2004). A gay tourism market: Reality of illusion, benefit of burden? *Journal of Quality Assurance in Hospitality & Tourism, 5*(2/3/4), 57–74. https://doi.org/10.1300/J162v05n02_04

Hughes, H. L., & Deutsch, R. (2010). Holidays of older gay men: Age or sexual orientation as decisive factors? *Tourism Management, 31*(4), 454–463. https://doi.org/10.1016/j.tourman.2009.04.012

Hurst, C. E., Grimwood, B. S. R., Lemelin, H. R., & Stinson, M. J. (2020). Conceptualizing cultural sensitivity in tourism: A systematic literature review. *Tourism Recreation Research*. https://doi.org/10.1080/02508281.2020.1816362

InterPride. (n.d.). *PrideRadar 2016/2017*. Retrieved June 15, 2021, from https://interpride.org/prideradar.html

Jeffrey, H., Vorobjovas-Pinta, O., & Sposato, M. (2017, June 26). *It takes two to Tango: Straight-friendly Buenos Aires*. Paper presented at Critical Tourism Studies Conference. Palma de Mallorca, Spain.

Johnston, L. (2005). *Queering tourism: Paradoxical performance at gay pride parades*. Routledge.

Kama, A. (2000). From *Terra Incognita* to *Terra Firma*: The logbook of the voyage of gay men's community into the Israeli public sphere. *Journal of Homosexuality, 38*(4), 133–162. https://doi.org/10.1300/J082v38n04_06

Kama, A. (2011). Parading pridefully into the mainstream: Gay & lesbian immersion in the civil core. In G. Ben-Porat & B. Turner (Eds.), *The contradictions of Israeli Citizenship: Land, religion and state* (pp. 180–202). Routledge.

Kama, A. (2014). Calculating hedonism among gay men. In M. J. Leitner & S. Leitner (Eds.), *Israeli life and leisure in the 21st century* (pp. 281–290). Sagamore.

Kama, A., & Ram, Y. (2020). "Hot Guys" in Tel Aviv: Pride tourism in Israel. *Israel Studies Review, 35*(1), 79–99. https://doi.org/10.3167/isr.2020.350106

Kates, S. M., & Belk, R. W. (2001). The meaning of lesbian and gay pride day: Resistance through consumption and resistance to consumption. *Journal of Contemporary Ethnography, 30*(4), 392–429. https://doi.org/10.1177/089124101030004003

Knopp, L., & Brown, M. (2021). Travel guides, urban spatial imaginaries and LGBTQ+ activism: The case of *Damron* guides. *Urban Studies, 58*(7), 1380–1396. https://doi.org/10.1177/0042098020913457

Kutschera, S. (2018). *LGBTQ tourism: Travel trends and opportunities 2018*. Retrieved June 20, 2021, from www.trekksoft.com/en/blog/lgbtq-tourism-2018

Lewin, E., & Leap, W. L. (1996). Introduction. In E. Lewin & W. L. Leap (Eds.), *Out in the field: Reflections of lesbian and gay anthropologists* (pp. 1–28). University of Illinois Press.

Luongo, M. (2002). Gay and lesbian travel resources guide. In S. Clift, M. Luongo & C. Callister (Eds.), *Gay tourism: Culture, identity and sex* (pp. 267–275). Cengage Learning.

Meyer, I. H. (2003). Prejudice, social stress, and mental health in lesbian, gay, and bisexual populations: Conceptual issues and research evidence. *Psychological Bulletin, 129*(5), 674–697. https://doi.org/10.1037/0033-2909.129.5.674

Morris, J. F. (2008). Lesbian coming out as a multidimensional process. *Journal of Homosexuality, 33*(2), 1–22. https://doi.org/10.1300/J082v33n02_01

Outright Action International. (2001). *Egyptian justice on trial: The case of the Cairo 52*. Retrieved June 16, 2021, from https://outrightinternational.org/content/egypt-egyptian-justice-trial-case-cairo-52

Peters, W. (2011). Pink dollars, white collars: *Queer as Folk*, valuable viewers, and the price of gay TV. *Critical Studies in Media Communication, 28*(3), 193–212. https://doi.org/10.1080/15295036.2011.559478

Poria, Y. (2006). Tourism and spaces of anonymity: An Israeli lesbian woman's travel experiences. *Tourism, 54*(1), 33–42.

Pritchard, A., Morgan, N. J., Sedgley, D., Khan, E., & Jenkins, A. (2000). Sexuality and holiday choices: Conversations with gay and lesbian tourists. *Leisure Studies, 19*(4), 267–282. https://doi.org/10.1080/02614360050118832

Puar, J. K. (2002). A transnationalist feminist critique of queer tourism. *Antipode, 37*(5), 935–946. https://doi.org/10.1111/1467-8330.00283

Ram, Y., Kama, A., Mizrachi, I., & Hall, C. M. (2019). The benefits of an LGBT inclusive tourist destination. *Journal of Destination Marketing & Management, 14*, 1–8. https://doi.org/10.1016/j.jdmm.2019.100374

Sears, J. T. (1997). Thinking critically/intervening effectively about homophobia and heterosexism. In J. T. Sears & W. L. Williams (Eds.), *Overcoming heterosexism and homophobia: Strategies that work* (pp. 13–48). Columbia University Press.

Sedgwick, E. (1990). *The epistemology of the closet*. University of California Press.

Seidman, S., Meeks, C., & Trascshen, F. (1999). Beyond the closet? The changing social meaning of homosexuality in the United States. *Sexualities, 2*(1), 9–34. https://doi.org/10.1177/136346099002001002

Troiden, R. R. (1993). The formation of homosexual identities. In L. D. Garnets & D. C. Kimmel (Eds.), *Psychological perspectives on lesbian and gay male experiences* (pp. 191–217). Columbia University Press.

Vikena, A., Höckertb, E., & Grimwood, B. S. R. (2021). Cultural sensitivity: Engaging difference in tourism. *Annals of Tourism Research, 89*. https://doi.org/10.1016/j.annals.2021.103223

Vorobjovas-Pinta, O., & Hardy, A. (2016). The evolution of gay travel research. *International Journal of Tourism Research, 18*(4), 409–416. https://doi.org/10.1002/jtr.2059

Waitt, G., & Markwell, K. (2006). *Gay tourism: Culture and context*. Routledge.

Waitt, G., Markwell, K., & Gorman-Murray, A. (2008). Challenging heteronormativity in tourism studies: Locating progress. *Progress in Human Geography, 32*(6), 781–800. https://doi.org/10.1177/0309132508089827

Want, P. (2002). Trouble in paradise: Homophobia and resistance to gay tourism. In S. Clift, M. Luongo, & C. Callister (Eds.), *Gay tourism: Culture, identity and sex* (pp. 191–213). Cengage Learning.

Weeden, C., Lester, J.-A., & Jarvis, N. (2016). Lesbians and gay men's vacation motivations, perceptions, and constraints: A study of cruise vacation choice. *Journal of Homosexuality, 63*(8), 1068–1085. https://doi.org/10.1080/00918369.2016.1150045

Index

Note: Page numbers in *italics* denote figures and in **bold** denote tables.

#blacklivesmatter *see* Black Lives Matter

accessibility 1, 8, 113–114, 117, 119–120, **120**, 122, *123*, 124–125, 163, 171
accessible tourism 8, 113–125
African American 5, 62–74, 84, 168, 170; business owners 63; resorts 68; travel writers 70; *see also* Black (people); Black and brown; people of colour
agricultural tourism (agritourism) 22, 24, 78–91, **85**
agriculture 7, 20, 22, 33, 64, 78–91, *81*, **85**; *see also* United States Department of Agriculture
anonymity 7, 135, 150, 164, 166, 167, 170, 195
assimilation 15, 199
assumption 3, 50, 65, 162, 164, 189, 199
attractions 3, 68, 69, 70, 71, 114, 119, 161, 163, 167, 171, 195; museum 8, 120, 121, 162, 164, 165–166, 167, 168, 170; night club 136, 183; theme park 8, 164, 165, 166, 167, 168, 171; *see also* restaurants

barrier 34, 36–38, 48, **49**, 89, 90, 101, 120, **120**, 122, 124, 144; African American 72; employment 5, 36, 38; obesity 161–172; women 47–57
bias 3, 4, 6, 56, 102, 192, 193; implicit 2, 3, 9; institutional 7, 9, 73, 79, 91; unconscious 72, 73, 200
bigotry 15, 62
bisexual *see* LGBTQ(IA)
Black (people) 4, 78, 79, 84, **85**, 89, 94, 103, 168; history of 5, 62–74; *see also* African American; Black and brown; people of colour

Black and brown 4, 40; *see also* African American; Black (people); people of colour
Black Lives Matter 5, 63, 69, 70–71, 94, 97
body (the) 161, 163, 169, 170, 172, 196; and disability 116; image 163, 172; male/female 51–52, 147, 148; size 4, 162–171; in travel and tourism 162–164
branding 3–4, 115; brand image 131; place-based 13–26; *see also* marketing
BSDM (bondage and discipline, dominance and submission, sadism, and masochism) 7, 176–184
bullying 163

capitalism 199; capitalistic 1, 9, 98, 163
cisgender *see* gender
civil rights 5, 63, 68–69, 78, 91, 199; Civil Rights Act 5, 66, 68, 69; movement 5, 69
colonial 4, 33, 40, 104; colonies 54; knowledge 94, 99, 100; postcolonial 96, 98, 99, 104; stereotypes 70; villages 133
colonialism 2, 41, 94, 95, 98, 102, 103; *see also* decolonization
community 2, 14, 15, 25, 68, 90, 100, 102, 105, *122*, *123*, 165, 169; African American 70; BSDM 7, 180–181, 184; community-based organisations 87; community building 102; development 47, 83; diversity of 15; education 79; expatriate 20; gardens 87; leaders 90; LGBTQ 7, 78, 130, 131, 133, 138, 140, 190, 194, 196, 197, 198, 199
community supported agriculture 86

Index

COVID-19 1, 30, 34, 39, 41, 71, 73, 89, 98, 124, 130, 135, 194
critical race 2, 99; tourism 2
critical theory 2, 96
cuisine 14, 18; French 18; Mexican 133; *see also* food; gastronomy; restaurant
culture 2, 3, 5, 14–15, 16, 17, 18, 19, 21, 22, 23, 24, 25, 26, 51–52, 57, 64, 79, 90, 115, 118, 131, 133, 135, 139, 146, 172, 191, 194; black 69, 70; consumer 199; destination 3; dominant 49, 64, 177; food 25, 26; male 49, 152, 155; minority 13, 24; national 20, 26; organisational 1, 48, **49**; subculture 180, 181, 182, 183, 195; work 50

decolonization 162; tourism 7, tourism education 9, 94–105, *97*; *see also* colonialism
destination 3–4, 14, 16, 17, 20, 21, 26, 63, 68, 79, 113, 117, 118, 119, **120**, 122, 123, 124, 130, 131, 133, 134, 135–136, 137, 139–140, 166, 192; competitiveness 4; gay friendly 131, 132, 133, 134, 136, 140, 194, 197; managers 8; *see also* branding
disability 2, 3, 8; obesity as 161–163, 167, 168, 169, 170, 171; people with 8, 113–125, *122*, 161; social model of 161, 164, 170; travellers/tourists 8, 113–125, 170
discrimination 2, 3, 6, 7, 26, 31, 35, 36, 38, 40, 41, 62, 64, 70, 72, 73, 78, 79, 89, 91, 115, 116, 117, 118, 129, 130, 153, 163, 167, 171, 176, 180, 181, 183–184, 189; anti 15; gender-based 6, 31, 47, 56, 156; institutional 3, 7–8, 9, 70; LBGTQ 132, 133, 134, 135–140, 193, 197; race-based 3, 4–5, 31, 64, 66, 68; structural 129, 130; work-place 31, 47, 50; *see also* exclusion; racism
diversity 1, 2–3, 5, 15, 51, 63, 72, 73, 74, 87, 89–90, 94, 95, 96, 102, 104, 131, 139, 162, 199; of knowledge 33

ecotourism 22, 24
education 3, 7, 8, 35, 36, 37, 38–39, 40, 47, 48, 49, 51, 54, 62, 64, 66, 69, 79, 82–83, 114, 117, 120, 124, 134, 135, 146, 156, 163; higher education 94–105, 144
employment 30, 34, 35, 36, 38, 39, 40, 41, 47, 48, 49, 64, 69, 71, 73, **149**, 163; contracts 181; division of labour 48, 146; recruitment 1, 48, 56, 72, 74; women 48, 51, 53–56; workforce 3, 41, 48, 50, 54, 55, 56, 71, 72, 144
empowerment 48, 53, 54
entrepreneur 6, 24, 53, 54, 56, 84, 153, 155; entrepreneurship 38, 40, 53, 54, 69, 153, 155; self-employment 38
epistemology 9, 94, 95, 104; Western 2, 7, 98, 99
equality 1, 5, 63, 94, 96, 104, 157, 171; Equality in Tourism Organization 51; gender 5, 6, 47–53, 54–55, 56, 156, 157; inequality 1, 53; LGBTQ 133, 190, 198; racial 65, 66, 69, 98, 144
equity 1, 5, 6, 9, 63, 89, 90, 105; inequity 56
ethics 2, 8, 17, 96, 103, 150, 165; framework 1, 2; marketing 16–17, 26, 162; theory 161; work 163
ethnicity 2, 15, 64, 105, 146, 200
events 1, 6, 15, 17, 22, 24, 71, 89, 100, 113, 118, 156, 157, 194, 198, 199; festival 6, 15, 20, food/wine 22, 24, 25; kink 7, 180–182, **182**, 183, 184; Pride 198–199
exclusion 30, 35, 50, 68, 70, 103, 115, 116, 118, 122, 157, 162, 167, 169; *see also* discrimination
exploitation 2, 4, 13, 30, 31, 32, 34, 40, 47, 66, 100; commercial 180–181

farmers 24, 79, **85**, **121**; Black 78, 84, 89; Native American/indigenous 78, 84; socially disadvantaged 78–91; women 78
feminine *see* gender
feminist theory 50, 51–53
food 18, 22, 23, 24, 25, 26, 39, 64, 67, 131, 168, 169, 183; and agriculture 78–91; and beverage 5, 39, 55, 113, 119, **182**; local 23; Slow Food 22; tourism 7, 79, 82–83, 91; *see also* agricultural tourism; events; gastronomy; wine

gastronomy 18, 20, 23; tourism 21, 22; *see also* food; wine
gay *see* LGBTQ(IA)
gaze 8, 70, 167, 168, 170–171
gender 1, 2, 3, 5–6, 38, 39, 47–57, **49**, 115, 118, 129, 139, 144–157, 166, 170, 171, 189, 190; binary 145, 148, 149, 152, 155, 156; cis 5; feminine

51–52, 132, 144–148, 151, 153–154, 155; identity 2, 133, 155, 157, 191; masculine 52, 132, 144–148, 151–154, 155; neutrality 50; norms 154; pay gap 50; resistance 50; roles 5, 53, 55, 144, 145, 148, 151, 154, 156, 157, 176; stereotypes 5, 150, 151, 153, 155, 156; *see also* discrimination; equality; men; stereotypes; transgender; women
glass ceiling 5, 47–57, **48**
governance 16, 51, 56; feminist 52–53

harassment 7, 31, 40, 73, 134, 180, 197; sexual 47
hegemony 155, 199
heritage 14–15, 18, 20, 25, 67, 71; interpretation 70; minority 24
heterosexual *see* sexual orientation
homophobia 6, 8, 134, 138, 189, 191, 192, 193, 194, 195–197, 199; homophobic 132, 133; violence 189
homosexual *see* sexual orientation
hospitality 1, 3, 4, 8, 18, 24, 30–32, 33, 37, 39, 40, 41, 54, 63, 71, 96, 114, 161, 164, 171, 180, 182–183, 184; *see also* hotel/motel
hotel/motel 5, 8, 35, 50, 55, 67, 134, 145, 151, 164, 165, 166, 167, 168, 169, 170, 171, 172, 183, 189, 197–198; employees 119; managers 32, 147, **149**; women employment 55–56, 147, **149**, 151; *see also* hospitality

identity 2, 3, 13, 17, 24, 40, 52, 70, 79, 132, 144, 150, 181–182, 190–191, 192, 196; branding 17–21; cultural 4, 14–16, 17, 25, 26; gender 2, 52, 133, 148, 191; national 14; sexual 6, 129, 131, 135–140, 179, 191, 195, 196, 197, 198
image 3, 8, 41, 55, 144, 151, 157, 163, 170, 172; brand 131; promotional 3; *see also* body
immigration 4, 15, 18, 34–35, 37; policy 30–41; refugee 15, 33, 35, 79
inclusion 1–2, 4, 13, 14, 15, 50, 63, 72, 89–90, 95, 96, 104, 114, 117, 122, 140, 161, 166, 192, 195, 197
inclusive tourism 3, 8–9, 113
indigenous 23, 84, **85**, 94, 100, 103; knowledge 94, 98; *see also* Native American
inequality *see* equality
inequity *see* equity

institutional culture *see* culture
institutional discrimination *see* discrimination

Jim Crow 5, 62–74

knowledge 1, 16, 31, 32, 33, 87, 94–104, 164, 172, 184, 193; colonial 94, 97, 100; indigenous 94, 98; Western 2, 96

labour *see* employment
leadership 48, 57, 71, 72, 144, 145, 147–148, 153, 155, 156, 157; organisational 5; *see also* management
legislation 23, 25, 84, 87, 132, 161, 162, 181; *see also* regulation
leisure 7, 62, 63, 162, 165, 167, 168, 170, 180, 181, 182, 183, 190, 192, 193, 194–195; studies 179; travel 70, 130, 131, 134, 135, 136; *see also* recreation
lesbian *see* LGBTQ(IA)
LGBTQ(IA) (lesbian, gay, bisexual, transgender, queer, intersex, and asexual) 6, 7, 8, 78; bisexual 130, 132, 191, 193; gay 6, 129–141, 182, 189–200; lesbian 130, 131, 182, 191–192, 193, 198; queer 130, 199; transgender 130, 193

management 5, 7, 20, 31, 32, 40, 41, 47–48, 49, 50, 52, 53–57, 63, 72, 144–145, 147–156, 162, 169, 172, 191; change 95–98, 104; risk 83; *see also* leadership
marginalisation 1, 118
marketing 3–4, 13, 16, 32, 55, 63, 73–74, 78, 83, 84, 86, 89, 91, 124; *see also* branding
masculine *see* gender
men 31, 47, 48, 49, 51, 52, 55, 56, 115, 144, 145–146, 147, 148, 150, 151, 152, 153, 156, 165, 168, 170; gay 6, 129–141, 189–200; racialised 38, 168, 170; White 38, 64
minority 13, 14, 15, 19, 20, 23, 24–25, 26, 32, 38, 54, 72, 79, 80, 102, 103, 105, 154, 176, 182, 184, 191, 193

nationalism 8, 15, 98
Native American 78, 79, 81, 82; *see also* indigenous
norms 16, 17, 21, 51, 66, 103, 147, 164, 197

obesity 161–172
other 64, 100, 101, 114, *115*, 124, 146, 147, 190; othering 114–116

pedagogy 1, 7, 9, 96, 98, 99, 105
people of colour (POC) 2, 4, 7, 8, 62, 63, 71, 72, 73, 78, 84, 85, 89, 102
policy 4, 16, 18, 21, 22, 23, 25, 26, 35, 39–41, 50–53, 63, 74, 79, 86, 156; policymakers 40, 124; policymaking 18, 25, 50–53, 72; *see also* immigration
postcolonial *see* colonial
post-modern 52
power 2, 9, 13, 14, 16, 26, 36, 52, 53, 64, 65, 66, 71, 94, 98, 100–101, 102, 104, 129, 146, 148, 157, 178; Black 69; gender 144; purchasing 117, 118, 130, 170; relationships 51, 53, 144, 146, 157, 178; structures 3, 66, 100, 157
prejudice 6, 48, 49, 79, 81, 102, 117, 129–130, 132, 134–135, 136–137, 139, 140, 152, 156, 157, 163, 168, 170, 193, 197, 199
privilege 2, 9, 65, 67, 98–99

queer *see* LGBTQ(IA)

race 1, 2, 3, 4, 31–32, 35, 38–39, 64, 66, 67, 70, 73, 98, 99, 104, 105, 115, 118, 168, 170; critical 2, 99; typing 32; *see also* African American; Black (people); ethnicity; stereotypes
racism 1, 2, 4, 5, 6, 8, 31, 34, 38, 40–41, 62, 63–65, 66, 67, 69, 71, 72, 73, 89, 94, 98, 102, 163, 196; structural 2, 64, 65, 73; *see also* discrimination; race
ranchers *see* farmers
recreation 33, 119, 129, 135, 162; outdoor 63, 68; *see also* leisure
refugee *see* immigration
regulation 16–18, 22, 38, 48, 53, 56, 65, 117, 120, 121; regulatory institutions 4, 6, 14, 21, 23, 25–26; *see also* legislation
religion 14, 15, 17–18, 20, 25, 64, 133, 146; Christians 23; Greek Orthodox 20; Hindu 18; Muslim 20, 23
remittances 34
resistance 98, 104, 155; gender 50, 157
restaurants 5, 8, 18, 39, 67, 136, 164, 165–166, 168–169, 170, 171, **182**, 198; *see also* cuisine; food; gastronomy

risk 6, 57, 73, 83, 119, *123*, 124, 138, 139, 145, 148, 151, 163, 176, 182, 184, 199; adverse 37; *see also* management

same-sex 6, 132, 176, 177; *see also* LGBTQ(IA)
seclusion 8, 161, 163, 167, 168, 172
segregation 4, 31, 32, 50, 62, 64, 66–67, 69, 70, 144; labour markets 38–39; occupational 72
self-employment *see* entrepreneur
separate but equal 5, 62, 67
sex 2, 6, 52, 129, 131–132, 135, 136, 145, 176–184, 191, 195–198; as gender 117, 129, 133, 139, 144, 145–146, 147, 171, 176; harassment 31, 47; practices 176–184, **182**, 195; sexism 8, 152; sexual advances 153; sexuality 2, 51, 176, 191, 196, 197, 200; tourism 192; *see also* gender; identity; LGBTQ(IA); sexual orientation
sexual orientation 1, 2, 3, 5–6, 132, 133, 134, 136, 138–139, 140, 190, 191–192, 193, 197, 198; heterosexual 132, 134, 139–140, 176, 189, 193, 194, 197, 198, 199; homosexual 129–130, 132–133, 134, 135, 137, 138–139, 140, 191, 195, 196; *see also* gender; identity; LGBTQ(IA); sex
social exclusion 115, 118, 122, 169
social group 3, 7, 129, 182, 190, 191, 193; dominant 2
social justice 2, 71, 72, 96, 98, 105
social media 21; internet 184; online 3, 20, 54, 73, 135, 172, **182**, 198; reviews 124
social stigma 164
stakeholder 4, 5, 13, 14, 17, 18, 31, 53, 74, 86, 88–89, 90, 97, 114, 122, 124, 156, 171
stereotypes 49, 117, 200; gay 194; gender 5, **49**, 150, 151, 152, 153, 155, 156; racist 4, 32, 39, 40, 70
sustainability 4, 17, 24, 25, 26, 41, 47, 50, 51, *81*, 87, 96, 102
Sustainable Development Goals 48
sustainable tourism 50

theory 2, 16, 21; feminist 51, 52
transgender *see* LGBTQ(IA)
transparency 83, 100
travel agency 121, 149; accessible 120; Black 69

United States Department of Agriculture xi, 7, 78

violence 6, 7, 63, 66, 70, 71, 100, 101, 117, 129, 133, 134, 135, 136–139, 140, 180, 189, 196, 197, 199; domestic 47, 53, 132

wage gap 31, 37, 39, 47, 50
white supremacy 1, 2, 40, 41, 67, 71
wine 23, 24, 26; raki 20, 22–23, 26; *see also* food; gastronomy
women 5–6, 7, 30, 31, 38–39, 47–57, **49**, 78, 79, 81, 82, 102, 115, 144–157, 163, 165, 168, 169, 170; bisexual 191; freed 65, 67; pregnant 113, **121**; White 38; *see also* gender
workforce *see* employment
work-life balance 56, 152, 157
worldview 17

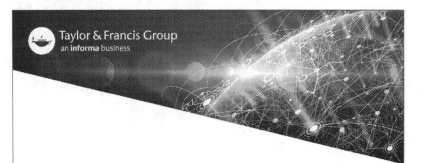